The Second Coming of the *Antichrist*

The Second Coming of the Antichrist

Peter D. Goodgame

Defense
Crane, MO

Defense
Crane, MO 65633

Printed in the United States of America.

ISBN 13: 978-0-9856045-1-6

A CIP catalog record of this book is available from the Library of Congress.

Cover illustration and design by Shim Franklin.

All Scripture quotations from the King James Version; in cases of academic comparison, those instances are noted; unless otherwise noted, all bolding, underlining, and italicizing of Scripture in this work is added by this author for specific emphasis.

To Louis King: my friend, brother, and fellow soldier for the Kingdom of Heaven.

—June 26, 1968 to February 4, 2012—

You will always be an inspiration to many
and an example of what is possible in the Holy Ghost.

Contents

FOREWORD

MOST PROPHECY EXPERTS today believe the Man of Sin spoken of in Scripture will soon emerge on the world scene as a savior. It is said this deceiver will possess mysterious, transcendent wisdom that enables him to solve problems and offer solutions for many of today's most perplexing issues. In truth, the source of his profound comprehension and irresistible presence will be the result of an invisible network of thousands of years of collective knowledge stemming from his embodiment of a very old, super-intelligent spirit. As Jesus Christ was the "seed of the woman" (Genesis 3:15), he will be the "seed of the serpent." And though his arrival in the form of a man was foretold by numerous Scriptures, the broad masses will not immediately recognize him for what he actually is—paganism's ultimate incarnation: the "beast" of Revelation 13:1.

This is where the very title of Peter Goodgame's fascinating new book, *The Second Coming of the Antichrist*, introduces an intriguing hypothesis—that Satan's seed was manifest once before in history and is now poised to return again in bodily form. People not familiar with biblical eschatology may find this idea fantastic, that the being who becomes the Antichrist was once alive, then was dead, and returns from the grave to rule the world in the end times. And yet, this appears to be exactly what Revelation 17:8 says will happen: "The beast that thou sawest was, and is not; and shall ascend out of the bottomless pit, and go into perdition [*Apoleia*; Apollo]: and they that dwell on the earth shall wonder…when they behold the beast that was, and is not, and yet is."

This entity—identified in the Greek New Testament as Apollo—was known to the Egyptians as Osiris, the same deity by different names according to numerous scholars, including Plutarch, the ancient Roman historian. Rudolf Steiner, in his *Egyptian Myths and Mysteries*, confirmed: "The Greeks… recognized that Osiris was the same as the god whom they called Apollo."[1]

But in identifying the ancient spirit that will be revived in the end-times Antichrist, the rabbit hole goes deeper. Convincing evidence exists farther back in time that the historical figure upon whom these myths were based was the legendary King Enmerkar of Uruk, known in the Bible as *Nimrod.* Goodgame first made this riveting connection in his online thesis *The Giza Discovery*:

> And just who is this Greek god Apollyon who makes his strange appearance in the book of Revelation? Charles

1. Rudolf Steiner, *Egyptian Myths and Mysteries*, Norman Macbeth, trans. (New York, NY: Steiner Books, 1990), 100.

> Penglase is an Australian professor who specializes in ancient Greek and Near Eastern religion and mythology. In his book, *Greek Myths and Mesopotamia: Parallels and Influence in the Homeric Hymns and Hesiod*, Penglase carefully and methodically demonstrates that the Greek myths and legends of Apollo were simply Greek retellings of the Babylonian myths involving the rise to power of the god Marduk, which were themselves based on earlier legends of the Sumerian hunter/hero known as Ninurta…whose historical identity can be traced back to King Enmerkar of Uruk, the very same figure who is known in the Bible as Nimrod.[2]

According to a key prophecy in the book of 2 Thessalonians, the Antichrist will be the progeny or incarnation of the ancient spirit, Apollo. Second Thessalonians 2:3 warns: "Let no man deceive you by any means: for that day shall not come, except there come a falling away first, and that man of sin be revealed, the son of perdition [*Apoleia*; *Apollyon*; Apollo]."

Numerous scholarly and classical works verify the biblical identity "Apollyon" as identical with the god "Apollo"—the Greek deity "of death and pestilence," and Webster's Dictionary points out that "Apollyon" was a common variant of "Apollo" until recent history. An example of this is found in the classical play by the ancient Greek playwright Aeschylus, The Agamemnon of Aeschylus, in which Cassandra repeats more than once, "Apollo, thou destroyer, O Apollo, Lord of

2. Peter Goodgame, "The Giza Discovery, Part Nine: The Mighty One," last accessed May 10, 2012, http://www.redmoonrising.com/Giza/Asshur9.htm.

fair streets, Apollyon to me." Accordingly, the name Apollo turns up in ancient literature with the verb apollymi or apollyo (destroy), and scholars including W. R. F. Browning believe apostle Paul may have identified the god Apollo as the "spirit of Antichrist" operating behind the persecuting Roman emperor, Domitian, who wanted to be recognized as "Apollo incarnate" in his day. Such identifying of Apollo with despots and "the spirit of Antichrist" is consistent even in modern history. For instance, note how Napoleon's name literally translates "the true Apollo."

Revelation 17:8 directly ties the coming of Antichrist with this destroyer demon known as Apollo, revealing that the Beast shall ascend from the bottomless pit and enter him:

> The Beast that thou sawest was, and is not; and shall ascend out of the Bottomless Pit, and go into perdition [Apolia; Apollo]: and they that dwell on the Earth shall wonder, whose names were not written in the Book of Life from the foundation of the world, when they behold the Beast that was, and is not, and yet is.

Not long ago, well-known researcher and leader of the Koinonia Institute, Dr. Chuck Missler, in an online article raised the appropriate question about this text and the connection between Antichrist and the spirit of Apollo/Nimrod when he asked, "Could it be that this final world dictator will be, in some sense, a return of Nimrod?"[3] Nationally

---

3. Chuck Missler, "An Alternative View: The Return of Nimrod?" *Koinonia House Inc.*, last accessed May 10, 2012, http://www.khouse.org/articles/2002/433/.

recognized prophecy expert Gary Stearman believes this is more than a possibility. Over the years, Stearman has written extensively about Nimrod and the connection this historical figure has with Babylonian Mystery Religion, Watchers, Nephilim, the spirit of the end-times Antichrist, and revival of paganism. He thinks that, in fact, the coming of Antichrist could represent a return of Nimrod. "But who is this Assyrian[?]" he asked in the July, 2001 *Prophecy in the News Magazine*. "He is none other than the spiritual inheritor of the first great post-Flood religious apostasy. He is the keeper of the great heritage that began at the Assyrian capital, Nineveh. Its founder was Nimrod.... He is the Antichrist, the future despot who comes in the name of the ancient mystery religion."

A year earlier, in June of 2000, Stearman had written in Prophecy in the News concerning Nimrod:

> He was a rebel who allowed himself to be worshipped as a god. After the Flood, his rebellion became the foundation of mankind's greatest religious apostasy. Down through the generations, this system of false worship became known simply as the "Babylonian Mystery Religion". Its basis is quite clear. **It attempts to channel the power of the ancient gods through the figure of one, powerful man. Nimrod became that god**. (emphasis added)

Alexander Hislop, in his classic text, *The Two Babylons*, substantiates Stearman's thesis that the Babylonian Mystery Religion was based on the worship of Nimrod. "It was to glorify Nimrod that the whole Chaldean system of iniquity was formed," he wrote.[4] Yet Stearman sees that the Mystery Religion continued secretly through the ages, shrouded in hiding by adepts of the occult in anticipation of a final moment when the ancient spirit should be awakened:

> Corrupt priesthoods have flourished, carrying with them the shadow of Nimrod and his ancient mysteries. Their inner secrets have been known by various names, including alchemy, magic, sorcery, conjuring, soothsaying and so forth…waiting for the prophesied day when it would rise once again. This movement will result in the reign of the Antichrist.

Does a curious verse in the book of Daniel support Stearman and Missler's thoughts concerning the rising into flesh again of the ancient demon seed? Speaking of the last days of human government, Daniel prophesied: "They shall mingle themselves with the seed of men: but they shall not cleave one to another, even as iron is not mixed with clay" (Daniel 2:43).

While Daniel does not explain who "they" that "mingle themselves with the seed of men" are, the personal pronoun "they" caused Chuck Missler and Mark Eastman, in their book, *Alien Encounters*, to ask: "Just what (or who) are 'mingling with the seed of men?' Who are these Non-seed? It staggers the mind to contemplate the potential significance of Daniel's passage and its implications for the future global governance."[5]

4. Alexander Hislop, *The Two Babylons*, 20.
5. Chuck Missler and Mark Eastman, *Alien Encounters* (Coeur d'Alene, ID: Koinonia House, 1997), 275.

Daniel's verse troubled Missler and Eastman also because it seemed to indicate that the same phenomenon that occurred in Genesis chapter 6, where non-human species or "non-seed" mingled with human seed and produced nephilim, would happen again in the end times ultimately producing a "reborn" Nimrod in the person of Antichrist. When this verse from Daniel is coupled with Genesis 3:15, which says, "And I will put enmity between thee and the woman, and between thy seed [*zera*, meaning "offspring," "descendents," or "children"] and her seed," an incredible tenet emerges—that Satan has seed, and that it is at enmity with Christ.

To "mingle" non-human seed with Homo sapiens while simultaneously returning the "King of the Nephilim" to earth has been the inspiration of the spirit of antichrists ever since God halted the practice during the Great Flood. According to Louis Pauwells and Jacques Bergier in *The Dawn of Magic*, this was certainly the goal of the antichrist Adolf Hitler:

> Hitler's aim was neither the founding of a race of supermen, nor the conquest of the world; these were only means towards the realization of the great work he dreamed of. His real aim was to perform an act of creation, a divine operation, the goal of a biological mutation which would result in an unprecedented exaltation of the human race and the "apparition of a new race of heroes and demigods and god-men."[6]

6. Louis Pauwells and Jacques Bergier, *The Dawn of Magic* (first published as *Le Matin des Magiciens*) (Paris: Editions Gallmiard, 1960), 68.

One cannot read the conclusion by Pauwells and Bergier regarding Hitler's antichrist ambition without calling to mind how from the Middle Ages forward, church leaders have believed the Antichrist would ultimately represent the return of the nephilim—the reunion of demons with humans. St. Augustine, himself, wrote of such demoniality in the *City of God*,[7] and in the *De Daemonialitate, et Incubis, et Succubi*, Fr. Ludovicus Maria Sinistrari de Ameno (1622–1701) also perceived the coming of Antichrist as representing the biological hybridization of demons with humans. "To theologians and philosophers," he wrote, "it is a fact, that from the copulation of humans with the demon… Antichrist must be born."[8]

The English theologian George Hawkins Pember agreed with this premise, and in his 1876 masterpiece, *Earth's Earliest Ages*, he analyzed the prophecy of Christ that says the end times would be a repeat of "the days of Noah." Pember outlined the seven great causes of the antediluvian destruction and documented their developmental beginnings in his lifetime. The seventh and most fearful sign, Pember wrote, would be the return of the nephilim, "The appearance upon earth of beings from the Principality of the Air, and their unlawful intercourse with the human race."

Consequently, if the Antichrist is the resurrection of the demon Apollo/Osiris/Nimrod as prophesied by the apostle

---

7. Augustine, City of God, 23:15.

8. Fr. Ludovicus Maria Sinistrari de Ameno, De Daemonialitate, et Incubis, et Succubi (1622–1701), English translation of this portion provided by Jacques Vallee in Passport to Magonia (Contemporary Books, 1993), 127–129.

Paul, not only will he be the exact opposite of Jesus (Son of God), but the forerunner of the return of the nephilim.

In *The Second Coming of the Antichrist*, Peter Goodgame employs his finely honed skills as a researcher to magnificently interpret the ancient history that evolved around these events as well as eschatological concepts in line with the Hebrew Bible, Greek, and Semitic languages that vividly warn how this offspring of fallen angels and humans may not remain a thing of the past; that in fact a repeat of the activity that gave rise to the ancient despot popularly known as Apollo, Osiris, and Nimrod was prophesied to return in the end of times in the personage of Antichrist.

Readers will be amazed how, along with this analysis, Goodgame asks all the right questions to reach his startling and original conclusions that fit the whole of the redemption story—from Satan's first attempt to corrupt all flesh, to his last similar plot, and finally his judgment.

—Thomas Horn, author,
Petrus Romanus: The Final Pope is Here

INTRODUCTION

THE BOOK THAT YOU NOW HOLD in your hands is the product of over three years of research (2005–2008). It draws from material that has been published at www.redmoonrising.com, first as the "Giza Discovery" series, and then in "Prophecies of 'The Assyrian,'" which was also posted on Tom Horn's www.raidersnewsupdate.com in January and February of 2008.

The format from which I present this information is new, however, and was developed over a ten-week Bible study on Genesis and Revelation that I was part of in the spring of 2011. That experience, as well as guidance and support from my wife and many close friends, helped to confirm for me that the time is right to release this information as a book that will reach a much wider audience. But before we begin, I want to share a few words about end-times research and the study of Bible prophecy in general.

End-times research, if not led entirely by the Holy Spirit, can easily produce depression, frustration, and fear. Those who focus their lives on uncovering the devil's plans without regard for heaven's plans can often develop a defeatist attitude toward the Christian life. The truth is, with our eyes on heaven there are absolutely no limitations on what the Church can accomplish in the last days. I want this reality to be crystal clear to every reader, because I believe that end-times research is an area of Bible study that has often been misused and abused over the years.

On one hand, Jesus did repeatedly command His followers to "Watch!" and to be ready to discern the signs of the times so that the Day of the Lord would not come as a surprise to His people. But on the other hand, "watching" was never given as an excuse to become idle regarding the activities of preaching the Gospel, healing the sick, loving ones neighbor, and otherwise expanding the Kingdom of Heaven throughout the earth.

It seems to me that there are two extremes regarding the end times in the Church today, and I hope to introduce this book by putting such study in its proper place and in proper balance with the *primary* emphasis of the Gospel.

On the conservative evangelical side, which emphasizes "Bible teaching," there seems to be a lot of speculation on current events and a lot of focus on the signs of the times as they relate to Bible prophecy. Those with this perspective seem to think, *We know things are getting worse, but that's a good thing, because we know that the worse it gets, the closer we are to that day when Jesus will enter our atmosphere and call His Church up and rescue us to heaven!*

On the charismatic/Pentecostal side, which emphasizes revival and the gifts of the Holy Spirit, the "rapture mentality" of evangelicals is often mocked because it seems to produce inactivity and a resistance to revival. Many charismatics now embrace a "partial preterist" perspective that downplays the judgments of Revelation and puts most of them in the past. An end-times perspective has even emerged that argues for a "victorious eschatology" in which the Church will triumph over the world's systems in the last days and prepare the way for the peaceful return of Jesus.

Now, rather than pointing out the negatives from each of these perspectives, let's look at the positives, and see how God is preparing His Church for the inevitable *unity* that is predicted by Paul in Ephesians 4:13.

Today, more than ever, we need to heed the command of Jesus to "Watch!" Jesus gave us some very important signs and some good information so that we would not be surprised when the time comes for God to judge the earth. This reality of an inevitable end-times judgment and the last days fulfillment of the seven Seals, seven Trumpets, and seven Bowls of Revelation, as well as the final period of a three-and-a-half-year global reign of the Antichrist is confirmed by Scripture itself. Not only are these truths confirmed by Scripture, but they are also confirmed by *apostolic tradition* in the writings of the early Church Fathers. The great martyr Polycarp who was appointed as the first Bishop of Smyrna was a disciple of the Apostle John. Irenaeus was a disciple of Polycarp, and Hippolytus was a disciple of Irenaeus. These two men, Irenaeus and Hippolytus, who trace their personal understanding of the end-times right back to the author of Revelation, wrote extensively[9] about the

Antichrist and the last days, and what they wrote confirms the basic tenets of the pre-millennial futurist perspective on the end-times that is accepted and taught by most conservative evangelicals. In fact, the very first complete commentary[10] on the book of Revelation that survives today, which was written by Victorinus of Poetovio around 260 AD, also confirms these very same truths.

Here is the basic reality of what this world is headed for, as explained by the great Chinese Bible teacher Watchman Nee, in his book, *Love Not the World*: "There is a spiritual force behind this world scene which, by means of 'the things that are in the world,' is seeking to enmesh men in its system. It is not merely against sin therefore that the saints of God need to be on their guard, but against the ruler of this world. **God is building up his Church to its consummation in the universal reign of Christ. Simultaneously his rival is building up this world system to its vain climax in the reign of antichrist.**"[11]

Christians are not misguided to *anticipate* and to take note of the many signs that are being fulfilled all around us that point to the coming "reign of antichrist." The problem comes in when Christians believe that they must *react* to every

9. For a good overview of the writings of Irenaeus and Hippolytus, see the book *The Antichrist* by Larry D. Harper (The Elijah Project, Mesquite, Texas, 2003). Also see www.voiceofelijah.org/ and http://voiceofelijah.org/library/antichristdl.pdf.
10. See "St Victorinus of Poetovio: Commentary on the Apocalypse" at http://www.bombaxo.com/victapoc.html.
11. Watchman Nee, *Love Not the World* (Fort Washington, PA: CLC Publications, 2009), 19.

new scheme of the devil by being worried or offended and by responding in fear or by force. The truth is, if our thinking remains this shallow then we will remain perpetually diverted and distracted by news reports right up until Judgment Day.

The charismatic side of the Church embraces the gifts of the Holy Spirit and the five-fold ministry of Apostles, Prophets, Evangelists, Pastors, and Teachers (Ephesians 4:11). Their end-times teaching is very wide in scope, but they generally are not carried away with conspiracy research, tribulation charts, and endless arguments about the timing of the rapture. Their emphasis continues to be the expansion of the Kingdom of Heaven into all aspects of society by the power of the Holy Spirit.

Yes, the devil has a plan for the end times, but so does Jesus! If we can remain aware of the signs of the times, but keep our focus on heaven and our ears open to the Holy Spirit, then we can move forward as the Body of Christ with a plan and a purpose that will *force the devil to react to us.*

I believe that conservative evangelicals need a wake-up call regarding the reality and the power of the Holy Spirit, whereas charismatics need to be grounded in solid end-times teaching and be aware of the signs of the times. My prayer is that this book will help to advance both of these goals and bring further understanding and unity to the Church of Jesus Christ.

I am absolutely convinced that the Gospel story that is found in the Bible from Genesis to Revelation is an amazing, epic drama, unparalleled by any work of fiction or by anything that the human heart could imagine. It is essentially a love story, with many plot twists and turns, filled with heroes and villains, defeats and triumphs, and true and false Saviors.

And the amazing thing is that we get to be a part of it! The story is coming to an end, to a final crescendo of supernatural conflict, and I truly believe that today is the most exciting time to be alive in the history of the world!

chapter one

DARK REFLECTIONS

THE ANTICHRIST HAS BEEN HERE BEFORE. When he returns again to fulfill his role as an instrument of the wrath of God against a Christ-rejecting world, it will be his *second* coming.

To begin to uncover his identity we have to have a mind with *wisdom*, as it says in Revelation 17:9, "And here is the mind which hath wisdom..." That statement was referring to the angel's explanation of the seven-headed Beast of Revelation, which is a perfect starting point for our investigation.

The seven heads that are described in the book of Revelation are not mentioned elsewhere in the Bible aside from a passing reference in Psalm 74:14 to the "heads" (plural) that are associated with the great beast known as Leviathan. Aside from that single mysterious reference all of the references in the book of Revelation to the "seven heads" constitute an entirely new realm of revelation from heaven to the people of God.

The "seven heads" first appear in Revelation 12, in connection with Satan himself, as he attempts to devour the Messiah brought forth by Israel: "And there appeared a great wonder in heaven; a woman clothed with the sun… And she being with child cried, travailing in birth, and pained to be delivered. And there appeared another wonder in heaven; and behold a great red dragon, having **seven heads** and ten horns, and **seven crowns** upon his heads…and the dragon stood before the woman which was ready to be delivered, for to devour her child as soon as it was born" (Revelation 12:1–4).

These "heads" are then shown as being a part of the Beast that comes up out of the sea, having been transferred from Satan to the Beast: "And I stood upon the sand of the sea, and saw a beast rise up out of the sea, having **seven heads** and ten horns, and upon his horns ten crowns, **and upon his heads the name of blasphemy**…and the dragon <u>gave him</u> his power, and his seat, and great authority" (Revelation 13:1–2).

The full explanation of these "heads" is not given until Revelation 17, where we find it alongside an explanation of the Great Harlot of Babylon:

> And the angel said unto me, Wherefore didst thou marvel? I will tell thee the mystery of the woman, and of the beast that carrieth her, which hath the seven heads and ten horns. The beast that thou sawest **was, and is not; and shall ascend out of the bottomless pit, and go into perdition**: and they that dwell on the earth shall wonder, whose names were not written in the book of life from the foundation of the world, **when they behold the beast that was, and is not, and yet is.** And here is the mind which hath wisdom.

> The seven heads are seven mountains, on which the woman sitteth. And there are seven kings: five are fallen, and one is, and the other is not yet come; and when he cometh, he must continue a short space. And the beast that was, and is not, even he is the eighth, and is of the seven, and goeth into perdition. (Revelation 17:7–11)

The seven heads of the Beast symbolize *two separate things*. The *first* relates to the Great Harlot: "…seven hills on which the woman sits." These seven hills are a subject for another book. The *second* relates to the Beast, and the seven heads are explained as "seven kings." Five of them were from the past, one of them existed at the time the angel spoke to John, and the seventh was yet to come. Notice that the angel describes them as "kings" and not as "empires" or "kingdoms," which is a popular but completely misleading man-made interpretation.

The seven heads are a revelation of the "kings" of Satan, whereas the revelation of the "kingdoms" of the world is given in chapter 7 of the book of Daniel, and further explained in Revelation 13:

"I saw in my vision by night, and, behold…four great beasts **came up from the sea**, diverse one from another…the first was like a lion…a second, like to a bear…another like a leopard…and behold a fourth beast, dreadful and terrible, and strong exceedingly…and it was diverse from all the beasts that were before it; and it had <u>ten horns</u>" (Daniel 7:2–7).

"The fourth beast shall be the fourth kingdom upon earth, which shall be diverse from all kingdoms, and shall devour the whole earth, and shall tread it down, and break it in pieces" (Daniel 7:23).

"**And I saw a beast coming out of the sea.** He had ten horns and seven heads, with ten crowns on his horns, and on each head a blasphemous name. The beast I saw resembled a leopard, but had feet like those of a bear and a mouth like that of a lion" (Revelation 13:1–2).

The "Beast from the Sea" of Revelation 13:1 is a kingdom; the very same as the fourth great and terrible kingdom that was revealed to Daniel, which conquers all of the other kingdoms of the world.

The "Beast from the Earth" of Revelation 13:11 is the religious leader known as the False Prophet who is also shown in Revelation 19:20. He deceives the world into worshiping the Antichrist.

The "Beast from the Bottomless Pit" is the king of the great and terrible kingdom that rises out of the sea. *He is the Antichrist himself.* Daniel 7 describes him as a little horn that rises out of the ten horns that initially rule over that kingdom. Revelation 13 describes him as a head (*a king*) that is healed of a deadly wound, who is then given a mouth to speak blasphemies against God and heaven and given temporary power to rule over the entire world.

Revelation 17 describes him as one of the seven kings who existed in the past, but who will one day return by coming up out of the Bottomless Pit (the Abyss) to rule as the eighth and final king: "And the beast that was, and is not, even he is the eighth, and is of the seven, and goeth into perdition" (Revelation 17:11).

There are ten kings (ten horns) who will *simultaneously* rule the final Beast Kingdom just prior to the reign of Antichrist, and there are also seven kings (seven heads) who are described as having ruled *sequentially throughout history,* culminating at the very end with the reign of the Antichrist. There are only seven of these uniquely satanic kings throughout human history, but there are eight appearances of them. This simply means that one of them has to appear *twice*.

It is the Antichrist himself who "was, and is not; and shall ascend out of the bottomless pit, and go into perdition." He is one of the seven, but will appear again as the eighth and final king. If the Antichrist king once "was" and now "is not," then that means that **he is now dead.**

The Death and Resurrection of the Antichrist

Throughout this book we will list the different ways in which the life and career of the Antichrist mimics the life and career of Jesus Christ. The Antichrist is merely a **dark reflection** of the true Messiah, and in an ironic way his life actually points all men towards Jesus. These dark reflections begin with the fact that both Jesus and the Antichrist were killed in the past, and they both experience a resurrection from the dead. Jesus was resurrected three days after His death, during which time He descended into hell, while the soul of the Antichrist remains locked in hell while he still waits for his resurrection.

Revelation describes how both were once dead:

Jesus Christ: Revelation 5:6, "And I beheld (*kai eidon*)… a Lamb as it had been slain (*hos esphagmenon*)…"

Antichrist: Revelation 13:1–3, "I saw a beast coming up out of the sea, having ten horns and seven heads… I saw (*kai eidon*) one of his heads as if it had been slain (*hos esphagmenen eis thanaton*)…"

In these texts, the fact that the Antichrist experiences death receives even more emphasis than Jesus by the Greek phrase *esphagmenen eis thanaton*, which translates literally as "slaughtered to death." *Thanaton... Dead!* Just like Jesus, the Antichrist was slaughtered and killed. (In later chapters we will show how the Antichrist's death long ago was an actual *sacrifice* that benefited a specific group of beings, but that is getting ahead of our story.)

Continuing with our dark reflections, we know that the body of Jesus was raised from the dead, and the following passages from Revelation show that the very same thing will happen to the dead body of the Antichrist:

13:3: "And I saw one of his heads as it were wounded to death (*esphagmenen eis thanaton*), and his deadly wound was healed (*etherepeuthe*)..."

13:14: "the beast, which had the wound by a sword, and did live."

The popular notion of some sort of "Revived Roman Empire" is misguided, as well as the heated debates over whether it will be the Western (European) or Eastern (Islamic) half. It is not an empire or a kingdom that is revived; it is a KING that is revived! In fact, the resurrection of the body of the Antichrist will be the primary reason why the people of the earth will embrace him and worship him as God!

"And I saw one of his heads as it were wounded to death; and his deadly wound was healed: **and all the world wondered after the beast**" (Revelation 13:3).

"The beast that thou sawest was, and is not; and shall ascend out of the bottomless pit, and go into perdition: and **they that dwell on the earth shall wonder**, whose names were not written in the book of life from the foundation of the world, when they behold the beast that was, and is not, and yet is" (Revelation 17:8).

From Heaven and Hell

We know that in the long absence since His time on earth, Jesus has been in heaven, seated at the right hand of the Father. Here is how John witnessed the Second Coming of Jesus Christ: "And I saw **heaven opened**, and behold a white horse; and he that sat upon him was called Faithful and True, and in righteousness he doth judge and make war" (Revelation 19:11).

In contrast to Jesus, since his death the soul of the Antichrist has been confined to the bottomless pit of hell, known as the "Abyss" in the book of Revelation. Before his body can be resurrected to begin the final portion of his earthly career, the Abyss must be opened and his soul released. Here is how John witnessed the second coming of the Antichrist: "And the fifth angel sounded, and I saw a star fall from heaven unto the earth: and to him was given the key of the bottomless pit. And he **opened the bottomless pit** [literally, "the Abyss"]; and there arose a smoke out of the pit, as the smoke of a great furnace; and the sun and the air were darkened by reason of the smoke of the pit" (Revelation 9:1–2).

Dark Reflection #1:

Jesus Christ and the Antichrist are both worshiped by their followers as "Dying and Rising Gods."

The Antichrist will appear on the world scene and cause everyone to be astonished when his soul ascends out of the Abyss and his body is resurrected: "The beast, which you saw, once was, now is not, and will **come up out of the Abyss** and go to his destruction" (Revelation 17:8).

Dark Reflection #2:

**The Second Coming of Jesus Christ will take place after heaven is opened and He descends down from the sky.
The second coming of the Antichrist will take place after hell is opened and his soul ascends up from the Abyss to re-inhabit his dead body.**

---

chapter two

THE FIRST AND THE LAST

TO DISCOVER WHO THE ANTICHRIST will be in the future we have to discover who he was in the past. This calls for a deeper investigation of the seven kings of Satan: "And here is the mind which hath wisdom. The seven heads are…seven kings: five are fallen, and one is, and the other is not yet come; and when he cometh, he must continue a short space. And the beast that was, and is not, even he is the eighth, and is of the seven, and goeth into perdition" (Revelation 17:9–11).

The explanation is simple: Five kings are from the past, one existed at the time of the Revelation, and the seventh was still in the future. There are only seven heads, but there are eight appearances, because one of them, the Antichrist, appears twice. The Antichrist must be one of the first five because, like them, he "once was" and is therefore from the past. He is "of the seven" but then comes *again* as the eighth after he comes up out of the Abyss, after which he goes on to his destruction.

It is not too hard to identify these kings throughout history. They are properly characterized as *satanic* because they first appear in Revelation 12:3 as heads of the great red dragon, who is Satan. *He owns and totally possesses them.* They are also characterized by blasphemy, hatred of God's people, violence, and often suicide. I have attempted to put together a theoretical list of them, and the most important one I have no doubts about.

The sixth king, the one who "now is" must certainly be one of the Roman emperors, either Nero or Domitian, depending on the dating of the writing of the book of Revelation. Both were psychotic persecutors of Christians who blasphemed God and carried out vicious acts of violence. Nero's career ended when he committed suicide.

The seventh king, the one who did not yet exist at the time of the Revelation and who would appear in the future and "continue a short space" was, I believe, Adolf Hitler. He satisfies the requirements of being a completely satanic king, given over to blasphemy and violence against God's people. He killed millions of Jews, as well as many Christians such as Dietrich Bonhoeffer who dared to stand up against him. Like Nero, Hitler died by suicide.

The lengthy gap between the sixth and seventh kings is explained by the dominance of the Christian era. Christianity, when it first appeared, overwhelmed the old pagan Roman Empire and dominated the West for many centuries. Hitler seems to have been the first globally influential king who wholeheartedly returned to Europe's violent pagan roots.

I do not subscribe to the view that the first Seal of

Revelation is a description of the Antichrist—the eighth king—for reasons that will be clear later on in this book, but perhaps it does describe the career of Adolf Hitler, Satan's *seventh* king and *precursor* to the Antichrist. If that is truly the case then the second Seal may very well be descriptive of World War II. This makes sense because according to Jesus, Himself, the very first noteworthy "birthpang" at the time of the end would be a world war of "nation against nation and kingdom against kingdom" (Matthew 24:7).

Jesus went on to say that the generation that saw the signs that begin with this world war would not pass away before the end comes (Matthew 24:32–34). My belief is that the "Greatest Generation" that witnessed and/or fought in World War II is actually the "Final Generation" that won't pass away before the return of Jesus.

This brings us now to the five kings who "have fallen" as stated at the time when Revelation was written. We will examine them as we go backwards in time.

The fifth king must certainly be Antiochus IV Epiphanes. Here is what I wrote about him in my "Giza Discovery" series online:

> The fifth of Satan's seven kings can only be King Antiochus IV Epiphanes. His career was predicted in Daniel 11:21–35, where he is described as a contemptible and vile person, scheming and deceitful, psychotic and possibly insane, who would focus his rage against the Jews, against God, and against Jerusalem and the holy temple.
>
> Antiochus obtained his throne in Syria by conspiring against the rightful heir and by flattering powerful

allies. After he took power he waged war against Ptolemy VI of Egypt, and after striking a treaty with Ptolemy he brought his army into Palestine. He received word that the Jews were rejoicing because of false reports of his death, so he attacked Jerusalem, killing 40,000 and capturing another 40,000 as slaves. He reinstalled his puppet Menelaus as the Jewish high priest who continued Antiochus' plan to hellenize the Jews. After another unsuccessful campaign into Egypt Antiochus sent 22,000 troops into Jerusalem to aid Menelaus and to eradicate traditional Jewish worship. His forces attacked Jerusalem on the Sabbath and massacred many worshipers. Antiochus then entered the Temple and consecrated it to Jupiter (Zeus), setting up an idol and sacrificing a pig on the altar. He passed a law that outlawed the Jewish religion, and he killed and tortured the violators that were caught.

The career of Antiochus is typical of Satan's kings. He was one of the greatest blasphemers against the God of Israel, and he minted coins that pictured himself with the inscription "Antiochus the Great, God Manifest." He committed the greatest outrage possible against the Lord when he violated His sanctuary and erected a pagan idol within, followed by the sacrifice of an unclean beast on the altar. These acts were an "abomination" against the Lord that will be matched by the Antichrist when he sets up the "abomination of desolation" predicted by Jesus (Matthew 24:15), Paul (2 Thessalonians 2), and Revelation 13…

The end came for Antiochus after his retinue was ambushed while plundering the temple of a goddess

> in Persia. Some accounts say that he was violently slain, while others say he died of a stomach ailment while in retreat. Given the trend followed by these kings it seems more likely that he died violently. In any case Antiochus must certainly be counted as one of Satan's seven kings…[12]

The interesting thing about the prophecies that Daniel gave of Antiochus is that they transition from predictions of Antiochus into predictions of the end-times Antichrist, beginning in Daniel 11:36. Portions of Daniel 11 have already been fulfilled but a good deal of it is still in the future. It is as if the angel delivering the prophetic message sees no difference between the person of Antiochus and the person of the Antichrist. This makes sense only if we understand the spiritual reality that all of the seven kings are ultimately connected into one body, because they are seven heads of the body of Satan, himself.

The fourth king is King Ithobaal II of Tyre. He ruled over a powerful city-state that was the dominant port and trading center of the Mediterranean. Ezekiel 28 has much to say about this king and his blasphemy, pride, violence, and oppression against Israel. The words against the King of Tyre transition (similar to Daniel 11) into words that many believe are descriptive of Satan himself: "Thou hast been in Eden the garden of God; every precious stone was thy covering… Thou art the anointed cherub that covereth; and I have set thee so:

12. Peter Goodgame, "The Giza Discovery, Part Seven: The Second Coming of the Antichrist," last accessed January 4, 2012, http://www.redmoonrising.com/Giza/SavDest7.htm.

thou wast upon the holy mountain of God; thou hast walked up and down in the midst of the stones of fire. Thou wast perfect in thy ways from the day that thou wast created, till iniquity was found in thee" (Ezekiel 28:13–15).

Again, this prophecy directed against the King of Tyre only makes sense if he is viewed as being of the same body as Satan, himself. He is one of Satan's seven kings and his very personality was taken over and possessed by Satan to the extent that his life *became one* with Satan. How else can it be logically said of this King of Tyre that *he once existed in the Garden of Eden*?

The third king is King Sennacharib of Assyria. Here is what I wrote in "The Giza Discovery":

> The story of [Sennacharib's] campaign against King Hezekiah and against Jerusalem is given in 2 Kings 18–19, 2 Chronicles 32, and Isaiah 36–37. It is an amazing story of the effectiveness of prayer and of the mercy, justice and power of God. When King Hezekiah resisted Sennacherib's demands Sennacherib responded through his messengers with ridicule and blasphemy against the God of Israel. King Hezekiah responded to Sennacherib's insults by going to the Temple to pray, and after hearing Hezekiah's prayers God responded through the prophet Isaiah. The story unfolds in Isaiah 37:
>
> > Then Isaiah son of Amoz sent a message to Hezekiah: This is what the LORD, the God of Israel, says: "Because you have prayed to me concerning Sennacherib king of Assyria," this is the word the LORD has spoken against him:

> "The Virgin Daughter of Zion despises and mocks you. The Daughter of Jerusalem tosses her head as you flee. Who is it you have insulted and blasphemed? Against whom have you raised your voice and lifted your eyes in pride? Against the Holy One of Israel! By your messengers you have heaped insults on the Lord. And you have said, 'With my many chariots I have ascended the heights of the mountains, the utmost heights of Lebanon. I have cut down its tallest cedars, the choicest of its pines. I have reached its remotest heights, the finest of its forests...'
>
> "But I know where you stay and when you come and go and how you rage against me. Because you rage against me and because your insolence has reached my ears, I will put my hook in your nose and my bit in your mouth, and I will make you return by the way you came..."

Therefore this is what the LORD says concerning the king of Assyria:

> "'He will not enter this city or shoot an arrow here. He will not come before it with shield or build a siege ramp against it. By the way that he came he will return; he will not enter this city,' declares the LORD. 'I will defend this city and save it, for my sake and for the sake of David my servant!'
>
> "Then the angel of the LORD went out

> and put to death a hundred and eighty-five thousand men in the Assyrian camp. When the people got up the next morning—there were all the dead bodies. So Sennacherib king of Assyria broke camp and withdrew. He returned to Nineveh and stayed there."[13]

King Sennacherib was violent, proud, and blasphemous. After retreating from Jerusalem, he was murdered in one of his temples by two of his own sons. The characteristics of his life make him a good candidate for one of the seven kings of Satan.

The second king is Pharaoh of Egypt from the time of the Hebrew Exodus. I cannot be dogmatic about this choice, but he is the primary villain in the story of Moses and the Hebrew release from Egyptian bondage. Pharaoh is characterized by pride, blasphemy, violence, and hatred, and he died in a vindictive and reckless act that turned into suicide as he drove his armies into the Red Sea. Surely he must be considered as one of the seven kings of Satan.

The first king is Nimrod. The name of Nimrod only appears four times in the Bible (Genesis 10:8 and 10:9, 1 Chronicles 1:10, and Micah 5:6), and the only passage that offers a detailed description of "Nimrod" is Genesis 10:8–12: "And Cush begat Nimrod: he began to be a mighty one in the earth. He was a mighty hunter before the Lord: wherefore it is said, Even as Nimrod the mighty hunter before the Lord. And the beginning of his kingdom was Babel, and Erech, and Accad, and Calneh, in the land of Shinar. **Out of that land went forth Asshur**, and builded Nineveh, and the

---

13. Ibid.

city Rehoboth, and Calah, and Resen between Nineveh and Calah: the same is a great city" (bold added).

There is not a lot of biblical information on "Nimrod," but Nimrod was also known as **Asshur**, as the text above shows, and it is through *this* name that the Old Testament comes alive with information about this famous and thoroughly *satanic* king.

Here is what I wrote about Nimrod's identity as Asshur in my online series "Prophecies of 'The Assyrian,'" which was published on Tom Horn's online news site at www.raidersnewsupdate.com back in the Spring of 2008:

> The KJV and Septuagint (LXX) translations of Genesis 10:11 give the impression that "Asshur" is an individual, but in most modern Bible versions "Asshur" is translated as "Assyria"—a place. They generally read, "From that land he [Nimrod] went to Assyria, where he built Ninevah…" The fact is that "Asshur" can be read either as an individual or as the region of Assyria—we just don't know for sure and the text alone does not prove either case. However, because the name "Asshur" is not modified by the preposition *el* or the directional *heh* (thus giving either "el Asshur" or "Asshurah"), which would confirm "Asshur" as a place, it remains a distinct possibility that Asshur is meant to be understood as an *individual* and as *another name for Nimrod.*
>
> Another objection that is raised against equating Asshur with Nimrod is that this would mean that there are two "Asshurs" in Genesis 10—one a descendent of Ham and the other a descendent of Shem.

However, this is a superficial objection. Just because Asshur is named as a descendent of Shem does not mean that Ham could not have had a descendent with the same name. The fact is there are many such cases in Genesis 10. There are two Meshechs—one from the line of Japheth and one from the line of Shem; there are two Shebas—one from Ham and one from Shem; and there are two Havilahs—again one from Ham and one from Shem. There is also the curious case of the Ludites descending from Ham, but Lud himself descending from Shem. The truth is that the descendents of Shem and the descendents of Ham shared several names in common and Asshur is simply another one of these cases.

Here is what the *Bible Knowledge Commentary* has to say about Nimrod, the post-flood world's first conqueror:

> "Because his name seems to be connected with the verb 'to rebel' (*mārad*), tradition has identified him with tyrannical power. He was the founder of the earliest imperial world powers in Babylon and Assyria. The table [Genesis 10] simply presents him as a mighty hunter, a trait found commonly in Assyrian kings. He was founder of several powerful cities. The centers he established became major enemies of Israel."[14]

---

14. John F. Walvoord; Roy B. Zuck; Dallas Theological Seminary, *The Bible Knowledge Commentary: An Exposition of the Scriptures* (Wheaton, IL: Victor Books, 1983–c1985, S. 1:43).

> It is well accepted that Nimrod built Ninevah as well as the Biblical city of Calah which is the modern site of Nimrud. This ancient city, once a capital of Assyria, has been excavated by archaeologists who have uncovered numerous artifacts including the stele… of the god Asshur holding a flail and a club. If it is accepted that Nimrod built the great city of Ninevah then it is quite logical to assume that he also gave his name to the kingdom that was established. He was remembered as Nimrod but known also as Asshur who founded the kingdom of Asshur, which later built a capital city known as Asshur, whose people worshiped the terrible war-god known as Asshur.[15]

In Genesis 10:11 Nimrod, the original builder of Babel (Babylon), is also referred to as Asshur, and in Isaiah 23:13 (KJV) it is Asshur who is identified as the founder of the Chaldean (Babylonian) civilization: "Behold the land of the Chaldeans; this people was not, till the Assyrian [**Asshur**] founded it for them that dwell in the wilderness: they set up the towers thereof, they raised up the palaces thereof; and he brought it to ruin."

In Micah 5:6, the "Land of Asshur" is used as synonymous with the "Land of Nimrod." The form of this poetic prophecy is typical of that used throughout the Old Testament, where the same idea is repeated using different words. From the Micah passage we can conclude that "the land of

---

15. Peter Goodgame, "Prophecies of 'The Assyrian': The Mighty Hunter," last accessed January 4, 2012, http://www.redmoonrising.com/Giza/raiders3.htm.

Nimrod" is the very same as "the land of Asshur"[16]: "And they shall waste the land of Assyria [**Asshur**] with the sword, and the land of Nimrod in the entrances thereof: thus shall he deliver us from the Assyrian [**Asshur**], when he cometh into our land, and when he treadeth within our borders."

The very earliest surviving *complete* commentary on the book of Revelation was written by St. Victorinus of Poetovio in the second half of the third century. In his commentary on the eighth chapter of Revelation, he refers to Micah 5:6 as an end-times prophecy, stating very bluntly that *Asshur is the Antichrist.*[17]

One of the most comprehensive biblical expositions of the Antichrist was written by Arthur Pink and first published in 1923. Here is what he had to say about Nimrod and his connection to the biblical Antichrist:

> To sum up, in Nimrod and his schemes we behold Satan's initial attempt to raise up an universal ruler of men. In his inordinate desire for fame, in the mighty power that he wielded, in his ruthless and brutal

---

16. For instance, see the online entry of the Jewish Encyclopedia entitled, "Parallelism in Hebrew Poetry," by I. M. Casanowicz, located at: http://www.jewishencyclopedia.com/articles/11902-parallelism-in-hebrew-poetry.
17. "And he says before: then there will be peace in the earth, when seven shepherds will arise in it, and eight attacks (lit. 'bites') of men, and they will encircle **Assur, that is, Antichrist,** in the ditch of Nebroth." From *Victorinus Poetovionensis: Commentarius In Apocalypsin*, last accessed January 4, 2012, http://www.bombaxo.com/victapoc.html.

> methods, in his blatant defiance of the Creator, in his founding of the kingdom of Babel, in his assuming to himself Divine honors, in the fact that the Holy Spirit has placed the record of these things just before the inspired account of God's bringing Abraham into Canaan… we cannot fail to see that we have a wonderfully complete typical picture of the person, the work, and the destruction of the Antichrist.[18]

Our search for the historical Antichrist ends at the beginning of our list of Satan's seven kings. Nimrod, also known as Asshur, was not just a perfect *type* of the end-times Antichrist, he *is* the Antichrist. The one who started it all at the very beginning of the Pagan Era will rise again at the time of the end to *finish it all.* In Revelation 1:11, when Jesus appeared to John to give him the messages for the seven Churches, He identified Himself saying, "I am Alpha and Omega, the first and the last." In a similar way, we see that the Antichrist is the first and the last of Satan's seven kings to rule and reign on earth.

Dark Reflection #3:

Jesus Christ is the first and the last of all creation. The Antichrist was the first and will reappear again as the last of Satan's seven kings.

18. Arthur W. Pink, *The Antichrist: A Systematic Study of Satan's Counterfeit Christ* (Grand Rapids, MI: Kregel Publications, 1988 [1923]), p.224. For the online version see http://www.biblebelievers.com/Pink/antichrist.htm.

Dark Reflection #4:

Jesus Christ, as God, is the One "which is, and which was, and which is to come, the Almighty," (Revelation 1:8).

The Antichrist is the one who "was, and is not; and shall ascend out of the bottomless pit, and go into perdition" (Revelation 17:8).

SATAN'S SEVEN KINGS			
Past	**Present**	**Future**	**Past and Future**
Five *"have fallen"*	The Sixth *"is"*	The Seventh is *"yet to come"*	The Eighth *"once was, now is not,"* and is one of the seven
1. Nimrod	6. Nero Caesar or Domitian	7. Adolf Hitler	8. Nimrod (Asshur)
2. Pharaoh			
3. Sennacharib			
4. King of Tyre			
5. Antiochus			

"And here is the mind which hath wisdom. The seven heads are…seven kings: five are fallen, and one is, and the other is not yet come; and when he cometh, he must continue a short space. And the beast that was, and is not, even he is the eighth, and is of the seven, and goeth into perdition" (Revelation 17:9–11).

chapter three

THE BEGINNING OF HISTORY

OUR INVESTIGATION into the identity of the historical Nimrod takes us back to the beginning of recorded history and to ancient Sumer, the world's first civilization. The Bible refers to Nimrod as the very first human being to have a "kingdom," as recorded in Genesis 10:10: "And the beginning of his kingdom was Babel, and Erech, and Accad, and Calneh, in the land of Shinar."

Nimrod's kingdom began in the land of Shinar, which is the region of ancient Sumer. The city of Babel was the original Babylon, and Erech is the city also known as Uruk, which was later ruled by the Sumerian king, Gilgamesh. The name of Erech/Uruk is preserved today in the name of the modern Mesopotamian nation known as Iraq.

History Begins At Sumer

Recorded history begins at Sumer because it was in Sumer that *writing* was invented. The first written language was Sumerian, and later on a similar language known as Akkadian became dominant. These Mesopotamians were the first human beings to write down their history as well as their religious beliefs and, fortunately for us, they wrote their stories down on tablets of soft clay which were then baked and transformed into stone. Scholars believe that writing first emerged around 3000 BC, which means that the earliest stories that have been preserved from the time of ancient Sumer are up to five thousand years old!

Now the interesting thing about these records is that they closely parallel the stories that we read about in the early chapters of Genesis. For instance, the Sumerians had a story of the creation of the first human being; stories of immortality denied to human beings, and of a woman that became involved with a snake and a tree; stories that seem to parallel the dispute between Cain and Abel; a history of the founding of the very first city and the invention of metal-working; stories of advanced beings who descended from the heavens to teach, rule over, and even mate with human beings; a very colorful and dramatic story of the great Flood that wiped out civilization; and also epic tales that match up with the career of Nimrod, his mighty empire, and the building of the Tower of Babel.

The book of Genesis was written by Moses around 1450 BC, yet we find that very similar stories began to be written down over one thousand years earlier by the ancient

Sumerians! This is amazing, right? And confirmation of the truth of the Bible!

Well, not really, as far as the secular academic geniuses are concerned. They simply assume that the book of Genesis could not have been *a revelation from God of historical events,* and could only have been the early Hebrews' recollection of a partially-faded memory that must have originated with Abraham who originally came from Sumer.

A good example of such secular thinking can be found in the books written by Walter R. Mattfeld: *The Garden of Eden Myth: Its Pre-biblical Origin in Mesopotamian Myths*, and *Eden's Serpent: Its Mesopotamian Origins*. Mattfeld began his research as a Christian believer, but because of his exposure to the arguments of secular experts, he soon lost his faith. His books document his belief that everything in Genesis was adopted by the Hebrews from earlier, *more accurate*, Mesopotamian sources.

Secular researchers like Mattfeld completely dismiss any possibility of the *supernatural*, and any possibility of the *element of deception* in the creation of the earliest Sumerian texts. Academics like him cannot comprehend the possibility that even though the Sumerian and Akkadian texts were written much *earlier* than the book of Genesis, this does not mean that they are *truer*, and it does not mean that they must have been the original source for the book of Genesis.

There is an amazing paradox when we compare the Mesopotamian myths with the book of Genesis. On one hand, we see that Genesis has more in common with the myths of Sumer (much of which were recorded over one thousand years earlier) than it does with the myths of any of the other cultures that existed *at the same time* as the Hebrews. Here is what Mattfeld writes: "After having studied the religious myths of the Egyptians, Phoenicians, Canaanites, Syrians, Hittites and Mesopotamians I have concluded, in agreement with earlier scholars, that it is Mesopotamia which possesses the 'closest parallels' to motifs appearing in the book of Genesis concerning the relationship between Man and God in the mythical Garden of Eden story."[19]

On the other hand, even though the stories are similar, we find that there is actually a theological war being waged between Moses and the Sumerian and Akkadian scribes. They believed in the same events, but they had a perspective on those events that was *completely opposite!* Mattfeld writes, "I understand that the Hebrews are recasting the earlier Mesopotamian motifs and concepts in such a way as to refute and deny them. Why did the Hebrews seek to deny, refute and challenge the Mesopotamian beliefs?"[20]

For instance, consider for a moment the truly *revolutionary* statement that marks the very beginning of the book of Genesis: "In the beginning God created the heaven and the earth" (Genesis 1:1).

This was a revolutionary statement because at the time that Moses dictated these words from God, all of the surrounding cultures believed that the "gods" had originally descended from a primordial pair of a deified "Heaven" and a deified "Earth." In other words, the pagans that surrounded the Hebrews believed that, "in the beginning heaven and earth gave birth to

---

19. Walter R. Mattfeld, *Eden's Serpent: Its Mesopotamian Origins* (Lulu, ebook edition, 2010), iv.
20. Ibid., iv.

the gods." In Mesopotamia, which was the very root of these polytheistic pagan ideas, this primordial pair was known as Anshar (a male "Heaven") and Kishar (a female "Earth"). This pair mated and produced Anu, the original "Father" of the gods who then brought forth the next generation.

When it was revealed to Moses that "God created the heavens and the earth," it was revealed that the God that Moses served and the God *that he had a personal relationship with* was the Creator of all, the God above all gods, the true master and ruler of *everything*. In this way, Genesis 1:1 was absolutely revolutionary and absolutely provocative when compared with the theological claims of the nations that surrounded the early Hebrews.

Consider as well the differences between the Hebrew and Mesopotamian beliefs concerning the *purpose* for which mankind was originally created. To put it bluntly, the Sumerians believed that humans were created to be slaves to the gods, while on the other hand it was revealed to Moses that Adam and Eve were originally created as a part of God's family, to be in relationship with Him, and to bear His image and enjoy the God-given responsibility to rule over the earth.

Mattfeld notices this fact and observes that the Genesis account "appears to be a polemic challenging the Mesopotamian view of the relationship between God and Man."[21] He then quotes from Old Testament scholar Gordon J. Wenham:

> Viewed with respect to its negatives, Gen 1:1–2:3 is a polemic against the mythico-religious concepts of the ancient Orient... The concept of man here is markedly

21. Ibid., x.

> different from standard Near Eastern mythology: man was not created as the lackey of the gods to keep them supplied with food; he was God's representative and ruler on earth, endowed by his creator with an abundant supply of food and expected to rest every seventh day from his labors. Finally, the seventh day is not a day of ill omen as in Mesopotamia, but a day of blessing and sanctity on which normal work is laid aside. In contradicting the usual ideas of its time, Genesis 1 is also setting out a positive alternative. It offers a picture of God, the world, and man…man's true nature. He is the apex of the created order: the whole narrative moves toward the creation of man. Everything is made for man's benefit…"[22]

Mattfeld also refers often to Joseph Campbell as one of the most influential voices who pointed out the paradox of the relationship between the stories of Genesis and the myths of ancient Mesopotamia. Here are a few quotes (emphasis mine) from Campbell's book, *The Masks of God: Occidental Mythology*, that also appear[23] in Mattfeld's book:

"No one familiar with the mythologies of the primitive, ancient, and Oriental worlds can turn to the Bible without recognizing counterparts on every page, *transformed, however, to render an argument contrary to the older faiths.*"[24]

---

22. Gordon J. Wenham, *Word Biblical Commentary, Vol. 1* (Waco, Texas: Word Books, 1987), 37.
23. Mattfeld, *Eden's Serpent*, xi–xii.
24. Joseph Campbell, *The Masks of God: Occidental Mythology* (New York, Arkana &Viking Penguin, 1961 [1964]), 9.

"The ultimate source of the biblical Eden, therefore, cannot have been a mythology of the desert—that is to say, a primitive Hebrew myth—but was the old planting mythology of the peoples of the soil. However, *in the biblical retelling, its whole argument has been turned, so to say, one hundred and eighty degrees*... One millennium later, the patriarchal desert nomads arrived, and *all judgments were reversed in heaven, as on earth.*"[25]

"The first point that emerges from this contrast, and will be demonstrated further in numerous mythic scenes to come, is that in the context of the patriarchy of the Iron Age Hebrews of the first millennium B.C., the mythology adopted from the earlier Neolithic and Bronze Age civilizations of the lands they occupied and for a time ruled *became inverted, to render an argument just the opposite to that of its origin.*"[26]

The secular perspective on this paradox only leads to more questions because this view is dependent on a materialistic foundation and has to rule out supernatural explanations. But if we accept the Bible and the book of Genesis as the Word of God then the explanation is readily apparent. God had chosen Abraham from out of Sumer and intended to make His own nation out of Abraham's descendants. Many generations later, after centuries in Egyptian exile, this nation had been formed. While camped at Mt. Sinai, God spoke to His nation through Moses and gave them the Torah, which included God's version of human history as recorded in the book of Genesis.

After centuries of darkness and deception, the moment had finally arrived for God to speak and to *set the record straight.*

---

25. Ibid., 103–106.

26. Ibid., 17.

Setting the Record Straight

In Genesis we find that God created the heavens and the earth, which contrasts with the Mesopotamian belief (eventually related in the epic Akkadian creation story *The Enuma Elish*) that somehow "Heaven" and "Earth" gave birth to the gods.

In Genesis we find that Adam and Eve were created to be partners with God in administering over His creation, whereas the ancient Sumerians believed that humans were created to labor in service to the gods, as related in the myths *Enki and Ninmah* and *Cattle and Grain*, as well as numerous others.

In Genesis, the story of the first murder involves Cain, a farmer, and Abel, a shepherd. The brothers bring offerings to God, who accepts the animal from Abel and rejects the produce offered by Cain. Out of resentment, Cain kills Abel and is then banished from his home. The Sumerians have a version of this story (*Emesh and Enten*), but in the Sumerian account, after they get into a violent quarrel and bring their case before the gods, the farmer is *accepted* and the shepherd is *rejected* and must offer tribute to the farmer: "In the struggle between Emesh and Enten, Enten, the steadfast farmer of the gods...proved greater than Emesh."[27]

In Genesis, after documenting the two genealogies of the descendants of Cain (who built the first cities and invented

---

27. Samuel Noah Kramer, *Sumerian Mythology* (Philadelphia, PA: University of Pennsylvania Press, 1972 [1944]), 51. This book can be read online at http://www.sacred-texts.com/ane/sum/index.htm.

the art of metal-working) and the descendants of Seth (who replaced Abel), the sixth chapter provides an amazing tale of angels descending from heaven, taking human women for wives, and producing giants as offspring. These *Nephilim* offspring, half-human and half-fallen-angel, are noted as the "mighty men of old, men of renown."

Following this descent of fallen angels and the appearance of the Nephilim, Genesis explains that God became distraught at the complete wickedness that had overtaken the earth: "And God saw that the wickedness of man was great in the earth, and that every imagination of the thoughts of his heart was only evil continually. And it repented the Lord that he had made man on the earth, and it grieved him at his heart. And the Lord said, I will destroy man whom I have created from the face of the earth; both man, and beast, and the creeping thing, and the fowls of the air; for it repenteth me that I have made them" (Genesis 6:5–7).

The Sumerians tell a similar tale, but in their eyes the "fallen angels" are a group of gods known as the Anunnaki, who were created by Anu the distant and rather dis-interested "God of heaven." These beings descended to the earth to help establish civilization in Sumer and teach, guide, and rule over mankind. They are mentioned throughout Sumerian myths, including texts such as *Cattle and Grain*, *The Creation of the Pickax*, *Enki and Sumer*, *Enki and Eridu*, and various others.

So the book of Genesis views these beings from the heavens as disobedient fallen angels ultimately responsible for bringing violence and wickedness, whereas the Sumerians viewed them as "gods" worthy of worship who brought technology and civilization.

The Atrahasis Epic

As in the book of Genesis, the Mesopotamians had a very distinct memory of a great flood brought about by a great god for the purpose of wiping out civilization. The primary source for this tale can be found in the Akkadian myth known as *The Atrahasis Epic* now located in the British Museum. Elements of this tale can also be found in the Sumerian texts *The Deluge* and *The Epic of Gilgamesh*. However, as should be expected, these Sumerian and Akkadian stories have some very key differences when compared with the biblical account. In these stories, the god responsible for sending the Flood is Enlil, and the god who saves mankind is Enki. Here is what I write in "The Giza Discovery":

> Atrahasis is the Akkadian name for the Noah-like figure who is known in similar Sumerian accounts as Ziusudra (*The Eridu Genesis*) or Utnapishtim (*The Epic of Gilgamesh*). According to all of these accounts the creation of mankind eventually became regretted by the chief god Enlil. *The Atrahasis Epic* reads,
>
> > And the country was as noisy as a bellowing bull.
> > The god grew restless at their racket,
> > Enlil had to listen to their noise.

He addressed the great gods,
The noise of mankind has become too much,
I am losing sleep over their racket.

To deal with the problem of human over-population Enlil causes first a plague, and then a famine, to strike the land. In each case Atrahasis calls upon Enki to help mankind and offer a solution to the calamity. Enki responds by giving advice to Atrahasis but his interference on mankind's behalf causes Enlil to become very angry. The final solution, which is agreed upon by the gods despite a passionate argument from Enki, is that a flood will be caused to wipe out mankind entirely. This decision is kept secret and Enki is forced to make an oath that he will not speak of it to any human being. In spite of his oath Enki cleverly conceives a plan to save Atrahasis and still remain true to his word. He contacts Atrahasis from behind a reed wall, and then gives instructions as if he were talking to the reed wall. In this way Atrahasis is informed of what is coming and told how he can prepare for the calamity. He is told to build a boat as long as it is wide and to build a solid roof over the top. The *Gilgamesh Epic* includes the instructions to "load the seed of every living thing into the boat."

After the flood passes Enlil becomes enraged after finding out that mankind survived through Atrahasis and his family. However the other gods and goddesses rejoice and praise the wisdom and compassion of Enki. The anger of Enlil is eventually subdued after Atrahasis reverently builds an altar and offers him sacrifices. In the end Enlil becomes reconciled with Enki, blesses Atrahasis, and gives Atrahasis the gift of immortality.[28]

So according to the Mesopotamian story, there was a wicked god, Enlil, who was irritated at the noise and human over-population of the earth, who decided to wipe them all out. He tried a plague and then a famine to no avail, before deciding to send the Flood. In response to Enlil's madness, the kind, wise, and merciful god Enki stood up to defend the blameless human victims. He tried to stop the Flood, but could not prevail over Enlil's agenda. Instead, Enki decided to disobey Enlil and save the righteous Atrahasis. Because of Enki's courage, mankind was saved from extinction, and in the aftermath Enlil and all the other Anunnaki gods recognized Enki's wisdom and honored Atrahasis.

The Genesis story, although following a similar pattern, brings several corrections to the tale. First of all, *God loves people* and was never irritated at noise or human over-population. In fact, God continuously commanded mankind to "be fruitful and multiply, fill the earth and subdue it." Secondly, the Flood was a response to sin and violence that was rooted in the fallen angelic (Anunnaki) influence over human society. It was not an impulsive act against blameless victims, but was justice against widespread wickedness. Furthermore, the saving of Noah, the last righteous man, was God's idea; it was

28. Peter Goodgame, "The Giza Discovery, Part Five: The Spirit World and Civilization," last accessed January 4, 2012, http://www.redmoonrising.com/Giza/SpiritCiv5.htm.

not something undertaken against God's wishes by a secondary and adversarial deity.

In the next chapter we will take a closer look at the religious beliefs of the people who wrote the original histories of mankind. What kind of spiritual influences were they under, to write stories that so blatantly contradicted those written down by Moses hundreds of years later? These answers will then provide a foundation for us to better understand the life and times of Nimrod in his historical setting.

chapter four

THE GODS OF SUMER

THE ANCIENT SUMERIANS had a supernatural worldview. There is no getting around this fact. The idea that this advanced civilization somehow emerged all by itself by applying human ingenuity alone, but then created an imaginative false history filled with supernatural encounters, is laughable, yet that is what modern secular scholars try to tell us. You cannot separate Sumerian history from their relationship with the "gods" and then come up with a plausible scenario of what must have *really* happened. The truth is that *we are not alone.* We never were, and the book of Genesis supports the basic elements of the Sumerian accounts and makes this fact abundantly clear.

Kingship Descended From Heaven

Recorded history for the Sumerians began with the establishment of the first city. Here is what the very first line of the

Sumerian King List says: "When the kingship was lowered from heaven, the kingship was in Eridug."[29]

The Sumerian King List (SKL) contains the recorded history of the kings and ruling cities of ancient Sumer from its beginnings before the Flood almost to the end of the third millennium BC. There are many different copies of it, recently excavated and now held at various museums and universities, but they all say the same things regarding the earliest events. The SKL has always been viewed as an important *historical* document and the Babylonian historian Berossos used the SKL in his translation of Babylonian history into Greek around 290 BC.

In the Sumerian King List, the first city is named as Eridug (also named as Eridu), which was the city where "kingship" descended from "heaven." From this we see that according to the Sumerians the very first event in their history seems to involve a supernatural event. The SKL continues and names

29. The Sumerian King List, as quoted in David Rohl, *Legend: The Genesis of Civilisation* (London, UK: Random House, 1998), 164.

various kings and cities that ruled for a period of time before the very first portion of it ends with the following lines: "In 5 cities 8 kings; they ruled for 241200 years. Then the flood swept over."

According to the Sumerians, the Flood was definitely a historical event (despite the fact that the reign lengths that add up to 241,200 years disagree with the biblical chronology and are greatly exaggerated).

Let's look at this pre-Flood history and see how it compares with the book of Genesis. First of all, according to Genesis, the very first city was built by Cain and inhabited by his descendants. This was the cursed line of Cain, who had killed Abel and been driven from his family.

The second city on the King List is the city of Bad-tibira. This name means "Settlement of the Metal-Worker." According to Genesis it was Tubalcain, a descendent of Cain, who first learned the craft of metal-working. Here is what secular scholar David Rohl says: "Badtibira means 'Settlement of the Metal Worker.' If we take the Hebrew consonants which make up the name Tubal we get T-b-l. We know that the soft consonant 'l' is often representative of 'r,' thus we might get an original T-b-r which could, in turn, stem from ancient Tibira. Interestingly enough the Semitic epithet 'Cain' in Tubal-Cain also means 'smith' which suggests that this epithet has been added as a clarification of a little-known Sumerian word by the Hebrew author of Genesis. So these are clues which suggest that Tubal-Cain and Badtibira are connected in some way."[30]

The invention of metal-working was a great leap in

30. Ibid., 200.

technology, but there are sources that give further insight into how humans received this knowledge. For instance, the *primary and original source*, the Sumerians themselves, say that every technological innovation they received came from the Anunnaki gods who came down from heaven. Why do secular scholars dismiss this claim so easily?

This claim is supported by the extra-biblical book of Enoch, which gives a much more detailed explanation of what happened in Genesis 6 when the fallen angels descended to the earth and took human women for wives. According to this source it was the fallen angels who taught metal-working to mankind, specifically for the purpose of creating weapons for war.

What all of these different sources seem to be telling us is that the city-dwelling ancient Sumerians traced their line of descent directly back to Cain. It was to *Cain's* descendants that the fallen angels appeared, and helped establish the first civilization that quickly degenerated into violence and corrupted the whole earth, leading to the Flood.

The final reference to the line of Cain in Genesis 4 offers further support for this hypothesis. This enigmatic reference describes the beginning of the carnal human tendency to fall into a cycle of violence based upon the principle of vengeance. According to the KJV: "And Lamech said unto his wives, Adah and Zillah, Hear my voice; ye wives of Lamech, hearken unto my speech: for I have slain a man to my wounding, and a young man to my hurt. If Cain shall be avenged sevenfold, truly Lamech seventy and sevenfold." Whereas, for the sake of comparison, the NIV says: "Lamech said to his wives, 'Adah and Zillah, listen to me; wives of Lamech, hear my words. I have killed a man for wounding me, a young man for injuring me. If Cain is avenged seven times, then Lamech seventy-seven times'" (Genesis 4:23–24, NIV).

The last line of this text reads somewhat differently in the Septuagint (LXX) translation of the Old Testament and opens our eyes to the actually meaning behind Lamech's words: "Because vengeance has been exacted seven times on Cain's behalf, on Lamech's it shall be **seventy times seven.**"[31]

After Cain killed Abel and was punished by God and made to leave his homeland, he protested to God saying that if he was ever found he would certainly be killed. God listened to Cain's complaint and to make him feel at ease He decreed that whoever killed Cain would suffer a punishment seven times worse. This was the Word of God attempting to restrain mankind's corrupt tendency to take vengeance by violence by actually threatening divine retribution against Cain's enemies.

We don't know exactly what happened to Cain but because of what Lamech said the text does seem to imply that Cain was killed and that the killer of Cain was then punished by God. Regardless of what happened to Cain, we find that Lamech takes the Word of God and twists it and tries to apply it to himself to justify his own act of violence. In effect, Lamech says, "A man tried to injure me, so I killed him. Don't mess with me! Cain's enemies suffered seven-fold retribution, but I am Lamech, and anyone who comes against me will suffer *seven times seventy* retribution!"

---

31. Genesis 4:24, *THE SEPTUAGINT WITH APOCRYPHA: ENGLISH,* Brenton's translation, available at http://ecmarsh.com/lxx/index.htm.

You might be seeing now where this is going. This carnal, prideful, wicked human tendency to resort to violence and vengeance against our enemies was overturned by Jesus when He came to announce the coming of the Kingdom of Heaven: "Then came Peter to him, and said, Lord, how oft shall my brother sin against me, and I forgive him? Till seven times? Jesus saith unto him, I say not unto thee, Until seven times: but, Until **seventy times seven**" (Matthew 18:21–22).

After saying this, Jesus then told a parable about forgiveness, explaining that vengeance has no part in the Kingdom of Heaven. He taught that we must never take vengeance, but must offer forgiveness to all men, even as God forgives us.

This final reference to the line of Cain shows that one of the primary reasons that God brought the Flood was because of the fact that the ancient Sumerians, descended from the line of Cain and corrupted by the fallen angels, had become caught up in a degenerative cycle of vengeance, violence, and bloodshed.

"The earth also was corrupt before God, and the earth was filled with violence" (Genesis 6:11).

"Woe unto them! For they have gone in the way of Cain" (Jude 1:11).

The Corrupting Influence

According to the Sumerians, the two primary gods that ruled over ancient Sumer and had an influence on the creation of mankind were the gods Enlil and Enki. They were the primary and most powerful sons of Anu, the distant "God of heaven." Anu played no role in human affairs and his authority was delegated to Enlil, who eventually relinquished it to Enki. Here is what it says about these two gods in the book *Gods, Demons and Symbols of Ancient Mesopotamia*:

"**Enlil** is one of the most important gods in the Mesopotamian pantheon. According to one Sumerian poem, the other gods might not even look upon his splendour. Sometimes he is said to be the offspring of An… The great centre of the cult of Enlil was the temple E-kur (the 'Mountain House') at Nippur, at the northern edge of Sumer, and Enlil is often called the 'Great Mountain' and 'King of the Foreign Lands'… Other images used to describe his personality are king, supreme lord, father and creator; 'raging storm' and 'wild bull.' "[32]

"**Enki** (Akkadian Ea) was god of the subterranean freshwater ocean (abzu), and was especially associated with wisdom, magic and incantations, and with the arts and crafts of civilisation.… Enki/Ea was a son of An/Anu… Enki's most important cult centre was the E-abzu ('Abzu house') at Eridu. As a provider of fresh water and a creator god and determiner of destinies, Enki was always seen as favourable to mankind… In the Sumerian poem 'Inana and Enki' he controls the *me* concerned with every aspect of human life, and in 'Enki and the World Order' he has the role of organising in detail every feature of the civilised world."[33]

The Sumerian word *en* means "Lord." The word *lil* refers to the atmosphere, sky, winds and heavens, while the word *ki*

---

32. Jeremy Black and Anthony Green, *Gods, Demons and Symbols of Ancient Mesopotamia* (Austin, TX: University of Texas Press, 2003), 76.
33. Ibid., 75.

means "earth." Therefore, the name *En-lil* means something like "Lord of the Sky" while *En-ki* means "Lord of the Earth."

Enlil seems to be a slanderous Sumerian representation of the God of Genesis. He exercises supreme authority and he is the one responsible for bringing the Flood. However, he is portrayed in Sumerian accounts as impulsive, irritable, cruel, and unjust.

Enki, on the other hand, emerges as the Sumerian favorite. Always portrayed as the great champion of humanity he was also known as the "Lord of the Abzu," which is the original word for the Abyss. He didn't necessarily reside in the Abyss, and he certainly wasn't confined there, but he did have authority over it. The Abyss was known as a fresh-water barrier under the earth that separated our world from the underworld where the souls of the dead were confined after death. Fresh-water springs were thought to be gateways to this underworld and were therefore sacred.

The city where "kingship" first descended from heaven according to the Sumerians King List was Eridu, the original cult headquarters for the god Enki. Eridu was located on an island on the Euphrates River near the Persian Gulf, and the original temple built to honor Enki was built over a fresh-water spring. This temple was known as the E-abzu or "House of the Abyss."

According to the Sumerian texts, it was Enki who came up with the bright idea to create human beings in the first place and he is often referred to as "Father Enki" who even has authority over the souls of human beings after death while they are held in the underworld. We could say that according to the Sumerians it was Enki who "held the keys of hell and of death."

Enki Takes Dominion

A concept unique to the ancient Sumerians was the concept of the *me*, which are the laws, arts, technology, science, and skills necessary for civilization. Here is the definition as given in *Gods, Demons and Symbols of Ancient Mesopotamia*:

> **me**: The Sumerian term **me** (pronounced "may") is a plural, inanimate noun, and expresses a very basic concept in Sumerian religion. The *me* are properties or powers of the gods which enable a whole host of activities central to civilised human life, especially religion, to take place. A related term, gis-hur ("plan, design"), denotes how these activities ought, ideally, to be: the me are the powers which make possible the implementation of the gis-hur and which ensure the continuation of civilised life. They are ancient, enduring, holy, valuable. Mostly they are held by An or Enlil, but they can be assigned or given to other gods of, by implication, lesser rank.[34]

The *me* were originally held by Anu and Enlil, but the Sumerians believed that these powers to rule over human civilization were eventually handed over to Enki and transferred to Eridu. This story is related in the myth known as *Enki and the World Order*:

> Lord who walks nobly on heaven and earth,
>   self-reliant, Father Enki,
> engendered by a bull, begotten by a wild bull,

34. Ibid., 130.

prized by Enlil, the Great Kur, loved by holy An,
king who turned out the mes-tree in the Abzu,
raised it up over all the lands,
great usumgal [dragon], who planted it in Eridu
—its shade spreading over heaven and earth…
Enki, lord of the hegal [abundance] the Anunna-gods possess…
Nudimmud [another name for Enki], the mighty
one of the Ekur,
strong one of the Anunna,
whose noble house set up in the Abzu is the mast of heaven and earth…
Enki, king of the Abzu, celebrates his own magnificence—as is right:
My father, ruler above and below, made my features blaze
above and below.
My great brother, ruler of all the lands,
gathered all the *me* together, placed the *me* in my hands.
From the Ekur, house of Enlil, I passed on the arts and crafts
to my Abzu, Eridu…
I am the first among the rulers. I am the father of all the lands.
I am the big brother of the gods, the hegal is perfected in me.
I am the seal-keeper above and below. I am cunning and wise in the lands.
I am the one who directs justice alongside An, the king, on the dais of An.
I am the one who having gazed upon the kur,
decrees the fates alongside Enlil:

> he has placed in my hand the decreeing of the fates
> at the place where the sun rises...[35]

Enki, God of the Abyss

Samuel Noah Kramer, the famous Sumerologist, provides the best investigation of the Sumerian god Enki in his book *Myths of Enki, the Crafty God.* It even seems that the title he chose betrays the professor's suspicions when we compare it with Genesis 3:1: "Now the serpent was more subtil than any beast of the field which the LORD God had made..." Compare these words to the NIV: "Now the serpent was more crafty than any of the wild animals the LORD God had made."

Here are two quotes from Kramer identifying a number of important characteristics of this beloved Sumerian god:

> The craft of Enki is nowhere better represented than in magic. The one who knows the secrets of the gods and the ways of the other world is, not surprisingly, the god who knows the words and rituals to control the spirits. A large number of texts preserved in the

35. Samuel Noah Kramer, *Myths of Enki, the Crafty God* (New York, NY: Oxford University Press, 1989), 39–42.

> 'stream of tradition' are incantation texts, and Enki is prominent in the tradition.[36]

> Enki is the "lord of the watery deep," the "lord of hidden, unfathomable knowledge" in the depth of his "house of wisdom." He was also the chief magician of the gods, the great exorcist. His purifying water was used in incantations and magic rites. Ruler of waters of the underworld, lord of rivulets and brooks, of plenteous harvests, Enki was also the god associated with other goods of the earth, metals and precious stones. He was the patron of metal works and crafts generally. Patron of foundations, he gave instructions for building things… The sacred water basin, an image of the Abzu, was set up in temples in honor of Enki. And the sacred tree grew up in his cult city of Eridu.[37]

If we put together all of the different characteristics of Enki, we have a very provocative picture. He is the one who assumed dominion over the earth and is known as "The Lord of the Earth"; he is also known as the "Lord of the Abyss"; he is the god of wisdom and magic; he is associated with a sacred tree; and he is often represented as a dragon. To me the evidence is clear that Enki is the Sumerian representation of Satan—*he is the historical Satan.*

When Adam and Eve sinned by eating from the forbidden fruit of the Tree of Knowledge, they fell from the high calling that they were created for, and the dominion that they

36. Ibid., 100.

37. Ibid., 123.

possessed was taken up by Satan. That is why he could tempt Jesus in Matthew 4:8–9 by offering Him all the kingdoms of the world, and that is why Jesus referred to Satan as "the prince of this world" in John 12:31 and 16:11, saying that the time has come for Satan to be driven out!

The Father of Lies

So this brings us back now to the paradox that exists when we compare the Sumerian accounts with the Hebrew accounts. Why do they describe the same events but offer conflicting perspectives that are theologically one hundred and eighty degrees apart? It's simply because one account, the book of Genesis, comes from God, and the other account comes from Satan.

It's really quite that simple. The Sumerian story of the beginning of human origins is "Enki's story." As the god who exercised dominion and controlled the *me*—the arts and sciences of civilization—he also controlled the art of writing. Here is what Samuel Noah Kramer writes: "Enki is, in addition to the lord of magic and the great problem-solver of the gods, the god of craftsmen, including what we would now call artists and writers… Enki was, perhaps more than any other ancient deity, essentially identified with the spoken and the written word."[38]

The respected Assyriologist Georges Roux makes the same observation: "Enki-Ea, the tutelary god of Eridu, was above all the god of intelligence and wisdom, the 'broad-eared one who knows all that has a name.' He stood as the initiator and protector of arts and crafts, of science and literature,

---

38. Ibid., 5.

the patron of the magicians, the Great Teacher and the Great Superintendent who, having organized the world created by Enlil, assured its proper functioning."[39]

The *Historical Atlas of Ancient Mesopotamia* recognizes that control over the art of writing brought with it a tremendous influence over human affairs: "Among these basic elements [the *me*] was writing, considered to be a divine decree from the deities and under the patronage of Enki, God of Wisdom. From its inception, writing was therefore considered a gift of the gods and carried with it both power and knowledge."[40]

If we go back to the earliest written records in human history, Satan is there, smiling at us, pretending to be mankind's "Father" and our great protector, benefactor, and champion. He is *a* Father, but not *our* Father.

Jesus Christ announced his doom and explained that the same one who is "the prince of this world" is also "the Father of Lies": "Ye are of your father the devil, and the lusts of your father ye will do. He was a murderer from the beginning, and abode not in the truth, because there is no truth in him. When he speaketh a lie, he speaketh of his own: for he is a liar, and the **father** of it" (John 8:44).

The last days of Satan's rule are described in Revelation 12:7–9:

> And there was war in heaven: Michael and his angels fought against the dragon; and the dragon fought and

39. Georges Roux, *Ancient Iraq* (New York, NY: Penguin Books, 1986 [1964]), 95.
40. Norman Bancroft Hunt, *Historical Atlas of Ancient Mesopotamia* (Singapore, Thalamus Publishing, 2004), 24.

his angels, and prevailed not; neither was their place found any more in heaven. And the great dragon was cast out, that old serpent, called the devil, and Satan, which **deceiveth the whole world**: he was cast out into the earth, and his angels were cast out with him.

chapter five

THE MIGHTY HUNTER

IN THE LAST CHAPTER we looked at the Sumerian version of events that took place right up to the coming of the Great Flood. We also solved the mystery of the conflicting perspectives between Moses and the Sumerian scribes. We saw that the Sumerians, under the influence of their god, Enki, identified themselves with the line of Cain and traced their history right back to the founding of Eridu, the first city and original cult headquarters of Enki.

Writing wasn't even invented until sometime after the Deluge that wiped out civilization. So something significant must have happened after the Flood to allow Enki to become dominant, to rebuild Sumer, and to deceive the nations by using the Sumerian scribes as his propaganda mouthpiece. The next few chapters will explain how it all goes back to Nimrod and the Tower of Babel.

The Sumerian King List

According to the Sumerian King List, there were two dynasties that emerged out of Sumer shortly after the Flood. The first was Kish:

> ...Then the flood swept thereover.
> After the flood had swept therover (and)
> when kingship was lowered (again) from heaven,
> The kingship was (re-established) in Kish.[41]

The Dynasty of Kish was ruled by a total of twenty-three kings after the Flood. The next dynasty that is documented on the SKL is the Dynasty of Uruk. It contains a total of twelve kings and begins with these five:

> 1- **Meskiagkasher**, son of Utu, became high priest and king—reigned 324 years. Meskiagkasher went down into the sea and came out at the mountains.
> 2- **Enmerkar**, son of Meskiagkasher, king of Uruk, the one who built Uruk—reigned 420 years.
> 3- **Lugulbanda**, a shepherd—reigned 1,200 years
> 4- **Dumuzi(d)**, the [...], his city was Kua[ra]—reigned 100 years.
> 5- **Gilgamesh**, his father was a *lillu*-demon, a high priest of Kullab—reigned 126 years. (brackets in original)[42]

---

41. David Rohl, *Legend*, 164.
42. Ibid., 165.

The Dynasty of Kish was ended when Gilgamesh of Uruk defeated King Agga, the last king of Kish, after which Uruk reigned supreme. But this leaves a question regarding the first four kings of Uruk. When did they reign? This is important because Enmerkar, Lugulbanda and Dumuzi (as well as Gilgamesh) are all well-known heroes of Sumerian literature, whereas the kings of Kish are all relatively anonymous.[43]

What we find is that the Dynasty of Uruk interrupted and eclipsed the Dynasty of Kish shortly after it began after the Flood. Enmerkar is the king who built Uruk, according to the SKL, and other texts explain that Enmerkar ruled over a great Empire that conquered and dominated the ancient world for an extended period of time. Then, after Enmerkar's death, the Dynasty of Kish returned to power until the last king, King Agga, was defeated by Gilgamesh.

The Table of Nations

The Table of Nations in Genesis 10 provides the Hebrew history of what happened after the Flood. If we are searching for an entry-point for Enki's spiritual influence we need to look to the line of Ham. He was the son of Noah who mocked his father's nakedness, causing his son Canaan to be cursed. There are many unanswered questions regarding this incident, but the pattern that has been established is that

43. The kings of Kish are relatively unknown, but the last two kings on the list, Enmebaragesi and Agga, are actually the earliest Sumerian kings to be authenticated by archaeology (as opposed to only "literature") and are therefore viewed as actually being "historical." See: Georges Roux, *Ancient Iraq*, 135.

anything God blesses, Enki curses; and anything God curses, Enki blesses.

In Genesis 10, Ham's line is continued by four sons: Cush, Mizraim, Phut, and Canaan. The line continues through Cush, who had five sons: Seba, Havilah, Sabtah, Raamah, and Sabtecha, and then through Ramaah who had two sons: Sheba and Dedan. Then the record jumps back to, apparently, Cush's sixth son (?), named as Nimrod, who established the first post-Flood kingdom.

If we compare Genesis 10 with the SKL I believe we find a match between the line of "Ham – Cush – Nimrod" and "Utu – Meskiagkasher – Enmerkar." The Dynasty of Uruk is key here because it begins with Meskiagkasher who is named as high priest and king, and son of Utu. To be recognized as a priest and king on the Sumerian King List, he had to have been a servant of the god Enki, their favorite god and "king-maker."

On the SKL it is said that Meskiagkasher "went down into the sea and came out at the mountains." That is exactly what the biblical Cush did when he left Mesopotamia and became established in the mountainous coastal region of Ethiopia, which became known as the biblical "Land of Cush."

Here is what scholar David Rohl has to say about equating Cush with Meskiagkasher:

> Enmerkar's father and predecessor on the throne of Uruk must be the biblical Cush… The first ruler of Uruk following the flood is called Meskiag**kash**er in the Sumerian King List. You will immediately see the name Cush or Kush here, embedded in the longer Sumerian name. It seems likely that Cush is a Semitic/

> Hebrew hypocoristicon of the older Sumerian name Mes-ki-ag-**ka-she**-er. (bold in original)[44]

If Meskiagkasher is Cush, then his father, named as Utu on the SKL, must be Ham, the disgraced son of Noah. The Akkadian version of the name "Utu" is "Shamash," and Akkadian and Hebrew are both Semitic languages, with Ham perhaps being a shortening of the name S**ham**ash.

In the Sumerian myth *Enki and the World Order*, we see how Enki endorses Utu, and by implication the dynasty that followed him: "Enki placed in charge of the whole of heaven and earth the hero, the bull who comes out of the as̆ur forest bellowing truculently, the youth Utu, the bull standing triumphantly, audaciously, majestically, the father of the Great City, the great herald in the east of holy An, the judge who searches out verdicts for the gods, with a lapis-lazuli beard, rising from the horizon into the holy heavens."[45]

Utu, also known as Shamash to the Akkadians, and as the disgraced Ham to the Hebrews, came to be viewed as one of the primary gods of Mesopotamia, a sun god "regarded as a god of truth, justice, and right."[46]

This brings us now to the biblical Nimrod, whose kingdom began with the cities of "Babel, and Erech [Uruk], and Accad, and Calneh, in the land of Shinar" (Genesis 10:10).

---

44. David Rohl, *Legend*, 217.

45. *Enki and the World Order*, lines 368–380, *ETCSL Corpus*, last accessed on January 6, 2012, http://etcsl.orinst.ox.ac.uk/cgi-bin/etcsl.cgi?text=t.1.1.3#.

46. Jeremy Black and Anthony Green, *Gods, Demons and Symbols of Ancient Mesopotamia*, 184.

Nimrod was known to the Sumerians as Enmerkar, the king who "built Uruk" according to the SKL, who expanded the Kingdom of Uruk throughout the known world and established the world's first superpower.

The Return of the Nephilim

So what was so special about Nimrod? He is definitely named as a *descendent* of Cush, but he is actually mentioned in an odd place right after the two *grandsons* of Cush that came through Ramaah. My hypothesis is that Nimrod was *also* a grandson of Cush, and not his literal son.

If the phrase "Cush begat [*yalad*] Nimrod" (verse 8) means that Nimrod was Cush's immediate son, then he should have been listed in verse 7 along with Cush's five other sons. The meaning of the Hebrew word *yalad* is controversial, but I agree with the Bible scholars who argue that it does not necessarily mean "fathered" in the sense of an immediate descendent. In other words, Nimrod carried the blood of Cush, and continued his royal line, but he was not Cush's genetic "son." One possibility, among many, is that Nimrod was Cush's *grandson* through one of Cush's daughters.

Why is this important? Well, it goes back to Genesis 3 and the very first prophecy that predicted the coming of both the Messiah and the anti-Messiah:

> And the Lord God said unto the serpent, Because thou hast done this, thou art cursed above all cattle, and above every beast of the field; upon thy belly shalt thou go, and dust shalt thou eat all the days of thy life: And I will put enmity between thee and

> the woman, and between thy seed and her seed; it shall bruise thy head, and thou shalt bruise his heel. (Genesis 3:14–15)

It is well known that the prophecy of the "seed of the woman" was the very first Messianic prophecy in the Bible. God was saying that one day a human being would be born, descended from Eve, who would "bruise the head" of Satan the serpent. However, God was also predicting that the serpent would produce a "seed" who would be an enemy of the "seed of the woman."

The "seed of the woman" was fulfilled by Jesus Christ, the *literal* Son of God; whereas the "seed of the serpent" was to be fulfilled by the Antichrist, the *literal* son of Satan.

Dark Reflection #5:

Jesus Christ is the literal Son of God. The Antichrist is the literal son of Satan.

What this means is that *the Antichrist has to be a Nephilim*, just like the Nephilim described in Genesis 6 who were the offspring of fallen angels who had mated with human women. If Nimrod is indeed the Antichrist, then Satan *has to be* his genetic father, and therefore he must be a Nephilim.

Evidence for this appears when we compare the description of the pre-Flood Nephilim with Nimrod. Genesis 6:4 says that the Nephilim were the "**mighty men** which were of old, men of renown." The Hebrew word for "mighty man" is **gibbor**. This is the same word used to describe Nimrod repeatedly in Genesis 10:8–9, "And Cush begat Nimrod: he began to be a mighty one [**gibbor**] in the earth. He was a mighty hunter [**gibbor tsayid**] before the Lord: wherefore it is said, Even as Nimrod the mighty hunter [**gibbor tsayid**] before the Lord."

There seems to have been such a strong emphasis on Nimrod's identity as a "mighty one" that it became a popular expression even down to the time of Moses: "Wherefore it is said, Even as Nimrod the mighty hunter" (Genesis 10:9).

Luke 3:23 says, "And Jesus himself began to be about thirty years of age, being (as was supposed) the son of Joseph…"

I think the same can be said of Nimrod: "And Nimrod being (as was supposed) the son of Cush, began to be a mighty one in the earth…"

Nimrod was raised as the son and heir of Cush, but there was something very special about him that caused him to be called a **gibbor**. I believe his father was in fact Satan, the chief of the fallen angels, and Nimrod himself was a Nephilim, a throwback to the days before the Flood.

Satan's Fateful Decision

Let's take a step back for a moment and analyze some of these key points that we are arriving at. First of all, let's look again at God's prophecy against the serpent in Genesis 3. God was predicting that one day Satan (identified as the serpent in Revelation 12:9) would take for himself a human wife and produce a seed who would be an enemy of the seed of Eve, the woman whom the serpent had just deceived. This was an incredible prophecy to have hanging over one's head, considering the fact that after the Garden of Eden and up to the Flood there were many fallen angels who took human women for wives and produced Nephilim. These Nephilim ruled over and ravaged the earth for a long period of time before God finally wiped the slate clean by bringing the Flood. The book of Enoch describes their violence and even their cannibalism that filled the earth with wickedness. The Flood destroyed the Nephilim and cleaned up the wickedness on the earth, and along with it, there was a heavenly "police action" against the angels that had "crossed the line," so to speak, and taken human women for wives. These angels were captured, chained up, and cast into the Abyss to wait for judgment, as explained in 2 Peter 2:4 and Jude 1:6:

"God spared not the angels that sinned, but cast them down to hell, and delivered them into chains of darkness, to be reserved unto judgment."

"And the angels which kept not their first estate, but left their own habitation, he hath reserved in everlasting chains under darkness unto the judgment of the great day."

We know that at the Flood Satan was not among these angels. He may have reacted in dismay to the destruction of his Nephilim-ruled kingdoms that had filled the earth, but up until this time he was not among those who had "crossed the line" and mated with human women. If he had done so before the Flood, then he would have been cast into the Abyss, yet we know that he still has access to the heavens even to this day.

After the Flood the family of Noah was given instructions for replenishing the earth. This "Noachide Covenant" can be summed up in three simple commandments:

1: Be fruitful and multiply (God loves having lots of humans around).
2: Eat whatever you want (plants *and* animals—vegetarianism was repealed).

3: Don't be killing each other! (Human life is sacred—Genesis 9:6: "Whoso sheddeth man's blood, by man shall his blood be shed: for in the image of God made he man.")

Everything went well until Noah got drunk on wine from his vineyard, and then there was a rift in the family. This created the opportunity, as mentioned earlier, for Satan to begin to influence the line of Ham, which culminated in the life of Nimrod.

Apparently Satan just could not restrain himself, and as he looked upon the brand new peaceful civilization forming on earth he thought to himself, *I can rule over all of that! All I have to do is produce a supernaturally gifted Nephilim son predisposed to violence, and the nations are mine for the taking!*

The downside, of course, was that Satan would eventually face the punishment of being chained up and thrown into the Abyss. In any case, the temptation was just too great for Satan and he decided to produce Nimrod, thus fulfilling the prophecy that had been hanging over his head from Genesis 3:15.

For this crime, Satan had to have known that he ultimately faced punishment, which comes at the very end of the book of Revelation:

> And I saw an angel coming down out of heaven, having the key to the Abyss and holding in his hand a great chain. He seized the dragon, that ancient serpent, who is the devil, or Satan, and bound him for a thousand years. He threw him into the Abyss, and locked and sealed it over him, to keep him from

> deceiving the nations anymore until the thousand years were ended. (Revelation 20:1–3)

Up until now, much of this may sound like an unreal scenario based on a limited amount of evidence, but stay with me; more evidence is on the way and *we're just getting started.*

chapter six

THE TOWER OF BABEL

THE BIBLE PROVIDES only a short synopsis of Nimrod's career in Genesis 10, and then in Genesis 11 it describes the mysterious event involving the attempt to build a tower to heaven:

> And the whole earth was of one language, and of one speech. And it came to pass, as they journeyed from the east, that they found a plain in the land of Shinar; and they dwelt there. And they said one to another, Go to, let us make brick, and burn them throughly. And they had brick for stone, and slime had they for morter. And they said, Go to, let us build us a city and a tower, whose top may reach unto heaven; and let us make us a name, lest we be scattered abroad upon the face of the whole earth. (Genesis 11:1–4)

The location of this tower is given as "Babel" in Genesis 11:9, and is known as the legendary "Tower of Babel." Extra-biblical sources, including the Jewish historian Josephus,[47] reveal that it was Nimrod, whose kingdom began at Babel in the land of Shinar, who was the mastermind behind this building project.

The Tower of Babel (1563) by Peter Bruegel the Elder

---

47. "Now it was Nimrod who excited them to such an affront and contempt of God…a bold man, and of great strength of hand… He…gradually changed the government into tyranny—seeing no other way of turning men from the fear of God, but to bring them into a constant dependence upon his own power. He also said he would be revenged on God, if he should have a mind to drown the world again… And that he would avenge himself on God for destroying their forefathers!" Josephus, *Antiquities*, Part I, 4:2. Online edition available at http://www.sacred-texts.com/jud/josephus/ant-1.htm.

The Sumerian records of King Enmerkar of Uruk support the biblical account. There are four primary Sumerian sources that document the career of Enmerkar, and they can all be read online at the Electronic Text Corpus of Sumerian Literature maintained by the University of Oxford, England.[48] These sources are:

Enmerkar and the Lord of Aratta
Enmerkar and Ensuhgirana
Lugulbanda in the Mountain Cave
Lugulbanda and the Anzu Bird

The most important of these source texts, which is also the longest piece of Sumerian literature in existence, is *Enmerkar and the Lord of Aratta*. In this story, Enmerkar the king of Uruk makes a plea to the goddess Inana, whom he refers to as his sister. He asks her for help in coercing the distant mountain kingdom of Aratta into supplying him with building materials for two specific projects: One is the renovation of the temple of Inana at Uruk, and the other is the rebuilding of the "great shrine" of the Abzu for the god Enki in Eridu.

Here is the text of Enmerkar's plea to the goddess Inana. Note that Eridu is translated as "Eridug" in this version, and Uruk is "Unug." The name "Kulaba" is another name referring to the city of Uruk, Enmerkar's political capital:

> My sister, let Aratta fashion gold and silver skilfully on my behalf for Unug. Let them cut the flawless lapis

48. The *ETCSL Corpus* "Catalogue of available texts" can be accessed at http://etcsl.orinst.ox.ac.uk/edition2/etcslbycat.php.

> lazuli from the blocks, let them…the translucence of the flawless lapis lazuli…build a holy mountain in Unug. Let Aratta build a temple brought down from heaven—your place of worship, the Shrine E-ana; let Aratta skilfully fashion the interior of the holy ĝipar, your abode; may I, the radiant youth, may I be embraced there by you. Let Aratta submit beneath the yoke for Unug on my behalf. Let the people of Aratta bring down for me the mountain stones from their mountain, build the great shrine for me, erect the great abode for me, make the great abode, the abode of the gods, famous for me, make my *me* prosper in Kulaba, make the *abzu* grow for me like a holy mountain, make Eridug gleam for me like the mountain range, cause the *abzu* shrine to shine forth for me like the silver in the lode. When in the *abzu* I utter praise, when I bring the *me* from Eridug, when, in lordship, I am adorned with the crown like a purified shrine, when I place on my head the holy crown in Unug Kulaba, then may the… people marvel admiringly, and may Utu witness it in joy.[49]

> …let them take the mountain stones, and rebuild for me the great shrine Eridug, the *abzu*, the E-nun; let them adorn its architrave for me… Let them make its protection spread over the Land for me.[50]

---

49. *Enmerkar and the Lord of Aratta*, lines 38–64, from the *ETCSL Corpus*, last accessed March 11, 2012, http://etcsl.orinst.ox.ac.uk/cgi-bin/etcsl.cgi?text=t.1.8.2.3#.
50. Ibid., lines 490–496, last accessed March 11, 2012.

Eridu: the Original Babylon

There are a number of similarities between the Sumerian *Arrata* epic and the Genesis accounts of Nimrod and the Tower of Babel. Nimrod's kingdom began at Babel and Erech (Uruk). The name Babel is related to the Akkadian word Bab-ilu, meaning "Gate of God." Eridu was the original "Gate of God" by being the first city where "kingship descended from heaven," according to the SKL. In fact, in his Greek translation of the Sumerian King List, the Babylonian high priest Berossos simply translated the name of the city of Eridu as "Babylon."[51]

Eridu was Enki's original city, the location of the *abzu* shrine, which was also known as the "great shrine," the "great abode," and the "abode of the gods." Enmerkar's plan was for it to be rebuilt and grow "like a holy mountain." Eridu was the original Babylon, the location of the Tower of Babel, which was an attempt by Nimrod to rebuild and enlarge on a massive scale Enki's original *abzu* temple-shrine that had existed before the Flood.

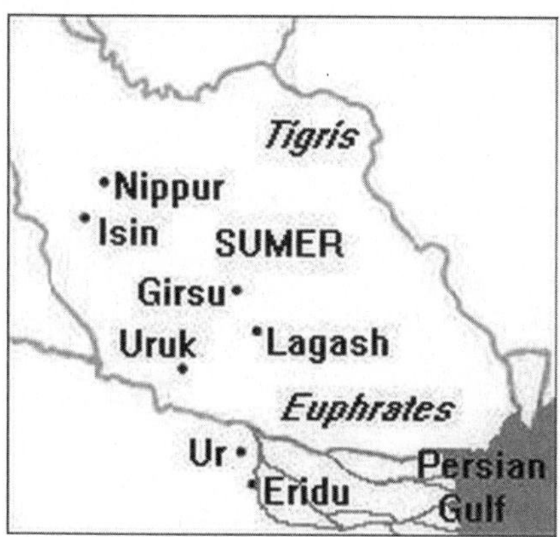

51. Gerald Verbrugghe and John Wickersham, *Berossos and Manetho* (Ann Arbor, MI: University of Michigan Press, 1996), 70.

Eridu was a Sumerian city located on the Euphrates River that was actually an island surrounded by canals. It was located in southern Mesopotamia near the Persian Gulf, which penetrated much further inland five thousand years ago.

Most scholars today believe that the Tower of Babel story was based on the memory of the temple located in the Akkadian city of Babylon in central Mesopotamia. This was the temple to Marduk built originally by King Hammurabi over one thousand years *after* the life of Enmerkar. It was known as the *Nun.ki* which means "The Mighty Place" in Sumerian, and also as *Bab-ilu*, the "Gate of God" in Akkadian. Here is David Rohl's explanation of how the original location of the Tower of Babel became obscured for such a long time:

> [Nun.ki] is otherwise known as Eridu—the very first royal capital in Sumer and the residence of the god of the abyss, Enki. Indeed, it seems that the sacred precinct at Babylon was named after that original Nun.ki, even going so far as to call the temple dedicated to Marduk, E-sagila or the "lofty house" and also known as the "mooring post of heaven and earth," after the original tower temple at Eridu. So, the biblical Tower of Babel/Nun.ki was not the second millennium Old Babylonian ziggurat at Babylon but rather the prototype third millennium ziggurat built at Eridu/Nun.ki in the Late Uruk period.[52]

52. David Rohl, *The Lost Testament* (London, UK: Century, 2002), 66.

To Make A Name

Remember that the Nephilim before the Flood were the "mighty men which were of old, men of renown." The phrase "men of renown" is literally translated as "men of the name." This implies that they had earned a reputation and gained recognition and fame.

Well, it seems that *fame* was also a motivating factor for the builders of the tower. In Genesis 11:4, they say, "...let us build us a city and a tower, whose top may reach unto heaven; *and let us make us a name*, lest we be scattered abroad upon the face of the whole earth."

In the same way within the *Aratta* epic, Enmerkar looks forward to the time when the *abzu* shrine is completed, when he will proudly wear the crown of Uruk saying, "...then may the people marvel admiringly, and may Utu witness it in joy."

Brick-built Kulaba

In Genesis 11:4, the people who begin building the tower also build a city: "Go to, let us build us *a city and a tower*..." The Genesis account explains that their primary building material was brick. The *Aratta* epic supports this, by referring to "brick-built Kulaba" *seven times* throughout the text. Kulaba is simply another name for Uruk. Brick works perfectly as a building material for single-story construction and for city walls, but building a multi-level tower with numerous floors, posts, beams, doors, and windows would require more than just baked mud-brick for structural support. That is why Enmerkar was so intent on having stone blocks delivered to him from

Aratta for the purpose of erecting the massive temple-tower at Eridu.

Archaeological Evidence

In my online series, "The Giza Discovery," I wrote at length about the archaeological evidence for the magnificent temple-tower that began to rise like a mountain in southern Mesopotamia during the reign of King Enmerkar of Uruk, the original King of Babylon:[53]

> In the late 1940s the ancient site of Eridu—modern Tell Abu Shahrain—was excavated by a joint British and Iraqi team led by Fuad Safar. What Safar found was evidence for a continuously maintained cult center of the god Enki. The very first shrine was a simple affair probably made of reeds, but a square brick structure was soon built and after this the inhabitants made continuous renovations and expansions. The excavation revealed seventeen different levels of construction for this temple, Enki's abzu, which during the Uruk Period became the holiest site in all of Mesopotamia.
>
> The most impressive discovery was known as Temple I, a massive structure with a huge temple built on a massive platform, with evidence of an even larger foundation behind it that would have risen up almost to the height of the temple itself. David Rohl believes

53. Peter Goodgame, "The Giza Discovery, Part Five: The Spirit World and Civilization," last accessed January 6, 2012, http://www.redmoonrising.com/Giza/SpiritCiv5.htm.

that whatever was built on top of this massive foundation was probably the structure that is described in Genesis as the Tower of Babel.

What was even more intriguing for the excavators was their discovery that precisely at its highest point of architectural achievement, the Eridu settlement was abandoned. Rohl writes that "quite suddenly, the island of Eridu suffered some unknown but cataclysmic fate."

Fuad Safar's academic analysis of the site states,

> ...the Uruk Period...appears to have been brought to a conclusion by no less an event than the total abandonment of the site... In what appears to have been an almost incredibly short time, drifting sand had filled the deserted buildings of the temple-complex and obliterated all traces of the once prosperous little community... At this point, there is a considerable hiatus in the history of the site, as it is known to us from the results of our excavations...the Jemdet Nasr epoch...is not represented at Eridu. During the Early Dynastic period also, there is reason to suppose that the fortunes of Enki's shrine at Eridu had reached an extremely low ebb. In fact, the only meager remains of this period, were indications on the slopes of the mound which now represented the ruins of the prehistoric shrine, that some kind of impoverished sanctuary still survived at its summit.[54]

54. David Rohl, *The Lost Testament*, 339.

The Confusion of Tongues

So what happened to virtually eliminate this ancient sacred site at Eridu? The Sumerian texts do not give a clear explanation for this mystery. However, the Bible does explain what happened at the Tower of Babel, and once again the biblical explanation finds support from the *Aratta* epic. Here are lines 134–155 of the text as translated by Samuel Noah Kramer:

> Once, then, there was no snake, there was no
> scorpion,
> there was no hyena, there was no lion,
> there was no wild dog, no wolf,
> there was no fear, no terror: human had no rival
> Once, then, the lands of Shubur-Hamazi, polyglot
> Sumer,
> that land great with the *me* of overlordship,
> Uri, the land with everything just so,
> the land Martu, resting securely,
> the whole world—
> the people as one—
> to Enlil in one tongue gave voice
> Then did the contender—the en (Lord)
> the contender—the master
> the contender—the king
> the contender—the en (Lord)
> the contender—the master
> the contender—the king
> Enki, en of hegal (Lord of Abundance),
> the one with the unfailing words, en (Lord) of
> cunning,

> the shrewd one of the land, sage of the gods, gifted
> in thinking,
> the en (Lord) of Eridu,
> change the speech of their mouths,
> he having set up contention in it,
> in the human speech that had been one.[55]

This passage within the *Aratta* epic is known as the "Incantation of Nudimmud," with Nudimmud being another name for Enki. It states that at one time the people lived in peace and spoke with one voice to the god Enlil, the Sumerian counterpart to the God of Genesis. However, in this text it is claimed that Enki was the one who appeared and changed the speech of mankind by bringing contention into the world. It is perfectly plausible that Enki was at the root of the problem, but the book of Genesis says that it was God, in agreement with other beings (whose identity we will reveal shortly), who caused the confusion of languages that brought a stop to the building of the tower which forced the abrupt abandonment of the site:

> And the Lord came down to see the city and the tower, which the children of men builded. And the Lord said, Behold, the people is one, and they have all one language; and this they begin to do: and now nothing will be restrained from them, which they have imagined to do. Go to, let us go down, and there confound their language, that they may not understand one

---

55. Samuel Noah Kramer, *Myths of Enki, the Crafty God* (New York, NY: Oxford University Press, 1989), 88–89.

> another's speech. So the Lord scattered them abroad from thence upon the face of all the earth: and they left off to build the city. Therefore is the name of it called Babel; because the Lord did there confound the language of all the earth: and from thence did the Lord scatter them abroad upon the face of all the earth." (Genesis 11:5–9)

Enmer the Hunter?

The name "Nimrod" is likely a Hebrew play-on-words, based on a phonetically related original name. The word-play is similar to the way in which the Hebrews connected the word *babel* (from *bab-ilu*, the "Gate of God") with the word *balal*, which means "confusion." Many believe the name "Nimrod" can be broken down to the prefix letter *nun* ("N") combined with the root word *marad* which means "to rebel," which aptly characterizes his relationship with God. This gives N-marad, or Nimrod, as it is translated today.

The name "Enmerkar" is a Sumerian name that is broken down into symbols transliterated as "En-me-er-kar2." David Rohl draws from the research of German scholar Werner Papke who believes the last sign (kar2) means "hunter," giving the Sumerian name "Enmer the Hunter." This conclusion offers support for equating Enmer-kar with "Nimrod the Mighty Hunter" from the book of Genesis, but it is really not necessary for proving the connection.

Near Eastern languages expert Michael S. Heiser informed me that this translation is suspect, so I did some research on my own by looking up the symbol in an online Sumerian lexicon. What I found is that *kar2* means either "to blow; to light up, shine; to rise," or "to insult, slander."[56]

I agree with Heiser and I doubt that "Enmerkar" is meant to be translated as "Enmer the Hunter." Perhaps it is better translated as "Enmer the Proud Blasphemer."

Whatever the case may be, the phonetic similarities of the consonant sounds N-M-R are undoubtedly there, and add further strength to the conclusion that King Enmerkar of ancient Sumer is the very same figure as the biblical Nimrod.

56. See the lexicon entries at http://psd.museum.upenn.edu/epsd/nepsd-frame.html.

chapter seven

HISTORY'S FIRST SUPERPOWER

SO FAR WE HAVE LOOKED at the *literary* evidence—the Bible, the Sumerian King List and the Sumerian myths—that place the biblical figure of Nimrod near the very beginning of Mesopotamian post-Flood history. Now we will look at the *archaeological* evidence of Nimrod's mighty empire that, through a ruthless strategy involving diplomacy, trade, and brute force, emerged as the world's very first superpower.

The rise of Uruk as the ancient world's pre-eminent city of power is referred to by modern archaeologists and anthropologists as the "Uruk Expansion." Here is how journalist Bruce Bower summarizes this phenomenon in his 1990 article "Civilization and its Discontents":

> [There is a] growing recognition among archaeologists that early Mesopotamian civilization experienced an unprecedented expansion between 3400 and 3100

B.C. The expansion occurred during the latter part of a phase called the Uruk period (named after the major city of the time), which began around 3600 B.C. Excavations conducted over the past 15 years indicate that southern Mesopotamian city-states, each consisting of one or two cities serving as political hubs and providing goods and services to thousands of people living in nearby farming villages, established outposts in neighboring territories lying within modern-day Iraq, Iran, Syria and Turkey. Even artifacts recovered at sites in the Transcaucasus of the Soviet Union show signs of Sumerian influence.

Such discoveries leave investigators pondering what made the Sumerians such hard-chargers in a world largely made up of subsistence farmers.

Many subscribe to the view of Robert McCormick Adams of the Smithsonian Institution in Washington, D.C., who calls the Uruk expansion "the first urban revolution." Adams says the economic demands of burgeoning Mesopotamian cities led to a great transregional civilization in the Near East.

Others, such as Henry T. Wright of the University of Michigan in Ann Arbor, contend the term "urban revolution" masks the fundamental significance of the Uruk expansion—the introduction, for the first time anywhere, of political states with a hierarchy of social classes and bureaucratic institutions that served powerful kings.

"Whatever the case, it was a revolutionary time, a moment of extraordinary innovations in art, technology and social systems," Adams says. For instance,

> in the late 4th millennium B.C., Mesopotamia witnessed the emergence of mass-produced pottery, sculpture as an art form and the harnessing of skilled craftsmen and pools of laborers by an administrative class to produce monumental buildings. The world's earliest clay tablets, portraying simple labels and lists of goods with pictographic symbols, also appeared, foreshadowing the birth of fully expressive writing around 3000 B.C.[57]

Much like the American superpower that emerged near the end of the twentieth century, the world's first superpower grew largely out of its materialistic pursuits and a desire to get rich through controlling trade.

Bower quotes from Harvard-based Assyriologist Piotr Steinkeller who explains, "The Sumerians wanted to become middlemen in international trade networks and reap big profits…they weren't forced to expand because of internal growth."[58]

The leading expert on "Uruk Expansion" studies is the University of San Diego-based Professor Guillermo Algaze. He is the author of two books on the subject: *The Uruk World System: The Dynamics of Expansion of Early Mesopotamian Civilization* (2005), and *Ancient Mesopotamia at the Dawn of Civilization: The Evolution of an Urban Landscape* (2008).

---

57. Bruce Bower, "Civilization and its Discontents: Why Did the World's First Civilization Cut a Swath Across the Near East?" *Science News*, March 3, 1990, last accessed March 11, 2012, http://findarticles.com/p/articles/mi_m1200/is_n9_v137/ai_8784921/.
58. Bruce Bower, "Civilization and its Discontents."

Journalist John Noble Wilford explains Algaze's view regarding Uruk's economic motivations: "Dr. Algaze compares Uruk's distant trading outposts to such modern examples as the Portuguese colony of Goa in India and the British colony of Hong Kong. The Uruk outposts, he said, 'reflect a system of economic hegemony whereby early emergent states attempted to exploit less complex polities located well beyond the boundaries of their direct political control and that this system may be construed as imperialistic in both its extent and nature.' "[59]

Economics provided the immediate impetus for Uruk's lust for power, but there was also a religious motivation behind it, much like today's American superpower is backed by the misguided religious notions that the expansion of capitalism represents the expansion of the Kingdom of Heaven, and that the accumulation of goods, worldly comfort, and material prosperity are essential doctrines of Christianity.

"Indeed," says Carl C. Lamberg-Karlovsky of Harvard University, "religious beliefs may have exerted an important influence on the Uruk expansion. Southern Mesopotamians believed their temple gods owned the land and humans were its stewards. Thus, Uruk city-states may have pursued a type of 'manifest destiny,' he suggests, claiming nearby lands in the name of their deities."[60]

"Globalization" is the term that is used to describe the rise

---

59. John Noble Wilford, "Trade or Colonialism? Ruins May Give Answer," *The New York Times*, May 25, 1993, last accessed March 11, 2012, http://www.nytimes.com/1993/05/25/science/trade-or-colonialism-ruins-may-give-answer.html.
60. Bruce Bower, "Civilization and its Discontents."

of the global "free market" and the decline of the sovereignty of nation-states throughout the world today. With global capitalism now backed up by the greatest military the world has ever seen, and over seven hundred American military bases across the globe, the world is now firmly controlled by the "merchants of the earth,"[61] the financiers, and corporate leaders who are the masters of the global marketplace.

In the book, *Globalizations and the Ancient World*, author Justin Jennings looks at the Kingdom of Uruk as history's first example of the "globalization" phenomenon that has periodically surfaced throughout earth's history, which today culminates with the American superpower:

> The rapid urbanization of Uruk-Warka during the Uruk Period must have sent shockwaves across the southern alluvium. By the Middle Uruk Period, the site's 100-hectare footprint was already ten times larger than any other site in the region and the city would more than double in size during the Late Uruk Period... The 50,000 people packed on the Uruk-Warka mound was a logistical nightmare. The city's frenetic growth would have quickly overwhelmed the exchange relationships that had previously supplied the towns of the southern alluvium, and the city's inhabitants would have had to increasingly rely on outside producers for food and other resources... A boisterous, informal economy likely formed; it would have brought agricultural products, animals, labor, spun wool, and other rural products into the city in exchange for exotic goods, copper

61. Revelation 18:23.

> tools, cloth, heavenly favor, and other urban products… Some of the towns closest to the city may have been tied to the site by tribute obligations at an early date, but it is likely most populations living outside of the city were initially connected more tenuously to Uruk-Warka through trade partners, family ties, cult allegiances, and other relationships…[62]

Uruk's dynamic expansion was indeed pushed along through economic and diplomatic means, but there is evidence that it also included a significant amount of violence and bloodshed, at least at the very beginning.

Journalist John Noble Wilford reports on the excavation of the ancient site of Hamoukar in northeast Syria that uncovered an ancient battleground. He writes that archaeologists describe it as, "the oldest known excavated site of large-scale organized warfare."[63] Hamoukar was a "flourishing urban center" before an army from the south conquered it near the very beginning of the Uruk Expansion:

> The discovery was reported by Clemens Reichel of the Oriental Institute of the University of Chicago, who was co-director of the Syrian-American excavations at the site…

---

62. Justin Jennings, *Globalizations and the Ancient World* (New York, NY: Cambridge University Press, 2010), 66.
63. John Noble Wilford, "Where War was Waged 5,500 Years Ago," *The New York Times*, December 16, 2005, last accessed March 11, 2012, http://www.nytimes.com/2005/12/16/world/africa/16iht-battle.html.

> The archaeologists reported finding collapsed mud-brick walls that had undergone heavy bombardment and ensuing fire. All around, they collected more than 1,200 oval-shaped "bullets" used with slings and some 120 larger round clay balls. The layer of ruins from that time also held vast amounts of pottery from the Uruk culture of southern Mesopotamia.
>
> "The picture is compelling," Reichel said.
>
> "If the Uruk people weren't the ones firing the sling bullets, they certainly benefited from it. They took over this place right after its destruction."
>
> Speaking by telephone from Damascus, Abdal-Razzaq Moaz, Syria's deputy minister of culture, said that Hamoukar was 'one of the most important sites not only in the Middle East but in the Old World,' and that the new discovery brought to light 'a kind of turning point in the history of civilization.' "[64]

This "turning point" was the regional triumph of the Empire of Uruk. Its extensive power and influence can be traced west to Egypt (which we will cover in future chapters), east to India, south to Arabia, north to Turkey and the Levant, and even throughout the Mediterranean Basin. This was the superpower that Nimrod ruled over prior to his fall from power.

We've already mentioned how the Bible seems to be silent regarding Nimrod's end, although the "confusion of tongues" helps to explain the disintegration of his kingdom. Archaeologists really can't explain what happened, although they clearly

---

64. Ibid.

see that the fall of Uruk happened very abruptly as a result of some sort of crisis or internal collapse:

> At the height of its development the Late Uruk culture included the following elements: a capital of indisputable preeminence, Uruk itself measuring one hundred hectares, with its sacred and organizational center at the Eanna precinct; a central territory that embraced all of Lower Mesopotamia (poorly known in this phase, unfortunately) and Khuzistan (Susa); a zone that we can define as the semi-periphery, Upper Mesopotamia, with a mixed culture; and a zone with commercial outposts distributed over the Anatolian and Iranian highlands. But this system had a short lifespan of only a couple of centuries. The settlements of the periphery were destroyed or abandoned, and the long development of the Eanna center was interrupted. It seems, therefore, that the first period of urbanization faced a crisis or a real collapse, after a long formative phase and the culmination of its internal organization (writing) and commercial expansion (colonies).[65]

This description of the Kingdom of Uruk having a "central territory" in Southern Mesopotamia and a "semi-periphery" in Upper Mesopotamia matches up perfectly with the description of Nimrod's empire in Genesis 10:10–12, which explains that it began in the south with Erech (Uruk)

---

65. Mario Liverani, *Uruk: The First City* (London, UK: Equinox, 2006 [1998]), 73.

and Babel (Eridu), and was then expanded to include Nineveh and several other cities in the north.

David Rohl summarizes Nimrod's career,

> By the end of his long reign the king of Uruk controlled much of Mesopotamia and had greatly enriched the cult centres of Sumer. He also controlled the donkey trade routes through the Zagros mountains and sea trade via the Persian Gulf. To the north, large heavily fortified colonies were established close to the main waterways and therefore connected the heart of the empire by means of fast-moving ships. Exotic goods and metals were pouring into the capital city of Uruk and, of course, Enmer's palace coffers. This really does make him the first potentate on Earth, just as the Genesis tradition states. In his guise of warrior-hero Enmer/Nimrod is remembered as the founder of the mightiest cities in Assyria and Babylonia, as well as a great builder in the old religious centres of Sumer.[66]

Dating the Uruk Expansion

The academic world of historians, archaeologists, and anthropologists is virtually unanimous in dating the end of the Uruk Expansion to a time right around 3100 BC. This may be viewed as problematic for some Christians who hold to the chronology of world history that is found within most English Bibles today. The Masoretic text is the basis of these translations, and according to this chronology, the Flood took

---

66. David Rohl, *The Lost Testament*, 63.

place in 2348 BC, long after the Uruk Expansion. If this is true, then we are looking at the wrong place in time for Nimrod. However, there is another biblical source for dating the early events of Genesis. This source is the Septuagint (LXX) translation of the Old Testament.

The Septuagint translation is a copy of the Old Testament that was translated from Hebrew into Greek by Jewish scholars in Alexandria, Egypt, sometime around 250 BC. The Masoretic text, on the other hand, was compiled (with significant changes) about 350 years later around 100 AD.

Barry Setterfield is a Bible scholar who provides an extensive argument for favoring the Septuagint chronology of the Old Testament over the Masoretic Text in his online article "Creation and Catastrophe Chronology."[67] Setterfield points out that, prior to 100 AD, the Jews used an authoritative text, known as the "Vorlage," which was written in a flowing cursive type of script known as paleo-Hebrew. This was the version of the Old Testament canon that was compiled by Ezra and Nehemiah and introduced at the "Great Synagogue" sometime around 440 BC. From this original Hebrew "Vorlage" text, which was used by Jesus and His disciples, there came three "recensions."

The first was the Samaritan Pentateuch, also written in paleo-Hebrew, which became the basis of the Samaritan version of Judaism. This version allegedly goes back to Tobiah the Ammonite who supposedly took a copy of the Torah from Jerusalem when he was cast out in 408 BC (see Nehemiah13:4–9).

---

67. Barry Setterfield, "CREATION AND CATASTROPHE CHRONOLOGY," September, 1999, last accessed March 11, 2012, http://www.setterfield.org/cchron/barrychron.html.

The second was the Greek Septuagint version of the Vorlage which was created around 250 BC which remains the official version of the Old Testament in the Eastern Orthodox Church to this day.

The third was the Masoretic text. This version was an "updated" version of the original Vorlage into a modern square Hebrew text type. Setterfield writes that this translation emerged out of the Council of Jamnia that took place in 100 AD, and afterwards older "Vorlage" versions were systematically destroyed by the leading Jews. This council was led by Rabbi Akiba ben Joseph along with Yohannan ben Zakkai. Rabbi Akiba was later involved in endorsing the false messianic claims of Simon Bar Kochba that led to the disastrous Bar Kochba Revolt against Rome in 132 AD. Akiba and Zakkai are both also known as early Kabbalists according to Jewish tradition.[68]

Setterfield analyzes all three of these recensions and compares them with portions of the Old Testament that appear in the Dead Sea Scrolls, in the New Testament, and in the works of Josephus. What he finds is that Jesus and the Apostles, as well as Josephus and the pre-70 AD Dead Sea Scrolls, all provide abundant evidence that the Septuagint (LXX) translation is more faithful to the original Vorlage text than the Masoretic text.

The Greek Septuagint version of the Old Testament was the Bible of the early Christian Church. According to Setterfield, this was precisely why the Jews at the Council of Jamnia repudiated it (and the Vorlage that it was based upon) and

---

68. See my online article, "The Divine Council and the Kabbalah," located at http://www.redmoonrising.com/agenda.htm.

created their own Masoretic version. Several centuries later, misguided Christian leaders led by Origen adopted the Masoretic text as the authoritative version of the Old Testament, from which it became the basis of our modern English Old Testament.

So why is all of this intrigue and debate important? Well, it has to do with dates. Based on the chronologies of the Septuagint (LXX) and the Masoretic text (MT) here are the dates of some important events in biblical history according to the two different sources:

Date of Creation:
MT – 4004 BC
LXX – 5810 BC

Date of the Flood:
MT – 2348 BC
LXX – 3536 BC

The Tower of Babel:
MT – 2100 BC (+/- 100 years?)
LXX – 3100 BC (+/- 100 years?)

The Calling of Abraham:
MT – 1921 BC
LXX – 2247 BC

Note that the Tower of Babel event cannot be dated precisely because it does not specifically fall within a biblical chronology. However, we can try to match Nimrod up with the third or fourth generations after Shem, who are Salah and Eber. According to the LXX chronology as calculated by Setterfield, these figures were born in 3399 and 3269 BC. If Nimrod was born anytime near these dates, then this means that the LXX translation of the Old Testament chronology offers a perfect fit if compared with the 3100 BC date for the end of the Uruk Expansion, which would have corresponded with the Tower of Babel event and the fall of Nimrod.

Regarding such an early date for Creation in the LXX, here is what Setterfield has to say, which is further evidence that the early church looked to the LXX as the authoritative version:

> Interestingly enough, a Creation date of 5793 BC is in broad agreement with the early church whose exegetes favoured dates of the order of 5500 BC. Thus Theophilus of Antioch (AD 115–181) gives a date of 5529 BC, Hippolytus (on some doubtful grounds) gives 5500 BC, while Julius Africanus (who died 240 AD) put it at 5537 BC. The Chronicle of Axum places it at 5500 BC while Talmudists (Petrus Alliacens) give a time around 5344 BC. Arab records quote 6174 BC.[69]

As we continue our investigation into the career of Nimrod, we will find that the Septuagint (LXX) version of the Old Testament, despite its idiosyncrasies, is actually *indispensable* to our research and reveals many mysteries that have been (purposefully?) written out of the Masoretic text.

---

69. Barry Setterfield, "CREATION AND CATASTROPHE CHRONOLOGY."

chapter eight

SHADOWS OF NIMROD

MODERN ARCHAEOLOGY and the Bible both agree on the dating of the fall of Nimrod and the end of the Uruk Empire sometime around 3100 BC. Before we move on to discuss the spiritual ramifications of the "Division of the Nations" that accompanied the end of the Tower of Babel, we will take a look at some interesting supporting evidence for this date.

In this chapter, we will look at ancient Indian (Hindu) records, and we'll also look at the myths of the Central American cultures of the Mayans and Aztecs. The ancient Hawaiians offer some interesting evidence in their myths as well. Later on we will open up another treasure trove of evidence when we delve into Egyptian history, mythology and religious beliefs.

The Age of Kali Yuga

The date of 3100 BC is hugely significant in the histories of ancient India. The *Mahabharata* and the *Ramayana* are the two major pieces of early Sanskrit Indian literature. Within the *Mahabharata* can be found the *Bhagavad Gita*, a discourse between Lord Krishna and Prince Arjuna in which Krishna reveals himself as a manifestation of God. The *Bhagavad Gita* has become known as "the concise guide to Hindu theology and also as a practical, self-contained guide to life."[70]

The context of the *Bhagavad Gita* is a battle known as the Kurukshetra War, and Krishna appears on the scene to convince Prince Arjuna that he has a duty to fight and defeat the opposing army, which happens to be led by Arjuna's cousins. Krishna appears only as Arjuna's chariot driver and councilor, although the stories make it clear that Krishna was himself a king and ruler of his own kingdom.

Arjuna and His Charioteer Krishna Confront Karna, c.1820

70. "Bhagavad Gita," *Wikipedia*, last accessed January 17, 2012, http://en.wikipedia.org/wiki/Bhagavad_Gita.

"The painting depicts the battle of Kurukshetra of the Mahabharata epic. On the left the Pandava hero Arjuna sits behind Krishna, his charioteer. On the right is Karna, commander of the Kaurava army."[71]

The truth is, the entire *Mahabharata* epic revolves around warfare and scholars have been divided regarding whether or not the greater Mahabharata War was truly historical or merely mythical.

One Hindu scholar, Dr. P. V. Holay, believes that the war definitely *was* historical and, based on astronomical evidence within the text, concludes that it began on November 13, 3143 BC.[72]

Using the same evidence plugged into computer software, in 2005 an Indian astrologer named Arun Kumar Bansal calculated that the birth of Krishna took place on July 21, 3228 BC.[73]

Modern-day Hindus believe that world history is divided up into four ages. We are presently within the age of Kali Yuga, an age of darkness characterized by violence and human selfishness. Of all the ages this one is the most "materialistic" and during this time mankind is separated from God by the widest possible gulf.

In addition to the other events dated in the *Mahabharata*, Hindu scholars also believe that they can pinpoint the starting

---

71. File: Arjuna and His Charioteer Krishna Confront Karna.jpg, PUBLIC DOMAIN, used by permission, last accessed January 20, 2012, http://en.wikipedia.org/wiki/File:Arjuna_and_His_Charioteer_Krishna_Confront_Karna.jpg.
72. Cr. Radhasayam Brahmachari, "Historicity of Mahabharata War," last accessed January 20, 2012, http://www.indianresurgence.com/history1.htm.
73. Ibid.

date for the age of Kali Yuga: "According to the Vedic scriptures, our current age, known as Kali-yuga, is one of spiritual darkness, violence and hypocrisy. Srimad-Bhagavatam (12.2.31) records Kali-yuga as having begun when the constellation of the seven sages (saptarsi) passed through the lunar mansion of Magha. Hindu astrologers have calculated this to have been 2:27 a.m. on February 18, 3102 BC. This took place some 36 years after Lord Krsna spoke Bhagavad-gita to Arjuna."[74]

Professor N. S. Rajaram appeals to ancient Greek sources to come up with a date that supports the astronomical calculations of these events in his article, "Search for the Historical Krishna":

> Amazingly, we even have Greek records pointing to the same approximate date. Greek travelers who came to India following Alexander's invasion have left us some tantalizing references to Krishna and also to Indian historical records as they existed in their time. Authors like Pliny referred to Krishna as Heracles, derived from Hari-Krishna. They record that the Indian Heracles—our Krishna—was held in special honor by the Sourseni tribe one of whose major cities was Methora. We can recognize them as Shuraseni and Mathura. (Shura was the father of Vasudeva and the grandfather of Krishna.)

---

74. "Kali-yuga and Sakabda," *Vedic Knowledge Online*, last accessed January 20, 2012, http://www.veda.harekrsna.cz/encyclopedia/kaliyuga.htm; also see: Satya Sarada Kandula, "Kali Yuga and Catur Yugas," last accessed January 20, 2012, http://www.harekrsna.com/sun/features/04-09/features1345.htm.

> Indian Heracles (Krishna) is recorded by the Greeks as having lived 138 generations before the time of Alexander and Sandracottos which we may take to be c. 330 BC. Taking 20 years per generation, which is known to be a good average when ancient Indian dynasties are involved, we are led to the computation 2760 + 330 = 3090 BC which is remarkably close to the Kali date of 3102 BC. So a reckoning based on ancient Greek records takes us again to the traditional date of c. 3100 BC.
>
> In summary, we may safely conclude that technical and literary evidence from several independent sources point to the traditional Kali date of 3102 BC as being close to the actual date of the Mahabharata War. We have therefore overwhelming evidence showing that Krishna was a historical figure who must have lived within a century on either side of that date, i.e., in the 3200–3000 BC period.[75]

According to Hindu tradition the age of Kali Yuga began with the death of Lord Krishna himself, when he broke free of his material shell and "dis-incarnated." The story goes that he died while resting under a tree, after a hunter who had mistaken him for a deer shot him with an arrow.[76]

---

75. N. S. Rajaram, "Search for the Historical Krishna," by N. S. *Vedic Knowledge Online*, last accessed January 20, 2012, http://www.veda.harekrsna.cz/encyclopedia/historical-krsna.htm.
76. "Story Matters: Relevant Lilas from Lord Krishna's Life," last accessed January 20, 2012, http://surrealist.org/gurukula/storymatters/krishna.html.

So, according to the most-revered Hindu texts, the world suffered a great blow and entered the ominous "Dark Age" of Kali Yuga on February 18, 3102, when Lord Krishna was killed.

I haven't spent a great deal of time researching the ancient Hindu texts, but for me the connections between Krishna and Nimrod seem to be too provocative to ignore. What must also be mentioned, however, is that there is also a widespread Hindu expectation of the *return* of Krishna in the near future, to rescue the world from its present chaos.[77]

The Mayan Calendar

According to the relevant experts, the world-famous Mayan calendar which, everyone knows, ends on December 21, 2012, *actually began back on August 13, 3114 BC.*

Central American calendar stone

77. "India Awaits Vishnu's Return," *Hinduism Today Magazine*, March 1, 1992, last accessed March 11, 2012, http://www.hinduismtoday.com/modules/smartsection/makepdf.php?itemid=908.

The Mayan sources that are available at this time are relatively silent regarding what happened at this early date, just as they are regarding the meaning of the end date. However, just as the Hindus expect the return of Krishna, whose death dates back to the same time-frame around 3100 BC, so, too, did the Mayans expect the return of one of their primary gods, Kukulcan, known later to the Aztecs as Quetzalcoatl.

Journalist Chris Tidwell explores this subject in his article "The Mayan Mystery: Who was Kukulcan and Quetzalcoatl":

> Kukulcan is one of the three gods that was thought to have created the Earth. He is a serpent in his natural form and was responsible for teaching the Mayan's about such things as how to run a civilization, agriculture, and medicine. After a brief period of being on Earth Kukulcan returned to the ocean telling the Mayans that he would return at some later date. Mayans perceived European settlers as the second coming of their god Kukulcan and this was eventually lead to the trust between the two cultures, and the eventual defeat of the Mayans culture…
>
> Aztecs worshiped a similar god, Quetzalcoatl, who also matches the description of Kukulcan. Quetzalcoatl taught many of the same things as Kukulcan and once Spanish conquistadors began to arrive in Mesoamerica they were also accepted as gods by the Aztecs. This would lead some to believe that both Quetzalcoatl, and Kukulcan were indeed the same deity, or man as it may be the case.[78]

78. Chris Tidwell, "The Mayan Mystery: Who was Kukulcan and Quetzalcoatl," *Yahoo Voices*, April 25, 2007, last accessed March

Lono and Captain Cook

According to ancient Hawaiian beliefs, the god Lono played a civilizing role similar to that of Kukulcan/Quetzalcoatl:

> In Hawaiian mythology, the deity Lono is associated with fertility, agriculture, rainfall, and music. In one of the many Hawaiian legends of Lono, he is a fertility and music god who descended to Earth on a rainbow to marry Laka. In agricultural and planting traditions, Lono was identified with rain and food plants. He was one of the four gods (with Kū, Kāne, and Kāne's twin brother Kanaloa) who existed before the world was created. Lono was also the god of peace.[79]

Just as the Aztecs at first embraced the Spanish conquistador Hernan Cortes as the expected return of their god Quetzalcoatl, so, too, did the Hawaiians at first embrace the British naval explorer Captain James Cook as the expected return of their god Lono.

As our research continues we will show that the return of an ancient god is an expectation that remains at the heart of nearly every pagan culture. I believe that all of these pagan expectations have their roots in the biblical Nimrod, a historical figure who ruled over the very first superpower in human history, who was killed sometime around 3100 BC, and who is, likewise, expected to return.

11, 2012, http://www.associatedcontent.com/article/217747/the_mayan_mystery_who_was_kukulcan.html?cat=37.

79. "Lono," *Wikipedia*, last modified October 24, 2011, http://en.wikipedia.org/wiki/Lono.

chapter nine

THE DIVISION OF THE NATIONS

THE BOOK OF GENESIS records that the ambitious agenda of the people building the Tower of Babel was brought to a halt by the divine decree to break up the peoples of the earth into different languages:

> And the Lord came down to see the city and the tower, which the children of men builded. And the Lord said, Behold, the people is one, and they have all one language; and this they begin to do: and now nothing will be restrained from them, which they have imagined to do. Go to, let us go down, and there confound their language, that they may not understand one another's speech. So the Lord scattered them abroad from thence upon the face of all the earth: and they left off to build the city. Therefore is the name of it called Babel; because the Lord did there confound

> the language of all the earth: and from thence did the Lord scatter them abroad upon the face of all the earth. (Genesis 11:5–9)

At this time the surrounding regions had all been subjugated to the political and economic power of the kingdom of Uruk. The whole world revolved around this city and there was nothing to prevent the world's rapid decline into the kind of situation that had existed before the Flood, just a few generations earlier. The world stood in awe of Nimrod, the Nephilim king, and was being forced into the worship of the god Enki, Nimrod's true father, whom we have identified as the historical Satan. The focal point of this new religion was the Tower of Babel, the massive *abzu* (Abyss)-temple that was being rebuilt at Eridu, Enki's cult headquarters, which was the original Babylon. Divine intervention was clearly called for.

We are very familiar with the fact that the division of the nations and the breakup of Nimrod's empire was brought about by the "confusion of tongues," which seems to have been a divine decree that brought about the spontaneous and supernatural appearance of many different languages at once. This was the *physical* aspect of God's decision to break up the kingdom of Uruk. However, what many don't realize is that the division of the nations also contained a very important *spiritual* aspect as well.

The Historical Origin of Polytheistic Paganism

When God decided to intervene at the Tower of Babel, He did so in agreement with a group of beings that surrounded Him: "And the Lord said… Go to, <u>let us go down</u>, and there confound their language, that they may not understand one another's speech" (Genesis 11:6-7).

Who was God speaking to? The extra-biblical book of Jasher explains that God was speaking to a particular group of *angels* who surrounded Him:

> And they built the tower and the city, and they did this thing daily until many days and years were elapsed. And God said to the seventy angels who stood foremost before him, to those who were near to him, saying, Come let us descend and confuse their tongues, that one man shall not understand the language of his neighbor, and they did so unto them. (Jasher 9:31–32)

What we see is that the decision to break up Nimrod's empire was made in a "divine council" setting, which included God and this group of angels who were part of God's chain of command that was particularly responsible for watching over the earth.[80] God descended to the earth to break up Nimrod's empire along with this specific group of *seventy* angels. Both God and these angels agreed that Uruk's agenda had to be brought to an end.

The extra-biblical source known as the *Targum Pseudo-Jonathan* explains:

---

80. We can't spend a great deal of time explaining and defending the doctrine and theology of this truly biblical "divine council" concept, which is an area of biblical research led by Dr. Michael S. Heiser, whose writings can be accessed at www.michaelsheiser.com/ and www.thedivinecouncil.com/.

> And the Lord said to the seventy angels which stand before Him, Come, we will descend and will there commingle their language, that a man shall not understand the speech of his neighbour. And the Word of the Lord was revealed against the city, and with Him seventy angels, having reference to seventy nations, each having its own language, and thence the writing of its own hand: and He dispersed them from thence upon the face of all the earth into seventy languages. And one knew not what his neighbour would say: but one slew the other; and they ceased from building the city.[81]

The account of the division of the nations that comes from these extra-biblical sources is actually supported in the Bible itself. In Genesis 10 there is the table of the seventy nations that descended from Noah and his three sons. Genesis 10:32 explains that, "These are the families of the sons of Noah, after their generations, in their nations [Goyim]: and by these were the nations [Goyim] divided [parad] in the earth after the flood."

The division that took place as a result of the Tower of Babel event in Genesis 11 eventually resulted in the creation of the seventy nations that are listed in full in Genesis 10. These nations were divided by different languages, but they were also divided by the fact that they were each handed over to, and became spiritually governed by, seventy different angels. This was the *spiritual* division that accompanied the *physical* division of the "confusion of tongues."

---

81. "Targum Pseudo-Jonathan," viewable here: http://uwacadweb.uwyo.edu/religionet/ts/pjgen611.htm.

Deuteronomy 32 explains, "When the Most High divided to the nations their inheritance, when he separated the sons of Adam, he set the bounds of the people according to the number of the children of Israel. For the LORD's portion is his people; Jacob is the lot of his inheritance. So the LORD alone did lead him, and there was no strange god with him" (Deuteronomy 32:8–9, 12). However, note the wording of the ESV translation: "When the Most High gave to the nations [Goyim] their inheritance, when he divided [parad] mankind, he fixed the borders of the peoples according to the number of the sons of God. But the Lord's portion is his people, Jacob his allotted heritage… the Lord alone guided him, no foreign god was with him" (underline added).[82]

The term "sons of God" *always* refers to angels in the Old Testament, as in the reference to the "sons of God" who disobeyed God and took human women for wives in Genesis 6. At the Tower of Babel, the entirety of humanity was divided up into tribes and eventually seventy tribes emerged who were "allotted" into the hands of seventy angels. These are the "sons of God" who Deuteronomy refers to as the "foreign gods" who are distinct from the "Most High," who Himself chose Israel as His own nation.

The "gods" of the pagan nations that surrounded Israel

---

82. Regarding Deuteronomy 32:8, most Bible versions read "Sons of Israel" which follows the Masoretic Text, but the Dead Sea Scrolls and the Septuagint (LXX), as well as most updated Bible versions read "Sons of God." See the article "Deuteronomy 32:8 and the Sons of God," by Michael S. Heiser, located at http://www.thedivinecouncil.com/DT32BibSac.pdf, for a detailed argument that "Sons of God" is the original and correct reading.

were *real.* The Tower of Babel event did not just mark the emergence of different languages; *it also marked the very beginning of polytheistic paganism as the dominant form of worship throughout the world.*

When God revealed the Torah through Moses this fact was emphasized by God's intense jealousy over His people. He had chosen Israel to be His own nation and He would not stand for any Israelite worshiping a foreign god. Deuteronomy 29 explains the punishment that would fall upon Israel for slipping into idolatry, and the response that would come from the foreign nations. The text speaks as if these pagan nations understood that they had been given other gods, but that Israel had been uniquely assigned to the Lord Most High:

> Even all nations shall say, Wherefore hath the Lord done thus unto this land? what meaneth the heat of this great anger? Then men shall say, Because they have forsaken the covenant of the Lord God of their fathers, which he made with them when he brought them forth out of the land of Egypt: For they went and served other gods, and worshipped them, gods whom they knew not, and <u>whom he had not given unto them</u>. (Deuteronomy 29:24–26)

The spiritual "division of the nations" into the hands of the various "gods" is understood in the histories of the pagan cultures themselves. For instance, the Greek view is summed up by Plato in his book, *Critias*, written around 360 BC,

> In the days of old the gods had the whole earth distributed among them by allotment... They all of them

> by just apportionment obtained what they wanted, and peopled their own districts; and when they had peopled them they tended us, their nurselings and possessions, as shepherds tend their flocks...[83]

The pagan culture that the Hebrews were closest to was the ancient Canaanites. They believed in a god that resembled Israel's God—Yahweh Elohim—but they placed him far removed from human affairs and mis-characterized and slandered him, just as the Sumerians slandered Enlil. The Canaanites and Hebrews both referred to him as the god "El," but the Canaanites believed that the world was ruled by Baal, who was the effective king of the gods. Here is what Bible scholar Lowell K. Handy writes about the Canaanite view:

> The division of the world into regions of authority is ascribed to El in the narratives related by Philo of Byblos. These regions were distributed to various deities to govern under the care of and with the consent of El. Both material and immaterial regions were allocated by El. Even the realm of the dead was assigned to Mot by El.[84]

What is interesting about the Canaanite records are the repeated references in their literature to the "seventy sons of El." This was the group of gods that they believed had been

---

83. Plato, *Critias*, online edition available, last accessed March 15, 2012, http://classics.mit.edu/Plato/critias.html.
84. Lowell K. Handy, *Among the Host of Heaven* (Winona Lake, IN: Eisenbrauns 1994), 83.

given authority to rule over the earth under the direct command of Baal. This spiritual reality that has long been understood within paganism all *began* at the Tower of Babel with the sacrifice of Nimrod and the breakup of his empire that allowed it all to happen.

The Fall of Nimrod

For the moment the Bible appears to be silent regarding the downfall of Nimrod, so let's attempt to construct a hypothetical scenario of what may have taken place between God, Satan, the seventy angels, Nimrod and his empire, and humanity in general.

There was a certain point in time when God looked down upon the earth and saw that things were getting out of hand. Uruk was so powerful that, barring intervention, the whole world was headed for enslavement under Nimrod's comprehensive political/economic/religious system. It had all started with Satan's decision to bring forth a son, and had been enabled by Nimrod's eagerness to engage in violence in direct violation of God's command against murder in Genesis 9:6.

As Nimrod's empire grew it seems that there was a group of angels who observed Satan's plan with a combination of fascination, resentment and jealousy. These weren't necessarily "fallen angels," and even Satan can't be described as a "fallen angel" at this time, seeing as they all continued to have access to the heavenly council room with God, both during and after this time. However, it does seem that these angels were somehow under Satan's command, which probably dated back to a time before the Flood and perhaps even to a time before the creation of Man. In any case, these angels were resentful of Nimrod's success and in their hearts they wanted a piece of the action.

The growth of Nimrod's empire also brought corruption into the earth, much like the Nephilim had corrupted the earth before the Flood. Remember that after the Flood, God had promised that He would not carry out such complete destruction ever again, despite the fact that He knew that "the imagination of man's heart is evil from his youth" (Genesis 8:21). Well it seems that Nimrod's empire, while initially resisted by many, actually succeeded in captivating and corrupting the hearts of men. For this reason mankind must also be held at least partially responsible for God's decision to hand the nations over to the authority of the seventy angels. In the end, the division of the nations seems to have changed mankind's situation from being "united under Nimrod, against God" to being "divided among the angels, against God."

As a result of the "division of the nations" God got what He wanted: an end to the reign of the Kingdom of Uruk, the original Babylon; the seventy angels got what they wanted: kingdoms of their own to rule; and mankind got what they wanted: to continue to indulge their wicked hearts. On the other hand, the parties that suffered the most from the decision were Satan and Nimrod, himself.

Uruk was fragmented at the Tower of Babel event, and Nimrod was killed, but Satan was appeased in this decision by being allowed to plan a resurgence of Babylon in the last days, which will, once again, be ruled over by the *resurrected* Nimrod.

chapter ten

GOD JUDGES THE "GODS"

THE POLYTHEISTIC PAGAN SYSTEM of spiritual control over humanity remained dominant for about three thousand years, from Babel until the coming of Jesus Christ; it has continued in the shadows, as well as openly within a few surviving ancient cultures, for the past two thousand years.

At the Tower of Babel, Satan's great empire of Uruk was dismantled and divided up, but he remained at his position of "lord of the earth" and continues to exercise authority over his own chain of command, which includes the seventy angels who were given the nations of the world.

We have already referred to Satan's end, when he will be chained up and cast into the Abyss for a thousand years, before being let out once again and then finally cast into the Lake of Fire (Revelation 20:10). His role and purpose seem to always remain mysterious. Leaving these questions aside we will now turn to examine the destiny of the seventy angels who were given their chance to rule when Nimrod was removed.

The End of the Pagan "Gods"

The Bible is clear that God gave these angels an opportunity to rule over the nations of the world. However, I don't believe that they were given this position without certain guidelines and restrictions attached. I believe that God actually expected them to rule well and to treat mankind with kindness and justice. I say this because of what it says in a Bible passage that is very well-known within the field of "divine council" scholarship—Psalm 82, written in the familiar repetitive poetic form:

> God standeth in the congregation of the mighty;
> he judgeth among the gods.
> How long will ye judge unjustly,
> and accept the persons of the wicked? Selah.
> Defend the poor and fatherless:
> do justice to the afflicted and needy.
> Deliver the poor and needy:
> rid them out of the hand of the wicked.
> They know not,
> neither will they understand;
> They walk on in darkness:
> all the foundations of the earth are out of course.
> I have said, Ye are gods;
> and all of you are children of the most High.
> But ye shall die like men,
> and fall like one of the princes.
> Arise, O God, judge the earth:
> for thou shalt inherit all nations.

The passage begins by saying, literally, "God stands in the 'council of God,' he judges among the gods." This is a "Divine Council" scene with God speaking to a group of angels that surround Him. The Psalmist was getting a heavenly view of God's judgment against the "gods" who had been given the authority to rule the nations. It ends with the plea for God to arise, judge the earth, and take possession of the nations that the "gods" had been mistreating.

This cry for God to judge the earth is similar to what is heard at the opening of the fifth Seal of Revelation: "I saw under the altar the souls of them that were slain for the word of God, and for the testimony which they held: And they cried with a loud voice, saying, How long, O Lord, holy and true, dost thou not judge and avenge our blood on them that dwell on the earth?" (Revelation 6:9–10).

This cry for judgment hasn't been answered yet, but in both Psalm 82 and Revelation 6:11 there is a promise that the judgment will come, and Psalm 82:7 predicts that these "gods" will fall from their positions of authority and die, just like human beings do.

Psalm 96 is another psalm that looks forward to God judging the nations of the world:

> For the Lord is great, and greatly to be praised: he is to be feared above all gods. <u>For all the gods of the nations are idols</u>: but the Lord made the heavens. Honour and majesty are before him: strength and beauty are in his sanctuary…for he cometh to judge the earth: he shall judge the world with righteousness, and the people with his truth. (Psalm 96:4–6, 13)

In the Septuagint (LXX) version, Psalm 96:5 reads, "For all the gods of the nations are *demons*."

The prophets Isaiah and Jeremiah also prophesied judgment against the "gods" of the nations, which will ultimately take place within the apocalyptic "Day of the Lord" just before the Second Coming of Jesus Christ:

> The earth is utterly broken down, the earth is clean dissolved, the earth is moved exceedingly. The earth shall reel to and fro like a drunkard, and shall be removed like a cottage; and the transgression thereof shall be heavy upon it; and it shall fall, and not rise again. And it shall come to pass in that day, that the Lord shall punish the host of the high ones that are on high, and the kings of the earth upon the earth. And they shall be gathered together, as prisoners are gathered in the pit, and shall be shut up in the prison, and after many days shall they be visited. Then the moon shall be confounded, and the sun ashamed, when the Lord of hosts shall reign in mount Zion, and in Jerusalem, and before his ancients gloriously. (Isaiah 24:19–23)

> But the Lord is the true God, he is the living God, and an everlasting king: at his wrath the earth shall tremble, and the nations shall not be able to abide his indignation. Thus shall ye say unto them, The gods that have not made the heavens and the earth, even they shall perish from the earth, and from under these heavens. (Jeremiah 10:10–11)

The final judgment against the "gods" of the nations, who are merely the devil's angels, will come after they are cast onto the earth during the Day of the Lord as predicted in Revelation:

> And there was war in heaven: Michael and his angels fought against the dragon; and the dragon fought and his angels, and prevailed not; neither was their place found any more in heaven. And the great dragon was cast out, that old serpent, called the Devil, and Satan, which deceiveth the whole world: he was cast out into the earth, <u>and his angels were cast out with him.</u> (Revelation 12:7–9)

God's Plan to Redeem the Nations

The angels that rule the nations were given their opportunity at the Tower of Babel. There is about a thousand years of history between this event in Genesis 11 and the calling of Abraham in Genesis 12, during which time God may have been observing how things were going. Psalm 82, as well as other texts, shows that these angels *failed* to rule justly and now stand *condemned*. This meant that God needed to initiate His original plan of bringing redemption to the entire world through the "seed of the woman."

It all started with Abraham, whom God called out from ancient Sumer saying that through him all the nations of the earth would be blessed:

> Now the Lord had said unto Abram, Get thee out of thy country, and from thy kindred, and from thy

> father's house, unto a land that I will shew thee: And I will make of thee a great nation, and I will bless thee, and make thy name great; and thou shalt be a blessing: And I will bless them that bless thee, and curse him that curseth thee: and in thee shall all families of the earth be blessed. (Genesis 12:1–3)

Abraham was the father of Israel, God's nation, which was completely set apart and unique from all the other nations of the world that were ruled by the seventy angels.[85]

After the nation of Israel emerged from Egypt, God gave Moses the Law to guide the young nation. Within it was included the early history of mankind that set the record straight and contradicted the distortions that had been purposely embedded in other pagan-influenced accounts.

Slowly, speaking through His prophets, the Lord began to reveal the plan of redemption that would take place through the appearance and sacrificial death of the Messiah, who would eventually judge all nations, defeat the devil and his hosts, and establish an eternal kingdom of righteousness throughout the earth.

The Hebrews knew they were unique and they also knew that the other nations of the earth ultimately depended upon them for salvation. The Feast of Tabernacles was an event that was celebrated every year in Israel, and through it the Hebrews remained aware of their important role.

The details for observing this Feast are given in Numbers

85. Michael the archangel was the angelic protector of Israel, but the Hebrews didn't worship him and they put all of their focus and devotion on God alone.

29:12–34, and they were given to Israel by God, Himself. The Lord took all seven of Israel's annual Feasts very seriously, because they pointed to the coming of the Messiah.

The Feast of Tabernacles, also known as Sukkot, was the bloodiest Feast in Israel's calendar because it involved the sacrifice, over seven days, of exactly *seventy* bulls on the altar, in addition to a variety of other animal sacrifices. Over time the Hebrews came to understand that the seventy bulls were offered on behalf of the sins of the seventy pagan nations of the world.

Of course the exact number of pagan nations has always fluctuated, but the number seventy has always stood as a symbolic number representative of the Gentile nations. Ancient Jewish commentaries on the book of Numbers support this understanding, and offer their opinion on what it meant when Jerusalem was destroyed by the Romans and the sacrifices were forcefully ended back in 70 AD:

> Said R. Eleazar, "What do these seventy bullocks stand for? They stand for the seventy nations..." Said R. Yohanan, "It's too bad for the idolators who suffer loss and don't know what they have lost. When the house of the sanctuary was standing, the altar would make atonement for them. And now who makes atonement for them?" (*Talmud*, Sukkah 55b)[86]

> If the nations of the world had only known how much they needed the Temple, they would have

86. "The Babylonian Talmud: Sukkah," last accessed March 13, 2012, at http://juchre.org/talmud/sukkah/sukkah3.htm.

> surrounded it with armed fortresses to protect it. (*Bamidbar Rabbah* 1, 3)[87]

What these commentators failed to understand was that when the Temple and its altar were destroyed the nations of the world had already been redeemed by the blood of Jesus, whose life was sacrificed around 33 AD.

"Like Lightning from Heaven"

The number seventy also appears within a symbolic act undertaken by Jesus, Himself, that relates to the Kingdom of God demonstrating its power over Satan and his angels.[88]

The account begins in Luke 10, when Jesus chooses exactly *seventy* of His disciples and commands them to go ahead of Him into the cities and towns, proclaiming the Kingdom of God, healing people and casting out demons, just as Jesus had earlier commissioned the Twelve.

The number seventy was, I believe, deliberately chosen by Jesus to symbolically demonstrate to the forces of darkness that the power of the Kingdom of God was greater than the power of Satan—the ruler of this world and leader of the seventy "gods" of the Gentile nations. Here is how Jesus

---

87. "Holiday Lessons: The Festival of Sukkot (Tabernacles)," by Rabbi Chaim Richman, last accessed March 13, 2012, at http://www.lttn.org/R5_Article4_Sukkot.htm.
88. The deeper meaning of this event was first brought to my attention through the research and interviews of Michael S. Heiser—www.michaelsheiser.com.

responded to the seventy disciples after they returned with an amazing report:

> And the seventy returned again with joy, saying, Lord, even the devils are subject unto us through thy name.
>
> And he said unto them, I beheld Satan as lightning fall from heaven. Behold, I give unto you power to tread on serpents and scorpions, and over all the power of the enemy: and nothing shall by any means hurt you. Notwithstanding in this rejoice not, that the spirits are subject unto you; but rather rejoice, because your names are written in heaven.
>
> In that hour Jesus rejoiced in spirit, and said, I thank thee, O Father, Lord of heaven and earth, that thou hast hid these things from the wise and prudent, and hast revealed them unto babes: even so, Father; for so it seemed good in thy sight. All things are delivered to me of my Father: and no man knoweth who the Son is, but the Father; and who the Father is, but the Son, and he to whom the Son will reveal him.
>
> And he turned him unto his disciples, and said privately, Blessed are the eyes which see the things that ye see: For I tell you, that many prophets and kings have desired to see those things which ye see, and have not seen them; and to hear those things which ye hear, and have not heard them. (Luke 10:17–24)

In the days of the early Church, exorcism was an essential part of Christian life, and spiritual authority over the devil and his demons was often demonstrated. Here is what Saint

Cyprian of Carthage wrote in a letter to a pagan unbeliever sometime in the early third century, AD:

> The gods whom you adore we exorcise in the name of the true God, and they are compelled to leave the bodies which they possessed... They howl terrifically, entreat of us to spare them, declare, in the presence of their adorers, whence they came, and confess a future judgment... Those whom you adore, fear us; those to whom you pray, entreat of us to spare them; those whom you revere as sovereigns, are as prisoners in our hands, and tremble as so many slaves.[89]

I think it is absolutely fitting that through Jesus Christ, human beings now have authority over the very same so-called "gods" who once taught *us* that we were created to be slaves to *them*.

89. Father Candide Chalippe (2004-08-01), *The Life and Legends of Saint Francis of Assisi* (Public Domain Books; Kindle Edition), 8. This translation is of Cyprian's *Treatices*, Treatice 5:15, which can be found online at http://www.newadvent.org/fathers/050705.htm.

chapter eleven

LEVIATHAN

THE PROPHET AMOS WROTE, "Surely the Lord God will do nothing, but he revealeth his secret unto his servants the prophets" (Amos 3:7). I found evidence for the truth of this passage while researching the meaning behind the legendary beast known as *Leviathan*.

There are only five passages in the Bible in which this word appears. Three of them describe a physical fire-breathing, water-dwelling creature of incredible toughness and great size (Job 3:8, Job 41, Psalm 104:26), whereas two others refer to Leviathan as an apocalyptic symbol of evil, saying that God crushes its heads (Psalm 74:14) and that Leviathan's final end comes in the Day of the Lord (Isaiah 27:1).

Setting aside the physical aspects of the real creature (which is probably a single-headed, dinosaur-like water-reptile) we will focus on the symbolic and spiritual meaning behind Leviathan.

The Seven-Headed Threat

The origin of Leviathan can be traced back to ancient Sumer and to an artifact that archaeologists say was produced in the Early Dynastic period between 2800 and 2600 BC. It is a small shell-inlay carving that depicts a seven-headed monster, with a hero-figure striking one of the snake-like heads.[90]

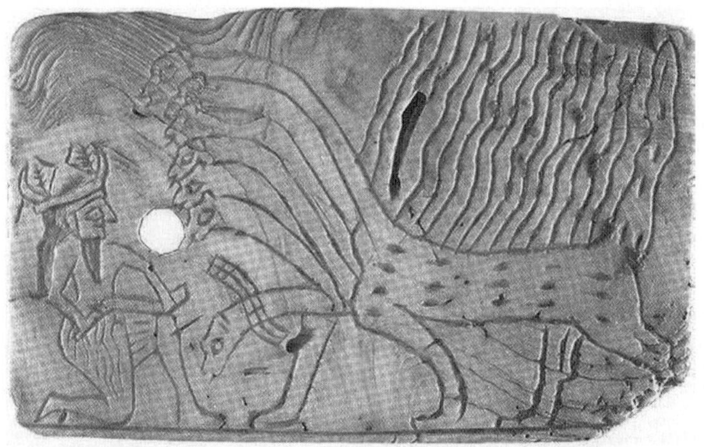

Here is what it says about this creature in the reference book *Gods, Demons and Symbols of Ancient Mesopotamia*: "A seven-headed musmahhu monster is referred to in mythological texts and depicted in Early Dynastic art as a kind of dragon with seven long snake necks and heads. This creature

90. For further information on this shell-inlay artifact, see Adela Yarbro Collins, "Satan's Throne," *Biblical Archaeology Review*, May/June 2006, 37. Also see "From Whence the Beast" by Simo Parpola, *Biblical Archaeology Review*, December, 1999, from www.biblicalarchaeology.org.

may be the seven-headed hydra killed by the god Ningirsu or Ninurta, also referred to in spells."[91]

When I first saw this artifact I was immediately struck by the similarities it has with the seven-headed beast described at the beginning of Revelation 13: "And I saw a beast…he had seven heads…and one of the heads of the beast seemed to have had a fatal wound…"

But why was this imagery appearing in Sumerian mythology that dates back to almost five thousand years ago? The answer, I believe, is that the truth about the seven kings of Satan (and their symbolic representation as a seven-headed beast) must have been revealed to mankind back at the Tower of Babel event.

The ancient Sumerians originally *knew* about the seven-headed threat. They knew that it was an enemy of God and man and knew that it was something terrible to be feared. However, over time, a mythology was created to alleviate those fears and to place it firmly in the past, whereas the Bible is clear that this threat will not be completely eradicated until the end-times Day of the Lord.

---

91. Jeremy Black and Anthony Green, *Gods, Demons and Symbols of Ancient Mesopotamia*, 168.

The ancient Sumerians were eventually convinced that their hero-god Ninurta, also known as Ningirsu, had slain the seven-headed beast, along with a host of other legendary monsters. One account is given in the Sumerian text known as *Ninurta's Return to Nibru*, which can be read at the ETCSL website.[92]

The slaying of the seven-headed serpent is also related on the famous artifacts known as the Gudea Cylinders. They document how the god Ningirsu appeared to a king in a dream to give him directions for building his temple. As part of the decorations the king was instructed to hang trophies on the wall, documenting Ningirsu's exploits:

> Facing the city, its place laden with awe, he had the Seven-headed serpent take its stand… Because these were warriors slain by Nin̂girsu, he set their mouths towards libation places. Gudea, the ruler of Lagaš, made their names appear among those of the gods.[93]

The legend of a hero slaying a multi-headed monster eventually made its way into Greek mythology through the story of Heracles slaying the Hydra as the second of his "Twelve Labors."

The Sumerian myths came from ancient antiquity while the Greek myths were developed much later. The bridge

---

92. "Ninurta's Return to Nibru," last accessed March 11, 2012, http://etcsl.orinst.ox.ac.uk/cgi-bin/etcsl.cgi?text=t.1.6.1#.
93. The Gudea Cylinders A and B, "The Building of Ningirsu's Temple," lines 696–721, *ETCSL corpus*, last accessed March 11, 2012, http://etcsl.orinst.ox.ac.uk/cgi-bin/etcsl.cgi?text=t.2.1.7#.

between them, which also connects the pagan seven-headed monster with the Hebrew *Leviathan*, comes from the myths of the ancient Canaanites.

The Baal Cycle

Modern-day scholars know a great deal about the ancient Canaanites because of the discovery, in 1928, of a collection of ancient cuneiform artifacts at a place called Ras Shamra on the Syrian coast. Experts have referred to these ancient texts as "the greatest literary discovery from antiquity since the decipherment of the Egyptian hieroglyphs and Mesopotamian cuneiform."[94]

The texts were part of an ancient collection held in a temple in the ancient city of Ugarit, a northern Canaanite capital, which was destroyed and buried around 1200 BC. The texts are written in the Ugaritic language, which is a Semitic language very close to Hebrew and also related to ancient Akkadian.

References to "Leviathan" appear in the Ugaritic creation myth known to scholars today simply as *The Baal Cycle*, which is similar to the Babylonian creation myth the *Enuma Elish*. Both describe the creation of the world and the exploits of their primary god (Baal for the Canaanites and Marduk for the Babylonians) as he rose to absolute power over the pantheon of gods and over heaven and earth.

One of the triumphs of Baal is given in these few lines within the *Baal Cycle*:

---

94. Wayne Jackson, "The Ras Shamra Discovery," *Apologetics Press*, last accessed January 20, 2012, http://www.apologeticspress.org/rr/reprints/Ras-Shamra.pdf.

When you smote Lotan the fleeting serpent,
Annihilated the tortuous serpent,
The tyrant with seven heads.[95]

Here we have a word that is directly related to the Hebrew word "Leviathan." The Canaanites referred to him as "Lotan," a serpent with seven heads who was a tyrant *annihilated* by their great god Baal.

Canaanite mythology also included a female counterpart/alter-ego of the great god Baal. She was the young warrior-goddess known as Anat, named as the sister of Baal, always depicted as young, strong, brave, fierce, and sometimes even as the *rescuer* of Baal, when he found himself in a tight spot.

In Greek mythology Baal is equivalent to Zeus, whereas Anat is equivalent to Athena, the warrior goddess of the Greek capital of Athens. In some of the Ugaritic texts Anat is named as the slayer of the seven-headed Lotan (along with a host of other monsters):

What enemy rises up against Baal,
What adversary against Him who Mounteth the Clouds?
Have I not slain Sea, beloved of El?
Have I not annihilated River, the great god?
Have I not muzzled the Dragon, holding her in a muzzle?

---

95. Passage taken from the article, "Behemoth and Leviathan—Creatures of Controversy," by Eric Lyons, *Apologetics Press*, last accessed March 11, 2012, http://www.apologeticspress.org/apcontent.aspx?category=9&article=184.

I have slain the Crooked Serpent,
The Foul-fanged with Seven Heads.[96]

Note that in the Canaanite passage above, the figures of Sea, River, Dragon and the seven-headed Lotan are all personified as gods or monsters that are subdued by Anat (which in the Baal Cycle are subdued by Baal). Now we will turn to Psalm 74 to show how the Hebrews and the Canaanites engaged in a literary competition with both claiming, "My God is bigger than yours!"

Scholars have noticed this polemical battle when they compare the writings of the Hebrew priests with the Canaanite priests. The Hebrews were always claiming that "El" was supreme, whereas the Canaanites often mocked "El" and claimed that Baal now had the very same power that the Hebrews ascribed to "El."[97]

Here is Psalm 74, with the very same figures appearing as in the Anat myth quoted above, but with the heroic acts attributed to God:

For God is my King of old, working salvation in the
midst of the earth.
Thou didst divide the **Sea** by thy strength:

---

96. *Myths of Anat*, as quoted in "Behemoth and Leviathan."
97. For an elaboration upon this polemical battle, see the article, "What's Ugaritic Got to Do with Anything?" by Michael S. Heiser, located at http://www.logos.com/ugaritic; also "Comparing the Baal Cycle with Isaiah 25," a blog located at http://epiginoskein.blogspot.com/2009/05/comparing-baal-cycle-to-isaiah-25.html.

thou brakest the heads of the **Dragons** in the waters.
Thou brakest the heads (plural) of **Leviathan**
(singular) in pieces,
and gavest him (singular) to be meat
to the people inhabiting the wilderness.
Thou didst cleave the fountain and the flood:
thou driedst up mighty **Rivers**.
The day is thine, the night also is thine:
thou hast prepared the light and the sun.
Thou hast set all the borders of the earth:
thou hast made summer and winter.
(Psalm 74:12–17)

Here we have a direct literary connection between the many-headed Leviathan of the Hebrews and the seven-headed serpent known as Lotan to the Canaanites. The psalmist seems to describe the defeat of Lotan as an *ongoing process*: "thou brakest the heads," rather than something that was completed in the distant past.

The prophet Isaiah appears to draw upon this foundation when he places the ultimate judgment of the "Crooked Serpent" Leviathan in the future, coming from the sword of the Lord during the apocalyptic "Day of the Lord":

Like as a woman with child, that draweth near the time of her delivery, is in pain, and crieth out in her pangs; so have we been in thy sight, O Lord. We have been with child, we have been in pain…

For, behold, the Lord cometh out of his place to punish the inhabitants of the earth for their iniquity:

> the earth also shall disclose her blood, and shall no more cover her slain.
>
> In that day the Lord with his sore and great and strong sword shall punish Leviathan the piercing serpent, even **Leviathan** that **crooked serpent**; and he shall slay the **Dragon** that is in the sea. (Isaiah 26:17–27:1; bold added)

All of this apocalyptic imagery is brought together in the book of Revelation. Starting with an image of a woman in labor, as in Isaiah, it then goes on to describe the Dragon and the seven heads that make up Leviathan:

> A great and wondrous sign appeared in heaven: a woman clothed with the sun, with the moon under her feet and a crown of twelve stars on her head. She was pregnant and cried out in pain as she was about to give birth. Then another sign appeared in heaven: an enormous red dragon with seven heads and ten horns and seven crowns on his heads. (Revelation 12:1–3)

In Revelation 12, the Dragon and the seven heads of Leviathan are pictured *as one*. This is true because these seven satanic kings truly are *one in spirit* with Satan, the Dragon. However, Isaiah and the Canaanite texts describe Leviathan and the Dragon as *separate*, which is also how they are presented as the vision continues in Revelation 13: "And I stood upon the sand of the sea, and saw a beast rise up out of the sea, having seven heads and ten horns…and the dragon gave him his power, and his seat, and great authority. And I saw one of his heads as it were wounded to death; and his deadly wound was healed: and all the world wondered after the beast" (Revelation 13:1–3).

The beast is Leviathan, the symbolic and allegorical representation of the seven earthly kings that Satan, the Dragon, uses throughout history. The head that is healed of a deadly wound is Nimrod, the first king of Leviathan who will also return as the last.

Mankind's knowledge of Leviathan dates back to Nimrod's culture of ancient Sumer, because it was at the death of Nimrod that the threat of Leviathan first emerged as a reality.

Seven Spirits

Satan's seven kings are seven individuals who are completely controlled by Satan. The spirits of these seven kings are at one with Satan's spirit. Similarly, the book of Revelation records that the Holy Spirit of God is made up of seven Spirits:

> Grace be unto you, and peace, from him which is, and which was, and which is to come; and from the seven Spirits which are before his throne. (Revelation 1:4)

> These things saith He that hath the seven Spirits of God. (Revelation 3:1)

> And out of the throne proceeded lightnings and thunderings and voices: and there were seven lamps of fire burning before the throne, which are the seven Spirits of God. (Revelation 4:5)

> And I beheld, and, lo, in the midst of the throne and of the four beasts, and in the midst of the elders, stood a Lamb as it had been slain, having seven horns and seven eyes, which are the seven Spirits of God sent forth into all the earth. (Revelation 5:6)

From these texts that speak about Jesus, and from what we have drawn from our study of Leviathan, we see that Leviathan is made up of the seven spirits of the seven kings of Satan, whereas Jesus possesses the seven Spirits of God.

It is often taught that the seven Spirits of God are named within a well-known Messianic passage of Isaiah that predicted the coming of Jesus:

> And there shall come forth a rod out of the stem of Jesse, and a Branch shall grow out of his roots: And the spirit of the Lord shall rest upon him, the spirit of wisdom and understanding, the spirit of counsel and might, the spirit of knowledge and of the fear of the Lord. (Isaiah 11:1–2)

Dark Reflection #6:

Leviathan is made up of seven satanic spirits.
Jesus Christ possesses the seven Spirits of God.

Many believe that this description of the Spirits of God in Isaiah is a perfect fit with the imagery of the menorah candlestick that was kept in the Temple of the Lord. It had a central lamp, surrounded by three pairs of lamps coming off each side. This makes sense when compared with what it says in Revelation 4:5 (page 136) because we know that the Jewish Temple was just an earthly copy of God's Temple in heaven. If the Jews had a menorah in Jerusalem then there is probably a menorah in heaven.

If Isaiah does describe the seven Spirits of God, that are as lamps burning before the throne of God, then "the Spirit of the Lord upon" is the central lamp, which is surrounded by the three pairs of Wisdom and Understanding, Counsel and Might, and Knowledge and the Fear of the Lord.

However, I have always regarded this interpretation with suspicion because in my reading of the text, I see not *seven* Spirits, but only *six* Spirits. Is "the Spirit of the Lord upon" really a Spirit? It seems to me to be only an *introduction* to the Spirits! All of this uncertainty was cleared away for me when I read this Isaiah passage in the *Septuagint* translation of the Old Testament:

> And there shall come forth a rod out of the root of Jesse, and a blossom shall come up from his root: and the Spirit of God shall rest upon him, the spirit of wisdom and understanding, the spirit of counsel and strength, the spirit of knowledge and godliness shall fill him; the spirit of the fear of God. (Isaiah 11:1–2, LXX)

In the LXX translation, we see that there are indeed seven Spirits. There are three pairs of Spirits: Wisdom and Understanding, Counsel and Strength, and Knowledge and Godliness; and the seventh and central Spirit is the "Fear of God."

This makes perfect sense because Solomon wrote that the "Fear of the Lord" is at the very beginning of coming into the knowledge of God. Indeed, it is the very first Proverb in the book of Proverbs: "**The fear of the Lord is the beginning of knowledge**: but fools despise wisdom and instruction" (Proverbs 1:7).

chapter twelve

THE MYSTERIOUS SIYYIM

THE SEPTUAGINT TRANSLATION of Psalm 96:5 tells us that, "…all the gods of the nations are demons." The demonic nature of the angels that were eventually brought into God's council room and condemned for not ruling over the nations with justice can be confirmed through a little bit of in-depth Bible study.

Consider the following Bible passages:

"He shall have dominion also from sea to sea, and from the river unto the ends of the earth. <u>They that dwell in the wilderness</u> shall bow before him; and his enemies shall lick the dust" (Psalm 72:8–9).

"Thou brakest the heads of Leviathan in pieces, and gavest him to be meat to <u>the people inhabiting the wilderness</u>" (Psalm 74:14).

"But <u>wild beasts of the desert</u> shall lie there; and their houses shall be full of doleful creatures; and owls shall dwell there, and Satyrs shall dance there" (Isaiah 13:21).

"Behold the land of the Chaldeans; this people was not, till the Assyrian [literally "Asshur"] founded it for them that dwell in the wilderness: they set up the towers thereof, they raised up the palaces thereof; and he brought it to ruin" (Isaiah 23:13).

"The wild beasts of the desert shall also meet with the wild beasts of the island, and the satyr shall cry to his fellow; the screech owl also shall rest there, and find for herself a place of rest" (Isaiah 34:14).

"Therefore the wild beasts of the desert with the wild beasts of the islands shall dwell there, and the owls shall dwell therein: and it shall be no more inhabited for ever; neither shall it be dwelt in from generation to generation" (Jeremiah 50:39).

Each one of the references above to the "inhabitants/wild beasts of the desert" is a translation of a four-letter Hebrew word—צײם—*siyyim* (or *tsiyyim*). Unfortunately, the English translations completely remove the supernatural and spiritual meaning behind this word.

Here is a definition for this word as given in the *Dictionary of Deities and Demons in the Bible*:

WILD BEASTS—צײם

I. **Siyyim**, ... is a plural derivative from the feminine noun siyya, which appears as an adjective to eres "land" with the meaning "dry land" (cf. sayon Isa 25:5; 32:2)...

II. In the conceptual world of the ancient Near East the "steppe/desert" and "ruins/ruined places" along with mountains and swamps were the habitations of the "counter-human world", not only were definite "desert animals" such as ostriches, gazelles and antilopes at home in the desert, but the desert also served as the habit of **various fabulous creatures which did not belong to any definable species. These were rather exponents of the powers that were associated with this sterile and barren realm...**

III. **The siyyim are evidently demonic beings (of the desert/dry land), whose exact definition is uncertain...** Thus the sinister animals which, together with demons, are listed in Job 38:39-39:30 inhabit all manner of accursed and ruined cities and regions. The animals which appear together with the siyyim in Isa 13:21; 34:14 and Jer 50:39 possess the same sinister connotations... They are joined in Isa 34:14 by the demon →Lilith. These beings populate former human settlements after they have been abandoned and returned to the desert whence they came... Like Isa 23:13, Ps 72:9 and Ps 74:14 are controversial pieces of evidence in understanding the siyyim. It is possible that in both cases **their embodiment of the chaotic or sinister forces is emphasized... the siyyim are not a zoologically identifiable species. The term is rather a collective designation for demonic desert beings... who represent a counter-human world of devastated habitations...** (bold and underline added)[98]

98. Pieter W. Van Der Horst, Karel Van Der Toorn, Bob Becking, *Dictionary of Deities and Demons in the Bible* (Leiden, The Netherlands: Brill Academic Publishers, 1999), 897–898.

In other words, what this dictionary is trying to say is that the *siyyim* (plural) are *demonic beings* of unknown origin. If we apply what we have learned over the preceding chapters to the passages listed above I believe we can find out exactly who they are.

Here is what I believe Isaiah 23:13 is trying to convey:

> Behold the land of the Chaldeans, they did not exist until Asshur founded it for the *siyyim*. The Chaldeans set up the towers and built the palaces, but then Asshur brought it to ruin.

From this perspective it seems that this passage is telling us that Asshur (Nimrod) built Babylon—the Land of the Chaldeans—for the *siyyim*, but then he brought it to ruin. This sounds like the *siyyim* may in fact be related to the seventy angels of the nations that are also referred to as "demons" in Psalm 96:5 (LXX).

From "Gateway of the Gods" to "Prison for Demons"

Isaiah 13:21 and Jeremiah 50:39 are both apocalyptic prophecies of the ultimate end of Babylon, when the city will be destroyed and thereafter inhabited only by monsters, wild animals and the *siyyim*. This prophecy of the aftermath of the destruction of Babylon is also repeated in Revelation, where we see that the *siyyim* can be directly equated with *demons*:

"But **the siyyim** shall lie there; and their houses shall be full of doleful creatures; and owls shall dwell there, and Satyrs shall dance there" (Isaiah 13:21).

"Therefore **the siyyim** with the wild beasts of the islands shall dwell there, and the owls shall dwell therein: and it shall be no more inhabited for ever; neither shall it be dwelt in from generation to generation" (Jeremiah 50:39).

"And he cried mightily with a strong voice, saying, Babylon the great is fallen, is fallen, and is become the habitation of **devils**, and the hold of every foul spirit, and a cage of every unclean and hateful bird" (Revelation 18:2).

Revelation seems to be telling us that Babylon, which was the original *gateway* for the seventy angels to come to the earth and receive their chance to rule over the nations, will in the end become their *prison*. The *siyyim* will be confined to the desolate wasteland of Babylon during the Millennial Kingdom of Christ, while the nations will enjoy the prosperity that will flow from Jerusalem.

Isaiah 34 gives a similar apocalyptic prophecy of the land of Edom, and once again the identity of the *siyyim*, when compared with the Septuagint translation, is proven as being *demonic*: "**The siyyim** shall also meet with the wild beasts of the island, and the satyr shall cry to his fellow; the screech owl also shall rest there, and find for herself a place of rest (Isaiah 34:14).

"And **devils** shall meet with satyrs, and they shall cry one to the other" (Isaiah 34:14, LXX).

King Solomon: Master of Demons

Psalm 72 records a prophetic prayer of King David for his son, Solomon. It predicts the glory of Israel's Golden Age under king Solomon, when prosperity and peace will reign and the kings of the nations will give him honor. It even says that the demonic *siyyim* will bow down to him:

> He shall have dominion also from sea to sea, and from the river unto the ends of the earth. The **siyyim** shall bow before him; and his enemies shall lick the dust. (Psalm 72:8–9; bold added)

This verse offers confirmation for the many legends that have sprung up in the Hebrew mystical tradition that say that Solomon was a great exorcist and was given authority over the demonic realm by God. The Midrashim, the Talmud, the Kabbalah, and various apocryphal and occult sources are full of tales of King Solomon's mastery over the demons.[99]

Here is what one source says about *The Goetia*, an occult manuscript known as a *grimoire* that instructs in the summoning of demons:

> *Ars Goetia* is the title of the first section of *The Lesser Key of Solomon*, containing descriptions of the seventy-two demons that King Solomon is said to have evoked and confined in a bronze vessel sealed by magic symbols, and that he obliged to work for him. The *Ars Goetia* assigns a rank and a title of nobility to each member of the infernal hierarchy, and gives the demons 'signs they have to pay allegiance to', or seals.[100]

---

99. For instance, see the article "Solomon and the Demons," by M.R. James, located at http://www.users.globalnet.co.uk/~pardos/ArchiveSolDemons.html.
100. "Goetia," *Wikipedia*, last modified January 13, 2012, http://en.wikipedia.org/wiki/Goetia.

In the occult world of pagan sorcery and Jewish Kabbalah it is generally recognized that the dark demons of the *Goetia* have their positive counterpart in the angels of the *Shem Ha'Mephorash*, which are described in a kabbalistic text:

> Rabbi Shimon said: There is a great and strong, tall supernal tree, which is Zeir Anpin. Those above and those below are sustained through it… And seventy branches, which are the seventy princes that are appointed over the seventy nations of the world, rise in it and are nurtured by it… When the time of dominion arrives for each branch, they all want to completely destroy the trunk of the tree, which is the mainstay of the branches, that rules over Yisrael who are joined with it. And when the domination of the trunk of the tree reaches them, which is the portion of Yisrael, it wants to guard them, and to arrange peace among them all. For this purpose, seventy oxen are offered during Sukkot to bring peace among the seventy branches in the tree, which are the seventy patron angels of the nations of the world.[101]

The name for these angels, *Shem Ha'Mephorash*, means "Names of Division." The occult world directly connects them with the angels of the Gentile nations that we have been tracing all the way back to their rise to power at the Tower of Babel.

Originally the number of these angels was known as seventy, but it later came to be known as seventy-two, probably

---

101. *The Zohar*, Volume 9 Beshalach, Section 24, verses 315–316.

because this was an easier number to work into astrology (for instance, 360/72 = 5). Within Greek Gnosticism we find evidence of this numerical transition:

> And before his mansion he created a throne, which was huge and was upon a four-faced chariot called 'Cherubim'. Now the Cherubim has eight shapes per each of the four corners, lion forms and calf forms and human forms and eagle forms, so that all the forms amount to sixty-four forms—and seven archangels that stand before it; he is the eighth, and has authority. All the forms amount to seventy-two. Furthermore, from this chariot the seventy-two gods took shape; they took shape so that they might rule over the seventy-two languages of the peoples.[102]

The occult world might be convinced that there is a difference between the seventy-two "demons" that King Solomon was able to command, and the seventy-two "angels" that rule the nations, but our study of these beings shows that this is clearly not the case. The angels of the *Shem Ha'Mephorash* <u>*are*</u> the demons of the *Goetia*. They are the very same beings! There is no such thing as "white magic," and the spiritual seekers that think they can safely make contact with the "good angels" of the Kabbalah are sorely deceived. The "angelic" and

102. *The Nag Hammadi Library*, edited by James M. Robinson (New York, NY: HarperCollins, 1990), 176, from a Greek Gnostic manuscript called *On the Origin of the World.*

"demonic" aspects of these seventy-two deceivers are merely two sides of the same coin.[103]

Our study of the mysterious *siyyim* that show up in all of these obscure Bible passages offers confirmation that the *siyyim* are indeed the seventy satanically-influenced angels that descended at the Tower of Babel to take authority over the seventy Gentile nations of the world. They were given their chance at the fall of the original Babylon, but their end will come *after* they are imprisoned within the desolation of end-times Babylon during the millennium, when they will finally be released and then judged by *Christians* (1 Corinthains 6:3).

A Sacrament for Demons

One of the most unpopular sermons Jesus ever gave can be found in the sixth chapter of the Gospel of John:

> And Jesus said unto them, I am the bread of life: he that cometh to me shall never hunger; and he that believeth on me shall never thirst. But I said unto you, That ye also have seen me, and believe not. All that the Father giveth me shall come to me; and him that cometh to me I will in no wise cast out. For I came down from heaven, not to do mine own will, but the will of him that sent me. And this is the Father's will which hath sent me, that of all which he hath given

---

103. For further research on these "72 angels" and their place in the occult world, go to: http://www.redmoonrising.com/Giza/DomDec6.htm.

me I should lose nothing, but should raise it up again at the last day. And this is the will of him that sent me, that every one which seeth the Son, and believeth on him, may have everlasting life: and I will raise him up at the last day.

The Jews then murmured at him, because he said, I am the bread which came down from heaven. And they said, Is not this Jesus, the son of Joseph, whose father and mother we know? How is it then that he saith, I came down from heaven?

Jesus therefore answered and said unto them, Murmur not among yourselves. No man can come to me, except the Father which hath sent me draw him: and I will raise him up at the last day. It is written in the prophets, And they shall be all taught of God. Every man therefore that hath heard, and hath learned of the Father, cometh unto me. Not that any man hath seen the Father, save he which is of God, he hath seen the Father.

Verily, verily, I say unto you, He that believeth on me hath everlasting life. I am that bread of life. Your fathers did eat manna in the wilderness, and are dead. This is the bread which cometh down from heaven, that a man may eat thereof, and not die. I am the living bread which came down from heaven: if any man eat of this bread, he shall live for ever: and the bread that I will give is my flesh, which I will give for the life of the world.

The Jews therefore strove among themselves, saying, How can this man give us his flesh to eat?

> Then Jesus said unto them, Verily, verily, I say unto you, Except ye eat the flesh of the Son of man, and drink his blood, ye have no life in you. Whoso eateth my flesh, and drinketh my blood, hath eternal life; and I will raise him up at the last day. **For my flesh is meat indeed,** and my blood is drink indeed. He that eateth my flesh, and drinketh my blood, dwelleth in me, and I in him. As the living Father hath sent me, and I live by the Father: so he that eateth me, even he shall live by me. This is that bread which came down from heaven: not as your fathers did eat manna, and are dead: **he that eateth of this bread shall live for ever.** (John 6:35–58)

After Jesus spoke these words we are told that many of His disciples were greatly offended and left Him. What kind of message was this, to advocate cannibalism to pious, law-abiding Jews?

Later on Jesus elaborated upon this teaching at the Last Supper, teaching His disciples to remember His death through the eating of bread and drinking of wine:

> And as they were eating, Jesus took bread, and blessed it, and **brake it**, and **gave it** to the disciples, and said, Take, eat; <u>this is my body</u>." (Matthew 26:26)

With these words, Jesus was establishing the Christian sacrament of Communion, based on the sacrificial death of Jesus on our behalf. Now compare this with what it says in Psalm 74:14, keeping in mind what we know of Leviathan and the demonic *siyyim*:

> Thou **brakest** the heads of Leviathan in pieces, and **gavest** him to be **meat** to the people, the siyyim.

What we see here is that God breaks the heads of Leviathan and gives them as meat as a sort of spiritual sustenance for the *siyyim*, the demonic angels of the Gentile nations. The death of Leviathan is thus portrayed as the sacrament of the gods of the pagan system, just as the death of Jesus is the sacrament for the "sons of God" of the New Covenant.

Dark Reflection #7:

The Body of Jesus Christ was broken and is offered as a sacrament on behalf of every human being that chooses to enter into the family of God.
The heads of Leviathan are broken and offered as a sacrament to the peoples of the world that reject Jesus and to the *siyyim* "gods" that rule over them.

Dark Reflection #8:

Nimrod was a human sacrifice on behalf of the "gods," giving them their chance to rule over all mankind.
Jesus was a divine sacrifice on behalf of all mankind, giving us the opportunity to receive freedom, dominion, and eternal life through Him.

---

chapter thirteen

THE APOTHEOSIS OF NIMROD

THE CIVILIZATION KNOWN as ancient Sumer began in the aftermath of the fall of Uruk. This is the time period (3100 BC to 2300 BC) during which writing became an art, when the Sumerians set down their understanding of the world on clay tablets that were baked into stone.

Eventually the spread of the Sumerian script, which likely began in the city of Nippur, gradually led to the adoption of Sumerian as the regional language, overcoming the "confusion of tongues" that had occurred at Babel. At the same time, religious beliefs were integrated as well and the culture of Sumer emerged with a common religion. As has been shown, this religion revolved around, and was guided by, the dark god Enki, who presented a distorted view of the history and purpose of mankind.

A Brief History

According to the Sumerian King List, the Dynasty of Kish was the first to emerge after the Flood. We have shown that this dynasty was interrupted by the Uruk Expansion and the reign of Enmerkar. After the fall of Uruk it seems that Kish again emerged as the regional power, which lasted until the appearance of Gilgamesh of Uruk, who defeated the final king of the First Dynasty of Kish around 2680 BC.

Ceremonial mask of Sargon of Akkad

The next major figure to emerge was Sargon of Akkad, whose kingdom arose out of middle Mesopotamia and lasted from c.2334–2279 BC. Sargon's conquests also brought his native language of Akkadian into prominence, which eventually superseded Sumerian as the dominant language of Mesopotamia. According to the LXX chronology, Abraham was called by God to leave the southern Sumerian city of Ur around the year 2247 BC, a few decades after Sargon's death.

Several centuries later another empire arose from central Mesopotamia, which was the Babylonian kingdom ruled by the famous *lawgiver*, King Hammurabi (c.1792–1750 BC), who briefly united all of Mesopotamia. Hammurabi's reign is important because he also made a major impact upon the *religious beliefs* of the entire region, which also affected many of the surrounding cultures. What I am talking about is the appearance of the *Enuma Elish,* in which a new young god, Marduk, takes over the pantheon and emerges as lord of heaven and earth. It was a *revolution* within the pagan pantheon.

The Memory of Nimrod

The word *apotheosis* means "to become a god." We already know that the seventy angels who descended at the Tower of Babel became worshiped as the "gods" of the Gentile nations. We have also identified the god Enki as the historical Satan, the ultimate leader of these angels. If Nimrod was the son of Satan/Enki then this means that he was "half-god" through his genetic father. So from the very beginning, due to his size, strength, cunning, and influence, Nimrod was undoubtedly worshiped as a "god."

After the fall of his kingdom, Nimrod's empire was broken up, but the nearby cities that were the greatest benefactors of the first superpower undoubtedly *remembered* and *revered* their great King Nimrod. The ancient Sumerians continued to worship Nimrod as a god even after his death. However, because of the initial "confusion of tongues," many of these cities knew him by different names. For instance, as Ninurta, Ningirsu, Zababa, Asarluhi, Assur or Marduk, as we will now explore.

The cities of Girsu and Lagash both honored the god Ningirsu as their primary god. He was very similar to the god Ninurta, who was the primary god of the cities of Kisurra and Marad. All four of these cities date back to 2700 BC or earlier. What is interesting is that Ningirsu and Ninurta are both names for the hero that was credited for slaying the seven-headed serpent, as discussed in a previous chapter. So it seems that Nimrod, himself, was credited with *ending* the symbolic representation of the threat that he actually *started.*

The possibility that the memory of Nimrod was preserved in the myths of the Sumerian god Ninurta is explored by K. van der Toorn and P. W. van der Horst, in their article "Nimrod Before and After the Bible":

> In several respects, then, Ninurta fits the description of Nimrod given in Gen 10:8–12. The literary tradition of Mesopotamia makes Ninurta indeed "the first on earth to be a hero." His heroism manifested itself mainly in his exploits as a formidable hunter (a gibbôr sayid) of mythical animals. Also the dominion (mamläkä) ascribed to Nimrod has its equivalent in the career of Ninurta... In cuneiform literature, Ninurta is celebrated as the founder of the Mesopotamian civilization. Though the texts at our disposal do not say that he built cities, they imply that he laid the foundations of all civilized life and thus created the conditions under which human settlements could prosper.
>
> According to the theology of Nippur, Ninurta not only stands at the beginning of agriculture, he detains all the MEs, the powers of civilized life. At the dawn of Sumerian society, our sources tell us, Ninurta made a journey to Eridu, the city of the god Enki. There the gods conferred upon him the supreme authority. He

> was entrusted with the leadership of the gods, that all the universe might be under his command. The composition *Angim dimma* relates his triumphant return from Eridu to Nippur, once the gods had proclaimed him king. There he is received in his temple… from where he is to exercise kingship unto the ends of the universe.[104]

It has already been related how the city of Kish eventually became dominant in the region after the Tower of Babel. Their primary god was known as Zababa, who is defined in the book *Gods, Demons and Symbols of Ancient Mesopotamia*:

> Zababa was the local god of the important city of Kish in northern Babylonia. His cult is attested already from the Early Dynastic Period. In the local tradition of Kish, his wife was Inana/Ishtar, and the worship of Inana of Kish was an important secondary cult of the goddess. The personality of Zababa appears to have been that of a god of war, and from the Old Babylonian Period he was identified with Ningursu or Ninurta. In a list of gods he is described as the 'Marduk of battle.' The principal cult centre of Zababa was the temple E-mete-ursag at Kish. An eagle-headed staff was his symbol.[105]

---

104. K. van der Toorn and P. W. van der Horst, "NIMROD BEFORE AND AFTER THE BIBLE," *Harvard Theological Review*, 1990, available at http://www.michaelsheiser.com/PaleoBabble/NimrodHTR.pdf.
105. Jeremy Black and Anthony Green, *Gods, Demons and Symbols*, 187.

Zababa was also the personal god of Sargon the Great of Akkad. Sargon's capital has yet to be found and excavated by archaeologists, but we know that he built magnificent temples there for the god Zababa and the warrior goddess Ishtar, his two favorite deities.

The memory of Nimrod was also held by the city of Kuara, where he was worshiped as the god Asarluhi:

> Asarluhi:
> Originally the god of Kuara, a village near Eridu, Asarluhi came to be associated with Enki (the god of Eridu), and with magical knowledge, the special preserve of Enki. Asarluhi was regarded as the son of Enki and Damgalnuna, and when Marduk was also accorded the title of son of Ea (the Akkadian name of Enki) it was natural for Asarluhi to be absorbed in the personality of Marduk. A hymn of the Old Babylonian Period addresses Asarluhi as the river of ordeal...as the first-born son of Enki and as Marduk. In the Standard Babylonian magical tradition Asarluhi is used as an alternate name for Marduk in incantations and prayers."[106]

Within the name Asarluhi we also see evidence of Nimrod's other biblical and historical name, which is Asshur or Assur.

After Babel, the kingdom of Assyria first emerged as a regional power around 1800 BC, only to be temporarily subdued a few decades later by Hammurabi. The name of their

106. Ibid., 36.

nation, city, and primary god was Assur. This makes sense because we know that Nimrod, named as Asshur, established cities in the region according to Genesis 10:11–12. We will speak more of Asshur in the next chapter when we begin our in-depth study of the prophecies of Isaiah.

The patron deity of the middle-Mesopotamian city of Babylon was the god Marduk. What was at first a local cult was spread throughout the region through the conquests of Hammurabi. This legendary king is known for establishing the famous Code of Hammurabi to govern his lands, and he also sponsored the creation and distribution of the *Enuma Elish*, the famous creation epic that promoted Marduk as the world's new and undisputed "King of the Gods."

In the *Enuma Elish* we see that Marduk, a deified memory of the long-dead Nephilim-king Nimrod, is clearly named as the "son of Enki":

> After Ea [Enki] had vanquished and trampled his foes, had secured his triumph over his enemies, and had rested in profound peace within his sacred chamber which he named "Abzu"... There in the chamber of fates, the abode of destinies, a god was born—the most able and wisest of gods... In the heart of holy Abzu, Marduk was created.
>
> At his names may the gods tremble and quake in their dwellings. Asar-luhi is his foremost name... Asar, bestower of the cultivated land, who establishes its boundaries, the creator of grain and herbs who causes vegetation to sprout forth.
>
> His body was beautiful; when he raised his eyes great lights flared; his stride was majestic; he was

> the leader from the first. When Ea [Enki] who begot him saw him he exulted, he was radiant and light-hearted, for he saw that he was perfect... when his lips moved a tongue of fire burst out. Titanic limbs, standing so high he overtopped the tallest god; he was strong and he wore the glory of ten, and their lightnings played round him. "My son, my son, son of the sun, and heaven's sun!"[107]

Babylonian frieze of Marduk battling Tiamut

Satan Reinvents Himself

With a new leader at the helm of the pantheon of gods a lot of spiritual confusion was erased, at least from the pagan perspective. All of the old gods became essentially irrelevant,

107. *Enuma Elish*, Tablet I, lines 73–102. From *The Babylonian Creation Myth*, last accessed March 15, 2012, http://frontpage.montclair.edu/alvaresj/JAMYTH/Enumaelish.html.

and the new generation, led by Marduk, stepped proudly into the spotlight.

The rise of Marduk to the head of the pantheon was paralleled in Canaanite religion by the rise of Baal over the god El; the Assyrians followed and adopted the *Enuma Elish* by simply substituting Assur for Marduk; later on the Greeks understood this change as the replacement of Kronos with Zeus, and for the Romans it was Jupiter (Jove) eclipsing Saturn.

It was a process of *generational layering*, and it distanced the pagan world from knowledge of an original "Creator God"—or at least made Him completely unimportant in the pagan mind. In fact, if you pay attention to the classical writers of the late Greek and Roman world, you will see that Zeus/Jupiter was being increasingly viewed as an old god, and the process of succession was ready to be repeated by Apollo, the son of Zeus. However, the coming of Jesus Christ halted any Apollonian change-over that may have been planned by the spiritual forces behind the pagan system.

So who was this new God, *really*? Were the priests of Marduk, Baal, and Zeus being manipulated by the spirit of Nimrod acting from beyond the grave? I suppose that is possible, because John writes in 1 John 4:3 that the "spirit of Antichrist" is in the world. However, in context I believe John was using "spirit" in a broader sense, as in the "spirit of rebellion" or "spirit of disobedience," and was not referring specifically to the actual spirit of Nimrod manipulating world events from where his soul is now held in the Abyss.

The book of Revelation offers, I believe, a glimpse into the spiritual force behind the central god of the pagan system. It comes from Jesus, Himself, in His message to the church in Pergamos:

> And to the angel of the church in Pergamos write; These things saith he which hath the sharp sword with two edges; I know thy works, and where thou dwellest, even where Satan's seat is: and thou holdest fast my name, and hast not denied my faith, even in those days wherein Antipas was my faithful martyr, who was slain among you, where Satan dwelleth. (Revelation 2:12–13)

According to Jesus, the "seat of Satan" was located in Pergamos, or Pergamum, the city "where Satan dwells." Scholars believe that this reference in Revelation was referring to the "Great Altar to Zeus" located in Pergamum.

Here is my description of this altar in my online series "Against World Powers":

> This great altar, called by historians "the finest altar ever built," was completed in about 180 BC. The structure stood forty feet high, measured over one hundred feet long, and the stairs that ascended to the upper level were sixty-five feet wide. The most impressive aspect of the altar, however, was its intricate imagery sculpted into the frieze work that surrounded the lower level of the altar. Altogether there were almost four hundred feet of this frieze-work that some experts say marked the climax of classical Greek sculpture.
>
> The sculptures depicted the defeat of the Titans by Zeus, Hercules and Athena, and the founding of Pergamum by the son of Hercules. The magnificent frieze-work is known as "the first known instance of continuous narrative in sculpture" and contained

representations of 34 goddesses, 20 gods, 59 giants and 28 animals.

This ancient monumental masterpiece was discovered by a German railroad builder, Carl Humann, in 1875, and several years later he began to excavate and uncover pieces of the intricate frieze, shipping them to Germany. In 1930 a replica of the entire massive altar was set up, with pieces of the original frieze work, in the newly-built Pargamum Museum in Berlin.[108]

The appearance of the ancient "Great Altar to Zeus" (pictured above[109])—which Jesus referred to as the throne of

108. Peter Goodgame, "Against World Powers," last accessed January 20, 2012, http://www.redmoonrising.com/worldpowers/awpIV.htm.

109. Picture © Raimond Spekking / CC-BY-SA-3.0 (via Wikimedia Commons), http://en.wikipedia.org/wiki/File:Pergamonmuseum_Pergamonaltar.jpg.

Satan—in Berlin, Germany, just prior to the rise of Hitler and the Third Reich, reinforces my view that Hitler was the seventh king of Satan and is the conquering figure shown at the first Seal of Revelation.

Jesus' words also show that He clearly viewed Zeus, the ruling god of the Greek pagan system, as the embodiment of Satan, himself.

The capital of ancient Greek culture was Athens, and its holiest site was the temple known as the Parthenon. Bible scholar Robert Bowie Johnson, Jr. has researched the Parthenon and written several books on the subject of Greek religion and how it relates to the book of Genesis, including *The Parthenon Code* (2004). I refer to Johnson's views in my article, "Against World Powers":

> Zeus was also known by the name Zeus Phanaios, which means "One Who Appears as Light and Brings Light." Johnson refers to 2 Corinthians 11:14 in which Paul states that "Satan himself is transformed into an angel of light." Johnson believes that this "Light," this "moment of lighting up" which brought "human consciousness," was for the pagan world the moment when Eve triumphantly accepted the forbidden fruit from the serpent in the Garden of Eden and gained the knowledge of good and evil for all humanity.
>
> Johnson explains that Zeus is characterized in the Parthenon and throughout Greek culture as a snake, and he refers to many ancient depictions, including one found at Athens harbor that dates to the fourth

century BC, that depicts a coiled, bearded snake, with the caption "Zeus Melichios"... Johnson quotes from an authoritative Greek scholar, Jane Ellen Harrison, an avowed atheist, who wrote the following in her study of Greek religion:

> We are brought face-to-face with the astounding fact that Zeus, father of gods and men, is figured by his worshipers as a snake...The human-shaped Zeus has slipped quietly into the place of the old snake-god. Art sets plainly forth what has been dimly shadowed in ritual and mythology. It is not that Zeus the Olympian has an "underworld aspect;" it is the cruder fact that he of the upper air, of the thunder and lightning, extrudes an ancient serpent-demon of the lower world, Meilichios.

Zeus was viewed by the Greeks as the father, savior and illuminator of the human race, and his primary symbol was that of the serpent, the very same creature that was cursed by God for deceiving Adam and Eve. Within the vast collection of ancient Greek religious art the representations of the second-tier gods and goddesses are often accompanied by snakes. In fact the gigantic gold and ivory statue of Athena that stood within the Parthenon was accompanied by a figure of a large snake, with head held high on Athena's left side, rising up next to her as if it were a pet.

Johnson explains that the appearance of snakes alongside the many Greek deities indicates that these deities are part of the serpent's "system of enlightenment and sacrifice." However, representations of the human figure of Zeus are never accompanied by a serpent. Johnson explains that this is because Zeus is not subordinate to the serpent's system—*he is the serpent.*[110]

110. Peter Goodgame, "Against World Powers."

chapter fourteen

ISRAEL'S GREAT APOSTASY

WHEN I WAS GROWING UP in Klamath Falls, Oregon, in the early 1980s I attended a small Seventh-Day Adventist elementary school. To this day I thank God for the biblical foundation that I received from my teachers during those years.[111] During that time every student was expected to have a favorite Bible verse that could be quoted from memory. Mine was Isaiah 9:6, "For unto us a child is born, unto us a son is given: and the government shall be upon his shoulder: and his name shall be called Wonderful, Counseller, The mighty God, The everlasting Father, The Prince of Peace."

Bible-believing Christians are fully aware that the prophet Isaiah wrote at great length about the coming of Israel's great Deliverer. It was he who predicted the virgin birth, as well as the sacrificial death of Israel's "Suffering Servant." He also

111. Thank you, Mr. Gibbons!

described the Messiah's triumph over Israel's enemies and the glory of His Messianic Kingdom.

What is not completely understood, however, is that Isaiah also wrote at great length about the anti-Messiah. *Often these prophecies are given in parallel with, and in contrast to, the prophecies of Jesus Christ.* This reality comes into clear focus once we understand, as Saint Victorinus claimed near the end of the third century, that Asshur is the Antichrist.[112] But before we turn to Isaiah we need to have some historical background on the events that caused the Word of the Lord to come forth from Isaiah.

The Great Assyrian Threat

Genesis describes the founding of the northern part of Nimrod's empire after he travelled north in his guise as "Asshur": "Out of that land went forth Asshur, and builded Nineveh, and the city Rehoboth, and Calah, and Resen between Nineveh and Calah: the same is a great city" (Genesis 10:11–12).

After the breakup of the great Empire of Uruk around 3100 BC we hear very little of the nation of Assyria until about 1800 BC. At this time a kingdom that called itself "Assur" began to expand in the same region where cities had first been established by Asshur. These people were the "people of Assur," who ruled from their capital city of Assur and worshiped the god Assur.

The early history of the nation of Assur was eclipsed by

112. "Assur is antichrist," *Victorinus Poetovionensis: Commentarius In Apocalypsin*, last accessed January 20, 2012, http://www.bombaxo.com/victapoc.html.

the Babylonian empire of Hammurabi, and Assur did not really emerge again as an aggressive regional power until shortly after the death of King Solomon (931 BC). Biblical historian Eugene H. Merrill describes the awakening of the great Assyrian threat:

> It is clear that the eyes of the world, including Aram and Palestine, were riveted on one nation—mighty Assyria. The revived empire had begun a sustained westward movement under Adad-nirari II (911–891). This was intensified under Tikulti-Ninurta II (890–884) and, by the time of Ahab and Jehoshaphat, had achieved extremely threatening dimensions under Aššur-nasirpal II (883–859). By about 875 he had pressed west as far as…the upper Euphrates, bringing all the Aramean states of that region under Assyrian control. It was his successor, Shalmaneser III (858–824), who first made it clear, however, that Assyria's objective was to extend her hegemony over the entire western world.[113]

In 931 BC the united kingdom of Israel was divided into the northern kingdom of Israel (ten tribes) and the southern kingdom of Judah (the tribes of Judah and Benjamin). Israel's capital was at Samaria and the nation was often referred to as "Ephraim" by the prophets, because Ephraim was the largest and most influential tribe in Israel. Judah's capital was

---

113. Eugene H. Merrill, *Kingdom of Priests: A History of Old Testament Israel* (Grand Rapids, MI: Baker Book House, 1988), 348.

in Jerusalem and they retained control over the Temple and the religious duties. Judah also carried with it the Messianic Promise of Genesis 49:10.

In the years after the breakup of Israel both nations alternated between periods of faithfulness to God and outright rebellion. It was during the period of 850–700 BC that God raised up many of the mighty prophets of the Old Testament: Elijah and Elisha, Jonah, Amos, Hosea, Isaiah, and Micah.

Through the prophets, God promised protection and prosperity for Israel and Judah if they would only turn to Him, but ultimately both nations fell due to a combination of pride, fear and the lack of both faith in, and faithfulness to, God.

The first Assyrian attempt to conquer the northern kingdom of Israel came in 853 BC, but the invaders were repulsed by the combined armies of King Ahab of Israel and the King of Aram who ruled from Damascus.

The Assyrians returned in 841 BC, but this time the new king of Israel, Jehu, betrayed the King of Aram and signed a pact with King Shalmaneser of Assyria, whose armies overran and plundered Aram and then took tribute from Samaria. The groveling of King Jehu on his knees before Shalmaneser is shown on the famous Black Obelisk (next page[114]). The carved text reads, "The tribute of Jehu, son of Omri: I received from him silver, gold, a golden bowl, a golden vase

114. File: Jehu-Obelisk-cropped.jpg, used by permission, Steven G. Johnson, last accessed January 20, 2012, http://en.wikipedia.org/wiki/File:Jehu-Obelisk-cropped.jpg.

with pointed bottom, golden tumblers, golden buckets, tin, a staff for a king [and] spears."[115]

Note the winged sun-disk in front of Shalmaneser, which represents the god Assur and appears throughout Assyrian inscriptions. Also note the the image of Assur holding the bow below, which was a common image of Assur and which compares with the bow held by the conqueror described at the first Seal of Revelation.

The spiritual force behind the overwhelming armies of Assyria is mentioned by the King of Assyria in an inscription that celebrates a subsequent conquest of Damascus that took place in 803 BC:

---

115. "The Jehu Relief," *Bible-History.com*, last accessed March 13, 2012, http://www.bible-history.com/black-obelisk/the-jehu-relief.html.

> Against Aram I marched. Mari, king of Aram, in Damascus his royal city, I shut up. **The terrifying splendor of Assur…overwhelmed him** and he laid hold of my feet, he became my vassal. 2300 talents of silver, 20 talents of gold, 3000 talents of copper, 5000 talents of iron, colored woolen and linen garments, an ivory bed, an ivory couch…his property and his goods, in immeasurable quantity, in Damascus, his royal city, in his palace, I received.[116]

Here is what I wrote about the years that followed in my online series "The Giza Discovery":

> For the next fifty years or so the kingdoms of Israel and Judah experienced a period of relative peace, even though they were led by kings who did not always obey God's commandments. The Assyrian Empire remained in a defensive posture and sometime during the reign of King Assur-dan III (772–755) the prophet Jonah fulfilled his mission to the city of Ninevah. Around this same time the prophet Amos began to speak words of warning to the children of Israel who had become comfortable and complacent, and who were forgetting to fulfill their obligations to the Lord. Amos prophesied against King Jereboam II saying that he would die in battle (fulfilled in 753),

116. Quote taken from a stela unearthed in 1905, mentioned in the article, "Israel and the Assyrians," *Quartz Hill School of Theology*, last accessed January 20, 2012, http://www.theology.edu/lec20.htm.

and Amos was the first to predict that Israel would be taken away into captivity: "...your sons and your daughters will fall by the sword, your land will be parceled up by a measuring line and you yourself will die upon unclean soil. Moreover, Israel will certainly go from its land into exile" (Amos 7:17).

The great prophet Isaiah's ministry began around the year 740 BC near the end of King Uzziah of Judah's reign. According to 2 Kings 15–16 both King Uzziah and his son King Jotham were faithful to the Lord. However, with Jotham's passing Judah became ruled by his son King Ahaz who turned away from God and embraced the pagan practices of the surrounding nations (2 Kings 16:1–4). For this reason we are told that God raised up the surrounding nations to punish Judah. At this same time Assyria was once again beginning to assert its dominance, and to resist this the nations of Israel and Aram (with its capital of Damascus) formed an alliance. However, King Ahaz refused to join this alliance and so, in 735 BC, the armies of Israel and Aram invaded Judah. With the appearance of this threat God called up the prophet Isaiah to speak to King Ahaz, but God's message was rejected by the king (Isaiah 7:1–12). Instead of putting his faith in God King Ahaz honored the gods of Damascus (2 Chronicles 28:23,) and he reached out to the kingdom of Assyria (Asshur) as his potential savior:

> Ahaz sent messengers to say to Tiglath-Pileser king of Assyria, "I am your servant and vassal. Come up and save me out of the hand of the

> king of Aram and of the king of Israel, who are attacking me." And Ahaz took the silver and gold found in the temple of the LORD and in the treasuries of the royal palace and sent it as a gift to the king of Assyria. The king of Assyria complied by attacking Damascus and capturing it. He deported its inhabitants to Kir and put Rezin to death. (2 Kings 16:7–9)

The destruction of Damascus took place in 732 BC, which marked the end of the ancient Kingdom of Aram (although the language of Aramaic, which was spoken by Jesus and His disciples, survived). Assyrian armies also ravaged Israel and took many captives. During this chaotic time King Pekah of Israel was assassinated and King Hoshea took his place. Hoshea immediately pledged his allegiance to Assyria and began paying a yearly tribute. However, some years later he stopped paying this tribute and turned to Egypt for protection. As a result of this disobedience King Shalmaneser V of Assyria swept into Israel with his armies in 722 BC and completely destroyed the kingdom of Israel, deporting hundreds of thousands of captives to Assyria. According to 2 Kings 17 this happened only because of the obstinate disobedience of the people of Israel.[117]

---

117. Peter Goodgame, "The Giza Discovery, Part Nine: The Mighty One," last accessed January 20, 2012, http://www.redmoonrising.com/Giza/Asshur9.htm.

This is the context from which to understand the prophecies of Isaiah concerning Asshur and the coming Messiah, but before we go there we must first take a look at the Assyrian understanding of their god Assur, and their national role as his willing and obedient servants in expanding Assur's territory on earth.

Assur is King! Assur is King!

The proclamation of "Assur is King! Assur is King!" is explained in a book by the same title, which is subtitled, *Religion in the Exercise of Power in the Neo-Assyrian Empire*, written by Steven W. Holloway. According to Holloway this was the proclamation uttered by the High Priest of Assur whenever a new king entered the Temple of Assur to be acknowledged as the ruling authority of the Assyrian Empire. Holloway writes:

> The god Assur, tutelary head of the ancient capital city and state pantheon…is publicly identified as king even as the new earthly king assumes power. The new king does not become a member of the state pantheon, still less is he absorbed into the godhead of Assur. The state, in creating a monarch, signifies through the implied *vox populi* that the divine imperial will to expand the borders of the Land of Assur is as one with the earthly king. It implies that his exercise of diplomacy, military force and administrative acumen shall magnify the Assyrian Empire, and, in context of ritual and imperial culture, communicates that the ideology of the new king shall satisfy the

> tutelary god and the people of the Land of Assur. The paradox of an earthly king who incarnates the imperial will-to-power of Assur is the ideological fulcrum to three centuries of Neo-Assyrian foreign relations.[118]

Holloway explains that one of the central beliefs of the Assyrian state cult was its belief in Imperial expansion under the direct control and guidance of Assur. A term that is found throughout Assyrian texts is the term "Yoke of Assur." Holloway writes that this was "propagandistic shorthand" for the regions and provinces that had been conquered and brought under Assur's control.[119]

In the chapter entitled "Terror in the Exercise of Empire," Holloway explains that "…every element of every victorious Assyrian campaign was an act of religious imperialism, since the entire enterprise of conquest was undertaken at the command of Assur and the great gods of Assyria…"[120]

The origin of the term "Yoke of Asshur" can be traced all the way back to the expansion of the Kingdom of Uruk under King Enmerkar, as related in the Sumerian epic, *Enmerkar and the Lord of Aratta*. In the narrative, Enmerkar asks the goddess Inana to cause the kingdom of Aratta to "submit beneath the yoke of Uruk" so that he could acquire the stones necessary to build the great temple-tower, the Abzu-house, for the god Enki. We have already put forth the evidence that

---

118. Steven W. Holloway, *Assur is King! Assur is King!: Religion in the Exercise of Power in the Neo-Assyrian Empire* (Leiden, The Netherlands: Koninklijke Brill NV, 2002), xv.

119. Ibid., 81.

120. Ibid., 99.

this was the Tower of Babel, built at Eridu the original site of Nimrod's city of Babylon. This is further evidence that Assur, the central god of the Assyrians, was in fact the satanically-controlled representation of Nimrod, the original founder of the Assyrian nation and builder of the Tower of Babel.

Israel Thinks the Unthinkable

In the early chapters of the book of Isaiah God directs the prophet to speak about things happening during the reigns of both the kings of Judah and the kings of Israel. In chapter 8, he predicts the fall of Samaria, the capital city of Israel, and Damascus, the capital of Aram, at the hands of the Assyrians. Isaiah ends the chapter by encouraging God's people to turn away from idols and occult sources such as mediums and spiritists, and to turn back to God. Isaiah says that if they don't repent, they will face darkness and anguish.

In the next chapter, Isaiah contrasts the previous negative word with a positive word of encouragement that looks forward to redemption and victory through the Messiah of Israel. He will be born to Israel as a child and grow up to defeat God's enemies and establish a kingdom that will last for eternity.

Following this glorious promise of the inevitable triumph of the Messiah and His Kingdom, Isaiah is then directed to turn his attention back to the northern kingdom of Israel, and explain why God has decided to punish the nation by handing them over to the Assyrians:

> The Lord has sent death upon Jacob, and it has come upon Israel. And all the people of Ephraim, and they

> that dwelt in Samaria shall know, **who say in their pride and lofty heart, The bricks are fallen down, but come, let us hew stones, and cut down sycamores and cedars, and let us build for ourselves a tower.** (Isaiah 9:8–10, LXX)[121]

What the Lord is saying to Israel at this time cannot be missed or misunderstood. Compare the LXX translation of the passage above with the New King James version of Genesis 11:3–4:

> **Then they said to one another, Come, let us make bricks and...let us build for ourselves...a tower...**

With this introduction to God's judgment against Israel He is saying that the apostasy of Israel is so deep and so complete that it is as if the people of Israel were saying in their proud and rebellious hearts, **"The bricks of the Tower of Babel have fallen down, but come, let us hew stones and cut timbers so that we can build it once again!"**

The Tower of Babel was the original and ultimate symbol of mankind's hubris and rebellion against God, and here God is comparing Israel's apostasy to the original post-Flood apostasy at Babel that had resulted in the creation of the entire pagan system. God's anger was kindled like never before, and judgment was sure to follow.

---

121. For a free pdf download of the Septuagint (LXX) Bible, go to http://ecmarsh.com/news/?p=226.

chapter fifteen

THE ROD OF GOD'S ANGER

THE ANGER OF GOD against Israel is initially expressed through four judgments that are given one after the other, each of them ending with the phrase, "For all this his anger is not turned away, but his hand is stretched out still."

Isaiah then explains that the fifth judgment that *completes* the punishment against Israel will come through Asshur, who is explained as the very rod that is held by the "outstretched hand" of God:

> O Assyrian, the rod of mine anger, and the staff in their hand is mine indignation. I will send him against an hypocritical nation, and against the people of my wrath will I give him a charge, to take the spoil, and to take the prey, and to tread them down like the mire of the streets. (Isaiah 10:5–6)

Modern translators don't truly understand the use of the name "Asshur" in its biblical-historical context, so the singular word "Asshur" is sometimes translated as *Assyria*, or *Assyrians*, and often confusingly as "the Assyrian." However, the Hebrew text rarely precedes "Asshur" with the definite article "the," and many of the translations are misleading. We should just take the Hebrew word "Asshur" to mean *Asshur*, and then let the verb tenses and context determine whether the name is meant to refer to the Assyrian nation, the Assyrian people, the Assyrian king, or the historical figure behind the Assyrians—Asshur himself.

Because the Assyrians believed that the king was the human voice of the god Assur and the expression of his will on earth, I believe that is how we need to understand the Isaiah passage above. It refers to the king and to the spiritual power behind the throne at the very same time. Asshur is the "rod" of God's anger, and God says "I will send him against a hypocritical nation…"

At this time the people of Israel were caught up in apostasy and had rejected God. They were pursuing idols, oppressing the poor and failing to keep the Law. When faced with the threat of Assyria the kings of Israel, against the direction of the prophets, repeatedly surrendered to Assur and offered to pay tribute. As far as the Assyrians were concerned, this proved that Assur was superior to the God of Israel. As far as God was concerned, these acts of submission were inexcusable.

On a good note, while Israel refused to heed the warnings from Isaiah, the southern kingdom of Judah under King Hezekiah *did* listen to Isaiah. The Lord heard Hezekiah's prayers and saw his repentance, and in response the angel of the Lord destroyed one hundred eighty-five thousand

Assyrian soldiers in a single night (Isaiah 37:36). As long as God's people honored and obeyed Him they had absolutely nothing to fear, even from the greatest military force on earth at the time.

However, the sins of the northern kingdom of Israel were piled up so high, and their hearts were so far from repentance and so full of pride and rebellion, that God's judgment eventually had to fall. His chosen instrument of punishment was Asshur, described as a man using terms that spoke of near events, as well as far events that will not be fulfilled until the Day of the Lord, when Asshur will rise again as God's instrument to provoke Israel's *final* repentance.

As we will show, this great prophecy against Israel and Asshur begins in Isaiah 9:8, but it doesn't *end* until Isaiah 14:27, when the themes that are introduced at the beginning are brought to their final conclusion.

God Judges Asshur

The five judgments against Israel that come from the "outstretched hand" of the Lord end with the predicted destruction of Israel at the hands of Asshur in Isaiah 10:6. From this point on, the Word of the Lord changes from being against Israel, to being against Asshur. God will use Asshur, a "proud and rebellious" figure, to punish Israel, a "proud and rebellious" people, and then God will punish Asshur himself. Here is what Isaiah writes:

> O Assyrian [Asshur], the rod of mine anger, and the staff in their hand is mine indignation. I will send him against an hypocritical nation, and against the people

> of my wrath will I give him a charge, to take the spoil, and to take the prey, and to tread them down like the mire of the streets.
>
> Howbeit he meaneth not so, neither doth his heart think so; but it is in his heart to destroy and cut off nations not a few.
>
> For he saith, "Are not my princes altogether kings? **Have I not taken the country above Babylon and Chalanes, where the tower was built? and have I not taken Arabia, and Damascus, and Samaria?**
>
> As my hand hath found the kingdoms of the idols, and whose graven images did excel them of Jerusalem and of Samaria; Shall I not, as I have done unto Samaria and her idols, so do to Jerusalem and her idols? (Isaiah 10:5–11; bold portion of text is found only in the LXX and is not included in the KJV.)

Once again the Septuagint translation provides, in verse 9 above, a reference to the Tower of Babel that is missing in the Masoretic text. "Babylon and Chalanes, where the tower was built," refers to the cities of Babel (Eridu) and Calneh that were two of the principal cities at the heart of Nimrod's empire as given in Genesis 10:10. Isaiah continues:

> Wherefore it shall come to pass, that when the Lord hath performed his whole work upon mount Zion and on Jerusalem, I will punish the fruit of the stout heart of the king of Assyria [literally: "King Asshur"], and the glory of his high looks. For he saith,
>
> "By the strength of my hand I have done it, and by

> my wisdom; for I am prudent: and I have removed the bounds of the people, and have robbed their treasures, and I have put down the inhabitants like a valiant man: And my hand hath found as a nest the riches of the people: and as one gathereth eggs that are left, have I gathered all the earth; and there was none that moved the wing, or opened the mouth, or peeped."
>
> Shall the axe boast itself against him that heweth therewith? or shall the saw magnify itself against him that shaketh it? as if the rod should shake itself against them that lift it up, or as if the staff should lift up itself, as if it were no wood.
>
> Therefore shall the Lord, the Lord of hosts, send among his fat ones leanness; and under his glory he shall kindle a burning like the burning of a fire. And the light of Israel shall be for a fire, and his Holy One for a flame: and it shall burn and devour his thorns and his briers in one day; And shall consume the glory of his forest, and of his fruitful field, both soul and body: and they shall be as when a standardbearer fainteth. And the rest of the trees of his forest shall be few, that a child may write them. (Isaiah 10:12–19)

This passage begins by shifting the scope of the prophecy to the time of the end. Isaiah writes that King Asshur will not be punished until after the Lord has performed "all His work upon mount Zion and on Jerusalem." The end of the passage gives the first reference of many in Isaiah that speak of Asshur the Antichrist perishing at the hands of the Messiah, the Holy One of Israel, who will destroy him by fire. Isaiah then continues:

And it shall come to pass in that day, that the remnant of Israel, and such as are escaped of the house of Jacob, shall no more again stay upon him that smote them; but shall stay upon the Lord, the Holy One of Israel, in truth. The remnant shall return, even the remnant of Jacob, unto the mighty God. For though thy people Israel be as the sand of the sea, yet a remnant of them shall return: the consumption decreed shall overflow with righteousness. For the Lord God of hosts shall make a consumption, even determined, in the midst of all the land.

Therefore thus saith the Lord God of hosts, O my people that dwellest in Zion, be not afraid of the Assyrian [Asshur]: he shall smite thee with a rod, and shall lift up his staff against thee, after the manner of Egypt. For yet a very little while, and the indignation shall cease, and mine anger in their destruction. And the Lord of hosts shall stir up a scourge for him according to the slaughter of Midian at the rock of Oreb: and as his rod was upon the sea, so shall he lift it up after the manner of Egypt. And it shall come to pass in that day, that his burden shall be taken away from off thy shoulder, <u>and his yoke from off thy neck, and the yoke shall be destroyed</u> because of the anointing.

For he shall arrive at the city of Angai, and shall pass on to <u>Maggedo</u>, and shall lay up his stores in Machmas. They are gone over the passage: they have taken up their lodging at Geba; Ramah is afraid; Gibeah of Saul is fled. Lift up thy voice, O daughter of Gallim: cause it to be heard unto Laish, O poor Anathoth. Madmenah is removed; the inhabitants of

> Gebim gather themselves to flee. As yet shall he remain at Nob that day: he shall shake his hand against the mount of the daughter of Zion, the hill of Jerusalem.
>
> Behold, the Lord, the Lord of hosts, shall lop the bough with terror: and the high ones of stature shall be hewn down, and the haughty shall be humbled. And he shall cut down the thickets of the forest with iron, and Lebanon shall fall by a mighty one. (Isaiah 10:20–34, bold portion of text is from the LXX)

At this point we need to shift our perspective completely to the end times before we can fully appreciate this part of Isaiah's prophecy against Asshur. The end times "Day of the Lord" will be fulfilled in connection with the final seven years of Daniel's "Prophecy of the Seventy Weeks" (Daniel 9:24–27). This seven-year period will begin with the "confirming" of a covenant that will be made between the resurrected Antichrist and the leaders of Israel. Halfway through that seven-year period we know that the Antichrist will establish himself in Jerusalem's Temple and proclaim himself to be God, as Paul writes in 2 Thessalonians 2:4.

The blasphemous takeover of the Temple will be the opening act of the Antichrist's final three-and-a-half-year period of global domination, which is a time period referred to throughout Revelation and in the book of Daniel.[122]

---

122. The final three and a half years: Daniel 7:25 and 12:7; Revelation 11:2, 12:6, 12:14 and 13:5. To further examine the end-times chronology, go to www.redmoonrising.com where the book *Red Moon Rising—The Rapture and the Timeline of the Apocalypse* can be read online or purchased.

In the Isaiah passage above we find an end-times reference to Megiddo in the LXX in verse 28, where Asshur will arrive before settling in Machmas and "laying up his stores." This is the region of Megiddo that is also referred to as Armageddon in Revelation 16:16, where Jesus Christ will destroy the Antichrist and his armies.

The Destruction that is Determined

The final end of the Antichrist is also alluded to within the context of the phrase, *consumption determined*, in Isaiah 10:23. This phrase is made by the two Hebrew words *kalah charats*. The word *kalah* is translated in *Strong's Concordance* as, "completion, termination, full end, complete destruction, consumption, annihilation."[123] The word *charats* appears in the Bible twelve times and the majority of these times it is translated as "determined."

In the three places in the Bible where these two words appear together **"the destruction that is determined"** speaks specifically of the end times in connection with the final judgment of the earth and the destruction of the Antichrist:

"For the Lord God of hosts shall make a consumption, even determined [kalah charats], in the midst of all the land" (Isaiah 10:23).

"Now therefore be ye not mockers, lest your bands be made strong: for I have heard from the Lord God of hosts

---

123. From www.blueletterbible.org: Strong's H2782—*charats*, http://www.blueletterbible.org/lang/lexicon/lexicon.cfm?Strongs=H2782&t=KJV.

a consumption, even determined [kalah charats] upon the whole earth" (Isaiah 28:22).

"And he shall confirm the covenant with many for one week: and in the midst of the week he shall cause the sacrifice and the oblation to cease, and for the overspreading of abominations he shall make it desolate, even until the consummation, and that determined [kalah charats] shall be poured upon the desolate" (Daniel 9:27).

A Covenant with Death and Hell

Many Bible scholars believe that Isaiah 28:14–22 describes the very same covenant that is confirmed in Daniel 9:27 between the Antichrist and Israel. If this is true, as our analysis of "the destruction that is determined" suggests, then Isaiah offers us further proof that we are correct in believing that the Antichrist will be the resurrected Asshur (Nimrod). Here is what Isaiah wrote about this covenant:

> Wherefore hear the word of the Lord, ye scornful men, that rule this people which is in Jerusalem. Because ye have said,
>
> "**We have made a covenant with death, and with hell are we at agreement**; when the overflowing scourge shall pass through, it shall not come unto us: for we have made lies our refuge, and under falsehood have we hid ourselves."
>
> Therefore thus saith the Lord God, Behold, I lay in Zion for a foundation a stone, a tried stone, a precious corner stone, a sure foundation: he that

> believeth shall not make haste. Judgment also will I lay to the line, and righteousness to the plummet: and the hail shall sweep away the refuge of lies, and the waters shall overflow the hiding place.
>
> **And your covenant with death shall be disannulled, and your agreement with hell shall not stand**; when the overflowing scourge shall pass through, then ye shall be trodden down by it. From the time that it goeth forth it shall take you: for morning by morning shall it pass over, by day and by night: and it shall be a vexation only to understand the report. For the bed is shorter than that a man can stretch himself on it: and the covering narrower than that he can wrap himself in it.
>
> For the Lord shall rise up as in mount Perazim, he shall be wroth as in the valley of Gibeon, that he may do his work, his strange work; and bring to pass his act, his strange act. Now therefore be ye not mockers, lest your bands be made strong: for I have heard from the Lord God of hosts **a consumption, even determined** upon the whole earth. (Isaiah 28:14–22)

The leaders of Israel will believe that they have made a "covenant with death and with hell" because the Antichrist, who will appear in the end times as a five-thousand-year-old corpse that has been resurrected from the dead by a soul that has come up out of the Abyss, will be looked upon as someone **who is the master of hell and even of death itself**.

This provocative possibility helps to clarify the awestruck reaction by the people of the earth to the appearance of the Antichrist, as described in Revelation:

> "And I saw one of his heads as it were wounded to death; and his deadly wound was healed: **and all the world wondered after the beast**" (Revelation 13:3).

> "The beast that thou sawest was, and is not; and shall ascend out of the bottomless pit, and go into perdition: and **they that dwell on the earth shall wonder**, whose names were not written in the book of life from the foundation of the world, when they behold the beast that was, and is not, and yet is" (Revelation 17:8).

The next chapter will provide even more evidence that Nimrod, known to Isaiah the Prophet as "Asshur," will be that resurrected Antichrist.

chapter sixteen

THE BREATH OF THE LORD

ISAIAH'S HARSH WORDS of judgment against Israel that begin in Isaiah 9:8 are preceded by a beautiful Messianic prophecy. Then, after dealing with Asshur in chapter 10, Isaiah again turns back to the subject of the Messiah in chapter 11:

> And there shall come forth a rod out of the stem of Jesse, and a Branch shall grow out of his roots: And the spirit of the Lord shall rest upon him, the spirit of wisdom and understanding, the spirit of counsel and might, the spirit of knowledge and of the fear of the Lord; And shall make him of quick understanding in the fear of the Lord: and he shall not judge after the sight of his eyes, neither reprove after the hearing of his ears: But with righteousness shall he judge the poor, and reprove with equity for the meek of the earth: and he shall smite the earth: with the rod of his

> mouth, and with the breath of his lips shall he slay the wicked. (Isaiah 11:1–4)

We have already looked at how the LXX translation of these seven "Spirits" of God adds to our understanding. The LXX also helps us understand the end of verse four: "…and with the breath of his lips shall he destroy **the ungodly one**" (LXX; bold added).

This translation makes it clear that the "ungodly one" is speaking of a specific *singular* person, rather than being a general reference to "the wicked," *plural*. Recall that in Isaiah 10:17 it was written that the Holy One of Israel would be a flame against Asshur. From this context I believe that Isaiah 11:4 is another prediction of the death of Asshur coming from the very breath of the Messiah. It is the very same thing that Paul predicted in 2 Thessalonians 2:8–9 (who was probably referring to this very Scripture), "And then shall **that Wicked** be revealed, whom the Lord shall consume with the spirit of his mouth, and shall destroy with the brightness of his coming: Even him, whose coming is after the working of Satan with all power and signs and lying wonders" (bold added).

Jesus Christ will destroy Asshur, the resurrected Nephilim King, by the breath of His mouth when He returns at His Second Coming. If any doubt about this remains, Isaiah gives another prophecy that says the very same thing in Isaiah 30:27–33:

> Behold, the name of the Lord cometh from far, burning with his anger, and the burden thereof is heavy: his lips are full of indignation, and his tongue as a

> devouring fire: And his breath, as an overflowing stream… And the Lord shall cause his glorious voice to be heard, and shall shew the lighting down of his arm, with the indignation of his anger, and with the flame of a devouring fire, with scattering, and tempest, and hailstones.
>
> For through the voice of the Lord shall the Assyrian [**Asshur**] be beaten down, which smote with a rod. And in every place where the grounded staff shall pass, which the Lord shall lay upon him, it shall be with tabrets and harps: and in battles of shaking will he fight with it. For Tophet is ordained of old; yea, for the king it is prepared; he hath made it deep and large: the pile thereof is fire and much wood; **the breath of the Lord, like a stream of brimstone, doth kindle it.**

Isaiah tells us that the judgment of Asshur has long been prepared, "ordained of old," just like a huge funeral pyre that has been built deep and large with wood, ready and waiting to be set ablaze. The Lord Jesus, here referred to as "The Name of the Lord," will kindle it with the breath that comes out of His mouth.

The Destroyer

A final passage that may speak of the fiery destiny of the Antichrist is found in Isaiah 33. It begins by saying, "Woe to thee that spoilest…" in the KJV. "Thee that *spoilest*" comes from the Hebrew root word *shadad*, which is translated as, "to deal violently with, despoil, devastate, ruin, destroy, spoil."

Here is how the NASB translates the passage: "Woe to you, **O destroyer**, while you were not destroyed; And he who is treacherous, while others did not deal treacherously with him. **As soon as you finish destroying, you will be destroyed**; As soon as you cease to deal treacherously, others will deal treacherously with you" (Isaiah 33:1, NASB; bold added).

The passage continues with apocalyptic images of the Lord coming in judgment on behalf of Zion, and then the text reads, "'Now I will arise,' says the Lord, 'Now I will be exalted, now I will be lifted up. You have conceived chaff, you will give birth to stubble; **My breath will consume you like a fire**'" (Isaiah 33:10–11, NASB; bold added).

From the overall context of this passage, it seems that the "Destroyer" will himself be destroyed by the breath of the Lord.

The name "Destroyer" as a title for the Antichrist makes perfect sense, considering what we read about Asshur's ruthless conquests in Isaiah 10. It also stands in contrast to the meaning of the name *Yeshua*, the Hebrew name for Jesus, which means "Savior." In fact, we find a version of the word *yeshua* in the passage right after the "Destroyer" is introduced: "O Lord, be gracious unto us; we have waited for thee: be thou their arm every morning, our salvation [yeshua] also in the time of trouble" (Isaiah 33:2).

The Antichrist is also named as the "Destroyer" in the book of Revelation when the Abyss is opened and his soul is released to re-inhabit his dead body:

> And the fifth angel sounded, and I saw a star fall from heaven unto the earth: and to him was given the key of the bottomless pit. And he opened the bottomless

> pit; and there arose a smoke out of the pit, as the smoke of a great furnace; and the sun and the air were darkened by reason of the smoke of the pit. And there came out of the smoke locusts upon the earth: and unto them was given power, as the scorpions of the earth have power…
>
> And they had a king over them, which is the angel of the bottomless pit, whose name in the Hebrew tongue is Abaddon, but in the Greek tongue hath his name Apollyon. (Revelation 9:1–3, 11)

Scholars have debated over the years whether or not Abaddon is the Antichrist. Some say that he is merely a fallen angel and could not be the actual Antichrist, but the word "angel" simply means "messenger" in Greek, and even Jesus is named as an "angel" in Revelation 10:10.[124]

Abaddon is the "Angel of the Abyss" and also the "King of the Abyss." He is the *leader* of the demonic host that will be released when the Abyss is opened at the fifth Trumpet of Revelation.

Abaddon's soul will be released to re-inhabit his body,

---

124. The strong angel is Jesus, whose description compares with Jesus as the "son of man" also shown in Revelation 14:14–16. The angel of Revelation 10 gives John a scroll to eat, just as Ezekiel was given a scroll to eat in Ezekiel 3:2. Both heavenly scroll-givers are described as having a rainbow around them. Ezekiel 1:28 says he was "the Lord," therefore the heavenly, mighty angel of Revelation 10 is most likely the Lord Jesus, whose infernal counterpart is the Antichrist —Abaddon the angel of the Abyss.

which will *cause the world to wonder* (Revelation 13:3 and 17:8). He will immediately be acknowledged and given authority by the ten kings that rule the world (Revelation 17:12–13), and shortly after that he will confirm the covenant with Israel of Daniel 9:27, which will be the starting point of the so-called Seven-Year Tribulation, or Daniel's Seventieth Week. This is the covenant that Isaiah 28 refers to as the "covenant with death and hell," for obvious reasons.

The name of the Antichrist is given as Abaddon in Hebrew and Apollyon in Greek. Both of these names mean "Destroyer." Here is what I wrote about the distinction between "The Savior" and "The Destroyer" in my online series "The Giza Discovery":[125]

> At one point during the earthly ministry of Jesus Christ He sent some of His disciples into a village in Samaria to make arrangements for Him to lodge there on His way into Jerusalem. However, the Samaritan village refused to host Jesus and His disciples, and after hearing of this James and John both approached Jesus angrily and said to Him, *"Lord, do you want us to command fire to come down from heaven and consume them?"* To this Jesus responded by rebuking them, saying, **"You do not know what kind of spirit you are of;** *for the son of Man did not come to* **destroy** *men's lives, but to* **save** *them."* (Luke 9:54–56, NASB)

125. Peter Goodgame, "The Giza Discovery, Part Nine: The Mighty One," last accessed January 20, 2012, http://www.redmoonrising.com/Giza/Asshur9.htm.

The very name of Jesus, which is Yeshua in Hebrew, comes from the Hebrew root word *yesha*, which means "to save." On the other hand, the two names of the Antichrist that are given in Revelation 9:11 are Abaddon and Apollyon, which can both be translated to mean "The Destroyer." Jesus the Messiah is the Savior of the world, while the Antichrist is the great Destroyer.

The Greek name Apollyon comes from the Greek verb *apollu*, which means "to destroy;" it is the word used in the Greek New Testament in the passage from Luke quoted above. The name Appollyon is also related to the Greek word *apoleia* which means "destruction." The Apostle Paul used this word when he referred in Philippians 3:18–19 to the people in the world who are *"enemies of the cross of Christ, whose end is* **destruction**.*"* The word *apoleia* is also found within the following well-known teaching of Jesus:

"Enter through the narrow gate. For wide is the gate and broad is the road that leads to **destruction**, and many enter through it. But small is the gate and narrow the road that leads to life, and only a few find it." (Matthew 7:13–14, NIV)

Several different forms of the word "destroy" can be found in a classical Greek play written by Aeschylus in reference to the Greek god Apollo, who is also referred to as Apollyon:

> CASSANDRA: O wail, wail, gods and Earth, woe, woe, Apollo, O Apollo.
> CHORUS: O why this wailing for the prophet king? He wants no wailer, far, far other he.

> CASSANDRA: O wail, wail, gods and Earth, woe, woe, Apollo, O Apollo.
> CHORUS: Again with lips of woe she calls the god, who has no part or parcel with the woeful.
> CASSANDRA: **Apollo, thou destroyer, O Apollo; Lord of fair streets, Apollyon to me; For thou hast clean destroyed me once again.**
> CHORUS: The prophetess is like to tell her sorrows; Heaven's spirit rests in her, albeit a slave.
> CASSANDRA: **Apollo, thou destroyer, O Apollo; Lord of fair streets, Apollyon to me**; Ah, where hast thou led me? Ah! Ah! To what home?[126]

And just who is this Greek god Apollyon who makes his strange appearance in the book of Revelation? Charles Penglase is an Australian professor who specializes in ancient Greek and Near Eastern religion and mythology. In his book, *Greek Myths and Mesopotamia: Parallels and Influence in the Homeric Hymns and Hesiod*, Penglase carefully and methodically demonstrates that the Greek myths and legends of Apollo were simply Greek retellings of the Babylonian myths involving the rise to power of the god Marduk, which were themselves based on earlier legends of the Sumerian hunter/hero known as Ninurta."[127]

---

126. Aeschylus, *The Agamemnon of Aeschylus*, translated by George Herbert Thring (London: Chiswick Press, 1904), 41.
127. Charles Penglase, *Greek Myths and Mesopotamia: Parallels and Influence in the Homeric Hymns and Hesiod* (London: Routledge, 1994), 76–125.

Dark Reflection #9:

Jesus Christ is the Savior; Asshur is the Destroyer.

Dark Reflection #10:

Jesus was given a three-and-a-half-year ministry with full authority on the earth, and He used it to preach, heal, and set people free.

Asshur will also be given a three-and-a-half-year period with full authority, but he will use it to deceive, destroy, and take people into captivity.

chapter seventeen

THE EVIL SEED

THE MESSIANIC PROPHECY that begins in Isaiah 11 speaks of the judgment against Israel's enemies and continues throughout Isaiah 12 as a poetic expression of thanksgiving to God for deliverance and salvation: "Sing unto the Lord; for he hath done excellent things: this is known in all the earth. Cry out and shout, thou inhabitant of Zion: for great is the Holy One of Israel in the midst of thee" (Isaiah 12:5–6).

Then Isaiah turns to prophesy the destiny of end-times Babylon during the Day of the Lord. Here is how it begins, as translated in the Septuagint:

> THE VISION WHICH ESAIAS SON OF AMOS SAW AGAINST BABYLON.

> Lift up a standard on the mountain of the plain, exalt the voice to them, beckon with the hand, **open the gates**, ye rulers. I give command, and I bring them: **giants are coming to fulfil my wrath**, rejoicing at the same time and insulting. A voice of many nations on the mountains, even like to that of many nations; a voice of kings and nations gathered together: the Lord of hosts has given command to a war-like nation, to come from a land afar off, from the utmost foundation of heaven; the Lord and his warriors are coming to destroy all the world. (Isaiah 13:1–5, LXX)

Open the Gates!

The original meaning of Babylon is "Gate of God," and Eridu was the location of the original Babylon and the Tower of Babel. Eridu was the location of the abzu-temple of Enki that included a gate to the Abyss accessed through the sacred fresh-water springs underneath it. This temple-tower was also built as a gate to heaven, which was probably meant to be within a sacred room at the very top of the temple structure. However, we can assume that this room was never completed. Nevertheless, the Tower of Babel did act as a heavenly "gate" because it provoked God's decision to allow the seventy angels to descend to rule over the nations of the world.

The reference to Babylon and to a "gate" in Isaiah 13:2 is following along with the tradition of Babel as the original "supernatural gateway" to both the heavens above and the Abyss below. Eridu was the location of the original *axis mundi*, also known as the "Great Mooring Post of Heaven and Earth" in Sumerian tradition.[128]

With this in mind, the opening lines of Isaiah 13 may be viewed as alluding to the opening of the Abyss, which will allow for the appearance of the demonic locusts and then the demonic cavalry of Revelation 9, the latter of which come out of the Euphrates River (Revelation 9:14). Recall that Eridu was a sacred site actually built on an island in the middle of the Lower Euphrates. *Perhaps the gateway to the Abyss will be opened once again at its original location.*

In addition to the giants that come forth from their "gate," Isaiah also seems to speak of the Lord's angels coming down out of a "heavenly" gate to do battle as well. As in the related "Joel's Army" prophecy that is found in Joel 2:1–11, it is hard to decipher the allegiance and the purpose of all the different supernatural forces that converge upon the earth, coming from both heaven and hell, during the end-times Day of the Lord. However, we do know that those forces that come up from the Abyss will be led by the "King of the Abyss," named as Abaddon and Apollyon in Revelation 9:11.

---

128. The myth *Enki and the World Order*: "Enki, lord of plenty of the Anuna gods, Nudimmud, mighty one of the E-kur, strong one of heaven and earth! Your great house is founded in the Abzu, **the great mooring-post of heaven and earth**" (bold added). Viewable online: last accessed January 24, 2012, http://etcsl.orinst.ox.ac.uk/cgi-bin/etcsl.cgi?text=t.1.1.3#. (Also see: "Axis mundi," *Wikipedia*, last modified January 17, 2012, http://en.wikipedia.org/wiki/Axis_mundi.)

Orion is Dimmed

Historically, Israel's primary enemies of Egypt, Assyria, and Babylon all worshiped their own versions of Nimrod, known as the gods Osiris, Asshur, and Marduk. Each of these gods are theologically connected with the constellation Orion, the great hunter in the sky. Isaiah's prophecy against Babylon includes a polemical statement against Orion, which I believe will be literally fulfilled during the Day of the Lord. In the Septuagint translation of the following passage, Isaiah specifies that even the great constellation Orion will be covered in darkness:

> For behold! the day of the Lord is coming which cannot be escaped, a day of wrath and anger, to make the world desolate, and to destroy sinners out of it. **For the stars of heaven, and <u>Orion</u>, and all the host of heaven, shall not give their light**; and it shall be dark at sunrise, and the moon shall not give her light. And I will command evils for the whole world, and will visit their sins on the ungodly: and I will destroy the pride of transgressors, and will bring low the pride of the haughty. (Isaiah 13:9–11, LXX)

After Isaiah introduces the forces that will appear after the gates are opened, and predicts the signs in the heavens that will take place during the Day of the Lord, he then goes on to describe the terrible conditions on the earth as the Day of the Lord is fulfilled. Jesus Christ, in Matthew 24:29, drew from the prophecy of Isaiah 13:10 in His description of the terrible Day of the Lord, therefore we know that the prophecies found in Isaiah's "Oracle Against Babylon" are meant to find their final fulfillment in the future.

The King of Babylon

After speaking of the great terrors of the Day of the Lord in Isaiah 13, the prophet then ends, once again, on a positive note, as he wraps up his "Oracle Against Babylon" in Isaiah 14. Note that the context is without a doubt the end times; specifically *after* Israel has been saved from the horrors of the Day of the Lord by the mercy of God:

> For the Lord will have mercy on Jacob, and will yet choose Israel, and set them in their own land: and the strangers shall be joined with them, and they shall cleave to the house of Jacob. And the people shall take them, and bring them to their place: and the house of Israel shall possess them in the land of the Lord for servants and handmaids: and they shall take them captives, whose captives they were; and they shall rule over their oppressors. (Isaiah 14:1–2)

Context is absolutely critical when it comes to properly understanding the important message of Isaiah 14. Here are the next two verses:

> And it shall come to pass in the day that the Lord shall give thee rest from thy sorrow, and from thy fear, and from the hard bondage wherein thou wast made to serve, That thou shalt take up this proverb against the king of Babylon, and say… (Isaiah 14:3–4)

Isaiah is predicting that *after* the Day of the Lord has passed *then* Israel will look back at what they have just experienced and taunt the very king that had led the forces that had oppressed them during the Day of the Lord.

This is a prophecy against Asshur, the original King of Babylon (Isaiah 23:13), who will rise as a king from the Abyss to fulfill his final destiny as Satan's eighth king during the Day of the Lord. Here is what Israel will say to the King of Babylon after he is defeated:

> Thou shalt take up this proverb against the king of Babylon, and say, How hath the oppressor ceased! the golden city ceased! The Lord hath broken the staff of the wicked, and the sceptre of the rulers. He who smote the people in wrath with a continual stroke, he that ruled the nations in anger, is persecuted, and none hindereth. (Isaiah 14:4–6)

This is the same description of Asshur that is found in Isaiah 10:5–7, who is given a rod and then goes out to ruthlessly conquer the nations of the world. Jesus is then shown giving Asshur a beating in Isaiah 30:31–32, before Jesus breathes on him and sets him ablaze like a funeral pyre.

Isaiah then continues his prophecy by offering various viewpoints on the cataclysmic fall of the great and terrible King of Babylon. First we hear from the trees:

> The whole earth is at rest, and is quiet: they break forth into singing. Yea, the fir trees rejoice at thee, and the cedars of Lebanon, saying, Since thou art laid down, no feller is come up against us. (Isaiah 14:7–8)

Next we hear from the long-dead kings of the world that are aroused to comment on the catastrophic end of the King of Babylon:

> Hell from beneath is moved for thee to meet thee at thy coming: it stirreth up the dead for thee, even all the chief ones of the earth; it hath raised up from their thrones all the kings of the nations. All they shall speak and say unto thee, Art thou also become weak as we? art thou become like unto us? Thy pomp is brought down to the grave, and the noise of thy viols: the worm is spread under thee, and the worms cover thee. How art thou fallen from heaven, O Lucifer, son of the morning! how art thou cut down to the ground, which didst weaken the nations! (Isaiah 14:9–12)

Note that Lucifer is not Satan. Lucifer is merely another name for Asshur, the King of Babylon. He is a Nephilim King, which is why the other kings are amazed that a man of such power has been reduced to such weakness.

Jesus says, "I am He who searches hearts and minds," in Revelation 2:23. Back in Isaiah 9:10, the Lord revealed the heart of Israel that was so far from God that it was as if they wanted to rebuild the Tower of Babel. In Revelation 18:7 Jesus reveals the heart of the Queen of Babylon. The next verse in Isaiah's prophecy reveals the heart of the King of Babylon, explaining his desires, motives, and purpose:

> You said in your heart, I will ascend to heaven; I will raise my throne above the stars of God; I will sit enthroned on the mount of assembly, on the utmost

> heights of the sacred mountain. I will ascend above the tops of the clouds; I will make myself like the Most High. But you are brought down to the grave, to the depths of the pit. (Isaiah 14:13–15)

The vain ambitions of the King of Babylon began with his desire to build the Tower of Babel. It was the "sacred mountain" that King Enmerkar intended to build as documented in the Sumerian epic *Enmerkar and the Lord of Aratta*. However, the heart of the king reveals an ambition that transcended far beyond a failed building project.

King of the Gods?

Let's consider once again the historical context and the time in which this "Word of the Lord" was first delivered by the prophet Isaiah. This was a message directed to Israel, but also to the proud nation of Assyria, which worshiped "Assur" as their god.

Israel was completely lost in apostasy and Assyria was on the verge of conquering and destroying Israel's capital of Samaria and taking the people into bondage. Israel was about to be brought under the "Yoke of Assur," and for many it may have looked like Assur, the god of the Assyrians, was stronger than the God of Israel. Isaiah's prophecy spoke against this false perception.

The god Assur was recognized throughout the region at the time as the "King of the Gods," comparable to the Babylonian god Marduk, whose supposed rise to heavenly leadership was documented in the Babylonian epic *Enuma Elish*. The heart of the King of Babylon as revealed in Isaiah compares perfectly with the descriptions of Marduk as found in the *Enuma Elish*.

The Assyrians recognized and honored the *Enuma Elish*, but they replaced the name of Marduk with the name of their god Assur. In fact, the very first copy of the *Enuma Elish* was excavated in modern times from the library of the Assyrian king Ashurbanipal in the ruins of the Assyrian capital of Ninevah, back in 1849.[129]

So I believe that Isaiah's prophecy against the King of Babylon must also be viewed as a Hebrew polemic against Assur, the god of the Assyrians who were on the verge of conquering Israel.

At the same time, however, it is also an important end-times prediction of the historical figure behind the Assyrian god, the original Asshur who died around 3100 BC, who will rise again at the beginning of the Day of the Lord.

Another item of evidence that helps to explain Asshur's vain ambition comes from a description of the Antichrist in the book of Daniel. Compare the two accounts:

Isaiah 14:13-14: "You said in your heart, <u>I will ascend to heaven; I will raise my throne above the stars of God; I will sit enthroned on the mount of assembly, on the utmost heights of the sacred mountain. I will ascend above the tops of the clouds; I will make myself like the Most High.</u>"

Daniel 8:9-12: "And out of one of them came forth a little horn, which waxed exceeding great, toward the south, and toward the east, and toward the pleasant land. And it waxed great, <u>even to the host of heaven</u>; and it cast down some of the

---

129. "Enûma Eliš," *Wikipedia*, last modified January 20, 2012, http://en.wikipedia.org/wiki/Enuma_Elish.

host and of the stars to the ground, and stamped upon them. Yea, he magnified himself even to the prince of the host, and by him the daily sacrifice was taken away, and the place of his sanctuary was cast down. And an host was given him against the daily sacrifice by reason of transgression, and it cast down the truth to the ground; and it practised, and prospered."

Daniel explains that on a certain level the Antichrist will be successful, if only temporarily. He will reach the "host of heaven," but then he will quickly be "cast down."

Our study of Isaiah continues with a final comment from the deceased kings of the earth that is directed towards Asshur:

> Those who see you stare at you, they ponder your fate: Is this the man who shook the earth and made kingdoms tremble, the man who made the world a desert, who overthrew its cities and would not let his captives go home? (Isaiah 14:16–17)

Cast Out of Thy Grave

The next few verses from Isaiah are filled with insight and compelling evidence that Asshur is the Antichrist, the original *and* end-times King of Babylon:

> All the kings of the nations, even all of them, lie in glory, every one in his own house. **But thou art cast out of thy grave** like an abominable branch, and as the raiment of those that are slain, thrust through with a sword, that go down to the stones of the pit; as a carcase trodden under feet. **Thou shalt not be joined with them in burial**, because thou hast destroyed thy

> land, and slain thy people: the seed of evildoers shall never be renowned. Prepare slaughter for his children for the iniquity of their fathers; that they do not rise, nor possess the land, nor fill the face of the world with cities. (Isaiah 14:18–21)

There is an apparent disagreement between Paul and Isaiah on the one hand, and the book of Revelation on the other, concerning the manner in which the Antichrist will be killed. Paul and Isaiah agree that the Antichrist will be one of the first casualties at the Second Coming when Jesus kills him by the very breath of His mouth. Revelation, on the other hand, states that after Jesus comes back, the Antichrist will be captured and cast *alive* into the Lake of Fire:

> And I saw the beast, and the kings of the earth, and their armies, gathered together to make war against him that sat on the horse, and against his army. And the beast was taken, and with him the false prophet that wrought miracles before him, with which he deceived them that had received the mark of the beast, and them that worshipped his image. These both were cast <u>alive</u> into a lake of fire burning with brimstone. (Revelation 19:19–20)

The apparent disagreement between these two sources is solved by the passage just quoted from Isaiah. Both sources are correct: Asshur will be *killed* by the breath of Jesus, and then he will be cast *alive* into the Lake of Fire. Isaiah explains that after Asshur is killed his soul will be *rejected* out of the grave. This means that Asshur will *again* be resurrected, <u>a</u>

second time, right after Jesus kills him. He will be resurrected to find himself *trodden down*, lying among the carcasses of his fallen army, only to be immediately captured and then cast fully alive, body and soul, into the Lake of Fire.

Bible scholar Arnold Fruchtenbaum explains how this all makes *perfect* sense:

> It is declared that the Antichrist will be cast *alive* into the Lake of Fire. In the previous chapter, passages were cited that state that the Antichrist will be killed as one of the first casualties of the Second Coming. Therefore, this verse requires that the Antichrist be resurrected at this time and then be cast alive into the Lake of Fire. It is for this reason that Isaiah 14:20 declared that the Antichrist will never see burial.
>
> There is some irony to be found in this fact. As will be seen later in this chapter, the term *the first resurrection* applies to the resurrection of all the righteous, although it comes in stages. The term *the second resurrection* applies to the resurrection of all the damned, and this, too, will come in stages. Jesus was the firstfruits of the first resurrection. The irony to be found here is that he who would be the counterfeit son will be allowed to act out the counterfeit role to completion by becoming the firstfruits of the second resurrection. But the result of his resurrection will be the Lake of Fire.[130]

---

130. Arnold Fruchtenbaum, *The Footsteps of the Messiah: A Study of the Sequence of Prophetic Events*, Revised Edition (Tustin, CA: Ariel Ministries, 2003), 363.

The Serpent's Seed

Isaiah gives us an important key to the true identity of the King of Babylon that is missed in English translations of the Masoretic text. Here is that key as it appears in the Septuagint:

> As a garment defiled with blood shall not be pure, so neither shalt thou be pure; because thou hast destroyed my land, and hast slain my people: thou shalt not endure for ever—thou an evil seed. (Isaiah 14:20, LXX)

The actual Greek reading of this text is even more blunt. The last sentence literally reads, *ou me meines eis ton aiona kronon* **sperma poneron** ("in no way should you abide into the eon of time –**seed of evil**").

The King of Babylon is the *evil seed.* He is the seed of the serpent whose birth was predicted in Genesis 3:15, who stands opposed to Jesus, the seed of the woman.

Dark Reflection #11:

Jesus Christ was the firstfruits of the First Resurrection; the Antichrist will be the firstfruits of the Second Resurrection.

Asshur is His Name

Isaiah's epic and all-important prophecy about the fall of the King of Babylon comes to an end with the following Words from the Lord:

> For I will rise up against them, saith the Lord of hosts, and cut off from Babylon the name, and remnant,

> and son, and nephew, saith the Lord. I will also make it a possession for the bittern, and pools of water: and I will sweep it with the Besom of destruction, saith the Lord of hosts.
>
> The Lord of hosts hath sworn, saying, Surely as I have thought, so shall it come to pass; and as I have purposed, so shall it stand: That I will break **the Assyrian** [Asshur] in my land, and upon my mountains tread him under foot: then shall his yoke depart from off them, and his burden depart from off their shoulders. This is the purpose that is purposed upon the whole earth: and this is the hand that is stretched out upon all the nations.
>
> For the Lord of hosts hath purposed, and who shall disannul it? **and his hand is stretched out, and who shall turn it back?** (Isaiah 14:22–27)

We can make no mistake about this prophecy. The Lord says literally, "**I will break Asshur in my land...and tread him underfoot.**" The Lord is speaking of an *individual* using *singular* verbs. This is not a nation being judged, but a *person.*

"The Assyrian" is *Asshur* the King of Babylon. He is Nimrod, the historical figure who became worshiped as Assur the Assyrian god.

Shortly after Isaiah penned this prophecy, the Assyrians, *by the delegated authority and in the name of Assur*, destroyed the northern kingdom of Israel and took the nation captive. Isaiah's prophecies predicted this, but they also predicted that God would inevitably prevail over Assur in the end time.

The end of this prophecy ties directly back to when it first began in Isaiah 9:8, when the Lord repeated, four times, the phrase "For all this his anger is not turned away, but his hand is stretched out still." It began as a Word of judgment against Israel that was fulfilled through Asshur, who was used as the *rod of anger* in God's outstretched hand against Israel.

In Isaiah 14:26, we are told that God will also use Asshur as His rod stretched out against **all the nations**. Asshur's *global government* will force the people of the world into choosing either Jesus Christ or the Antichrist. Everyone will receive the Mark of the Beast, or suffer the consequences of resistence. Once this "strange work" has been completed, then Jesus will return to judge the nations and bring an end to the violent reign of the Antichrist.

"For the Lord of hosts hath purposed, and who shall disannul it? And his hand is stretched out, and who shall turn it back?"

Dark Reflection #12:

Jesus Christ is the good seed, the seed of the woman; the Antichrist is the evil seed, the seed of the serpent.

chapter eighteen

EGYPT'S FIRST PHARAOH

SO FAR WE HAVE LOOKED at the legacy of Nimrod in the ancient records of Sumer, Babylon, Assyria and India, and within the cultures of the Canaanites and the Greeks. We now turn to ancient Egypt, where the discovery of Nimrod's legacy will reveal some important secrets about the life and death of this infamous king.

The *birth* of Egyptian history coincides with the *end* of the Uruk Expansion, around 3100 BC. The Mesopotamian influence on early Dynastic Egypt is a subject that is very politically incorrect today, because many modern Egyptians resist the idea that Egypt's origins can be traced to non-Africans, yet that is what the evidence clearly shows.

I cover this controversy in great detail in my "Giza Discovery" series in Part Four, "Egypt's Forgotten Origins."[131] I quote from the research of historian David Rohl, the author of *Legend: The Genesis of Civilisation*, who brings together all of the evidence that suggests that after the initial wave of settlers appeared in Egypt after the Flood, there was a second wave of colonists from Mesopotamia, who were actually unwelcomed invaders who *conquered* the land of Egypt. Rohl himself draws from the original research of the world's first modern Egyptologist, W. M. Flinders Petrie (1853–1942). Here now is a summary of the basic story.

The Falcon Tribe

The Uruk Expansion was led by a group of colonists designated by Petrie as "The Falcon Tribe." Their emblem can be traced back to Enki, the god of the Abzu-temple in Eridu. In the Sumerian cylinder-seal pictograph below Enki is shown with the "life-giving" waters of the Abyss flowing out of his shoulders while holding a falcon in one outstretched hand.

The Falcon Tribe's expansion was at first a sea-going adventure. Their ships came from Sumer and established bases and

131. Peter Goodgame, "The Giza Discovery, Part Four: Egypt's Forgotten Origins," last accessed January 23, 2012, http://www.redmoonrising.com/Giza/EgyptsOrigins4.htm.

friendly ports in the Persian Gulf, in Arabia and India, and on the Horn of Africa. Eventually they travelled north through the Suez and into the Mediterranean Sea, which was possible in antiquity because the water levels were higher, making the "Suez Canal" a natural waterway. Within the Mediterranean the "Falcon Tribe" established the port-cities of Tyre, Sidon, and Byblos in the Levant, as well as the port of Buto in Egypt.

In Africa, the sea-going *expansion* turned into a land *invasion* at two points. First, the Falcon Tribe settled in the mountainous area of Ethiopia traditionally known as the Land of Cush. Second, and sometime later, the Falcon Tribe dragged their ships overland from the Red Sea to the Nile River in Upper Egypt and established a presence in the settlement of Nekhen, today known as Hierakonpolis. According to Petrie, Nekhen means "City of the Falcon." This is the region that includes the sacred sites of Thebes, Luxor, and Abydos, which can all be dated back to the Falcon Tribe through the important "Nakada" archaeological digs undertaken by Petrie in this area.

The Nakada excavations provided evidence of the Mesopotamian origin of the invaders in numerous ways. They possessed Mesopotamian-type pottery, they possessed lapis-lazuli and cylinder seals, they fought with the Mesopotamian pear-shaped mace, and they also brought with them Mesopotamian architecture, as well as the knowledge of the art of writing in its early forms. Petrie also unearthed evidence of ritualistic cannibalism within the Falcon Tribe.

One of the most important early sacred sites in Egypt for the Falcon Tribe was the site known as Abydos on the Nile River, also known to Egyptologists as Abdju. Note that the "dj" sound is pronounced "z," and so we see that these invaders quickly established their own abzu-house for the god that they worshiped that we know as the Sumerian god Enki. Like Enki's original temple at Eridu, Abydos was built next to a river over a fresh-water spring.

Eventually the people of Nekhen emerged as the dominant force in Egypt, and they swept north and conquered all of Egypt, with the capture of the port city of Buto being the capstone of the campaign, as well as the starting point of Egyptian history. Here is how journalist Bruce Bower describes the historical circumstances at the time of this event:

> Investigators from the German Archaeological Institute in Cairo, Egypt, make an annual slog through the Nile Delta to the waterlogged site of Buto, the legendary ancient capital of Lower Egypt. Strategically located near the Mediterranean Sea, Buto was a major port during the 4th millennium B.C.—a poorly understood period of Egyptian history preceding the emergence of the pharaohs around 3100 B.C.…
>
> "We've found the first archaeological evidence of cultural unification in Egypt at the end of the 4th millennium B.C., before the first dynasty of pharaohs appeared," says project director Thomas von der Way. Excavations show that during the final stages of the predynastic era at Buto, local methods of pottery and stone-blade production were replaced by more advanced techniques that originated in Upper Egypt, which lay farther to the south. Apparently, Upper Egyptian invaders had conquered this prominent city and port, von der Way says…
>
> Even more intriguing is evidence of close contact between Buto's Egyptian residents and the Sumerians

of southern Mesopotamia (now southern Iraq), who fashioned the world's first full-fledged civilization and state institutions during the last half of the 4th millennium B.C. Not only does pottery at Buto display Mesopotamian features, but clay nails uncovered at the delta site are nearly identical to those used to decorate temples at sites such as Uruk—the largest Sumerian settlement and the world's first city. In Mesopotamia, workers inserted the nails to temple walls and painted their heads to form mosaics. The researchers also found a clay cone at Buto that closely resembles clay decorations placed in wall niches inside Mesopotamian temples.

Scientists have long argued over ancient Egypt's relationship to early Mesopotamia. Much of the debate centers on Mesopotamian-style artifacts, such as cylinder seals and flint knife handles, found in 4th-millennium-B.C. graves situated on slopes above the Nile Valley near Buto...

At Buto, however, Egyptians may have copied temple decorations shown to them by Sumerians more than 5,000 years ago...

Buto fuels the growing recognition among archaeologists that early Mesopotamian civilization experienced an unprecedented expansion between 3400 and 3100 BC.[132]

---

132. "Civilization and its Discontents: Why Did the World's First Civilization Cut a Swath Across the Near East?" by Bruce Bower, *Science News Magazine*, March 3, 1990, viewable here: last accessed January 24, 2012, http://www.findarticles.com/p/articles/mi_m1200/is_n9_v137/ai_8784921/pg_1.

The Narmer Palette

King Narmer: Egypt's First Pharaoh

Modern Egyptologists believe that the conquest of Buto that brought the unification of Egypt is an event that is celebrated on one of the most important artifacts that dates back to this time. This artifact is the famous "Narmer Palette," excavated at Nakada by Petrie's teams around 1897–98. Experts date the palette to the time period of pre-Dynastic Egypt around 3150 BC.

The front side of the palette (left) shows the king wearing the Red Crown that came to symbolize Lower Egypt bordering the Mediterranean in the north. On the back of the palette, the king wears the White Crown of Upper Egypt in the south. For this reason, among others, most scholars believe that this palette depicts the conquest of Lower Egypt by Narmer who came from the south, and the first time in history when all of Egypt became united under one ruler.

On the front side of the palette, the king is shown in the top scene as a giant within a procession led by soldiers holding standards. In front of them are the bodies of ten decapitated bodies.

The middle section shows a "hunting" scene of the capture of two great unknown beasts.

On the bottom there is an image of a bull that scholars believe represents Narmer. The bull is trampling a victim and breaching the walls of a city, continuing the representation of the mighty conquests of Narmer.

The back of the palette is dominated by an image of Narmer in a "smighting" pose (pictured on the back cover of this book). He holds an uplifted mace in one hand while his other hand clutches the scalp of a captured enemy. We get the clear impression that Narmer intends to kill the victim in the very next instant.

For a more comprehensive, scholarly analysis of the palette, readers can go to the article "Who Was Menes?" by journalist Jimmy Dunn.[133]

Two other ancient artifacts that date to the same time and record similar themes are the "Bull Palette" and the "Hunter's Palette." Egyptologist Nicolas Grimal describes them both:[134]

---

133. Jimmy Dunn, "Who Was Menes?" from the website *TourEgypt.net*, http://www.touregypt.net/featurestories/menes1.htm.

134. For a more comprehensive analysis of Narmer and the related artifacts, go to, "The Giza Discovery, Part Eight: The First Pharaoh," located at http://www.redmoonrising.com/Giza/AfricOrig8.htm.

The Bull Palette (Louvre) introduces [an] image of royal power, the bull, in the process of goring a man of northern ethnic type; below, a long line of prisoners is tied together with a single cord held by the personified standards of five federated kingdoms. The verso [opposite side] bears a depiction of two crenellated walls with the names of two conquered peoples written in the form of pictograms.[135]

The Hunter's Palette is quite explicit, depicting an organized expedition to slaughter and capture wild animals: lions are pierced by arrows, while deer and goats are driven along by dogs and taken captive. Men armed with bows and arrows, spears, axes, throwsticks and pear-shaped maceheads are shown organized in a military fashion, under standards representing a falcon on a perch and a version of the hieroglyphic sign that would eventually stand for the east. There are also depictions of a holy shrine and a bull with two heads recalling the upper section of the Narmer Palette.[136]

---

135. Nicolas Grimal, *A History of Ancient Egypt* (Cambridge, MA: Blackwell Publishers; UK: Oxford, 1988), 37.

136. Ibid., 36.

These ancient artifacts, depicting a conquering king, an aggressive bull, and a great hunting scene, all provide strong support for our thesis that the biblical Nimrod the "Mighty Hunter" led his forces in conquest, region-by-region, throughout the ancient Near East in the years leading up to 3100 BC.

Nimrod in Egypt

According to the Sumerian King List that was referenced earlier, Enmerkar of Uruk was the son of a king who "went down into the sea and came out at the mountains." We identified this figure as the biblical Cush who established the Land of Cush in Ethiopia. His heir, **Enmer**-kar, who built Uruk, is the biblical **Nimrod**. However, as a royal heir of Cush, it is quite likely that Nimrod was born among the original Falcon Tribe colonizers of Ethiopia, before he returned to the homeland of Sumer and initially established his kingdom of Uruk.

What the Egyptian evidence tells us is that right around *this very same time* a leader of the Falcon Tribe emerged, known as **Narmer**, who swept through Egypt with a mighty army, conquering and uniting the northern and the southern regions of Egypt. The evidence suggests that King Narmer was in fact the biblical Nimrod who, in addition to founding the civilizations of Sumer and Assyria, also became the first king and pharaoh of the great civilization of Dynastic Egypt.

The consonant sounds of N-M-R show up in all three historical accounts of this great king: the Sumerian Enmerkar, the biblical Nimrod, and the Egyptian Narmer. The names fit, as well as the *times* that date the end of his career on earth some time around 3100 BC.

The Egyptian King List

Modern Egyptologists have been able to put together a list of almost all of the historical kings of Egypt based on artifacts and Egyptian records. This list of kings using their original Egyptian names is then often compared with the Greek names of the kings listed in the writings of the Egyptian high priest of Ra known as Manetho. These writings were produced by Manetho for the Greek world after Egypt was taken by Alexander the Great in 332 BC.

According to Manetho, the Egyptians were first ruled by the gods; then there was a period when Egypt was ruled by the "dead and the demigods." After this shadowy period the first king appeared and established the great dynasties of Egypt. Here is what is written in Manetho's famous Egyptian King List:

> After the dead and the demigods comes the First Dynasty, with 8 kings of whom Menes was the first. He was an excellent leader. In what follows are recorded the rulers from all of the ruling houses in succession. Dynasty One, 1st King—Menes of Thinis, whom Herodotus calls Men, and his 7 descendents. He ruled

> 62 years. He led the army across the frontier and won great glory. He was killed by a hippopotamus...[137]

Today there is a debate among Egyptologists about the historical identity of King Menes. Some favor Narmer, while others favor the king known as Hor-Aha. Jimmy Dunn explains the dispute in his article, "Who Was Menes?":

> What seems clear to us is that Menes must have been another name given to one of the better attested kings of the 1st Dynasty, if he indeed was not a legendary figure composed of several of them. Many scholars do believe that he represents a specific king, but who exactly this might be is an argument almost as old as Egyptology itself. Today, the two primary candidates are Narmer and Aha. We are more certain, though not entirely, that these two individuals reigned successively, with Narmer preceding Aha. If Narmer is considered to be Menes, then Aha would be the second ruler of the 1st Dynasty. Otherwise, Narmer would be the last ruler of the Predynastic Period, or as some have suggested, Dynasty 0...
>
> Narmer's claim rests largely on his earlier historical position and on the Narmer Palette, which has been interpreted as showing the king in the act of conquering Lower (Northern) Egypt.[138]

---

137. Gerald Verbrugghe and John Wickersham, *Berossos and Manetho* (Ann Arbor, MI: University of Michigan Press, 1996), 131.
138. Dunn, "Who Was Menes?"

I think the evidence is clear that Menes, the founder of the First Dynasty, must be Narmer, and support for this can also be found in Manetho's description of Menes being killed by a hippo. As Egypt's high priest Manetho was privy to the most important secrets of their cult. I believe that the death of Menes, described by Manetho in *symbolic* terms, is a key to unlocking the circumstances surrounding the death of Nimrod. However, for this to be unlocked we first have to understand Nimrod's legacy in Egypt after he became worshiped as a god.

The divinity of Menes is something that is subtly hinted at in an ancient king list known as the Turin Canon, which is probably what Manetho drew from in publishing his king list in Greek. The canon dates back to around 1150 BC, and is described as, "a hieratic papyrus thought to date from the reign of Ramesses II, now in the Museo Egizio (Egyptian Museum) at Turin. The papyrus is believed to be the most extensive list of kings compiled by the Egyptians, and is the basis for Egypt's chronology before the reign of Ramesses II."[139]

Egyptologist Nicolas Grimal explains how this record provides further information on the first king of Egypt:

> [On the Turin Canon] the first "king of Upper and Lower Egypt" (*nsw bity*) is unequivocally named as Meni, his name actually being written twice, but with one important difference—the first time his name is written with a human determinative **and the second time with a divine determinative**... Is this Meni—or

139. "Turin King List," *Wikipedia*, last modified January 3, 2012, http://en.wikipedia.org/wiki/Turin_Canon.

> Menes according to Eratosthenes and Manetho—to be identified with Narmer, as is generally thought, or is it simply a literary method of designating "someone" in general, whose name is lost? ... It is difficult to see why Meni's name is repeated... (bold added)[140]

In the next chapter, we will show how Nimrod, known to Manetho as Menes, the first king of a united Egypt who led an army "across the frontier" and was allegedly killed by a "hippopotamus," came to be worshiped as Egypt's most important god.

140. Grimal, *A History of Ancient Egypt*, 47–48.

chapter nineteen

THE CULT OF OSIRIS

THE LIFE AND DEATH of the first king to unite and bring civilization to the ancient Egyptians emerged as the basis of the primary cult that dominated Egypt for close to four thousand years. The priests of this cult, however, remained very secretive about the exact details of the death of their god, and about the location of his corpse, which they claimed to possess. In this chapter we will begin to dig into these mysteries, penetrate past all of the smoke and mirrors, and get to the truth.

The memory of Nimrod was preserved in Egypt through the cult of the god Osiris. However, the name "Osiris" cannot be found in Egyptian records prior to c.2300 BC. This presents a mystery for Egyptologists, which is noted by best-selling author Robert Bauval:

> There is a great paradox in Egyptology that so far has not been properly explained. Although the earliest

> reference to Osiris is found in the Pyramid Texts which date from c.2300 BC, a cursory study reveals that the mythology, doctrines, liturgy and rituals which they contain could not possibly have developed overnight, but would have required a long process of intellectual and religious evolution long before that date…
>
> Furthermore, the Egyptologists are also at a loss to explain why in the large quantities of inscriptions that predate the Pyramid Texts, not one single mention of Osiris has been found. It is as if the cult of Osiris, with its rituals, doctrines, liturgies and mythology, suddenly materialised out of nowhere and, almost overnight, was readily adopted as the principle religion of the pharaonic state.[141]

This paradox disappears if the religion of Osiris is understood as the cult dedicated to a figure who died in 3100 BC. This cult took a few hundred years to incubate and develop within the Egyptian elite, and then at a certain point in time during the Fifth Dynasty, the cult "went public," choosing the name "Osiris" to designate their central figure. This was the time, c.2300 BC, when work began on the smaller pyramid complex at Saqqara, located about ten miles southeast of Giza.

The pyramids of Giza, which were built c.2600 to 2500 BC during the Fourth Dynasty, contained no symbols or hieroglyphs whatsoever. However, the interiors of the pyramids at Saqqara were *covered* with ritual inscriptions, which are today known as the "Pyramid Texts." These texts are a

141. Robert Bauval, *Secret Chamber: The Quest for the Hall of Records* (London, UK: Century, 1999), 95–96.

vast collection of spells that were meant to help protect the king and ensure his prosperity in the afterlife. It is within these spells that the name "Osiris" first appears as an integral part of Egyptian religion.

After the Pyramid Texts, the next source for studying the cult of Osiris was the Coffin Texts. Near the end of the Old Kingdom period (c.2000–1800 BC), and throughout the Middle Kingdom, kings began to leave inscriptions of spells within their burial chambers to aid them in the afterlife. Many of these spells were derived from the Pyramid Texts.

Around 1700 BC, the first spells written on papyrus began to emerge. By the time of the New Kingdom period (1550 BC) these spells became widely used in the chambers and coffins of kings and dignitaries and became collectively known as the spells of the "Book of Going Forth By Day." Today we know it as the *Egyptian Book of the Dead*.

These three sources: the Pyramid Texts of the Old Kingdom, the Coffin Texts of the Middle Kingdom, and the Book of the Dead of the New Kingdom, are the primary sources for scholars to piece together the various elements of the Osiris cult, as it gradually evolved over the centuries.

Here is a "Hymn to Osiris" from the *Book of the Dead*, which is typical of the many sacred Egyptian references to Osiris:

> Glory be to thee, Osiris Un-nefer, the great god who dwellest within Abtu [Abzu], thou king of eternity, thou lord of everlastingness, who passest through millions of years in the course of thine existence. Thou art the eldest son of the womb of Nut, and thou wast engendered by Geb, the Ancestor…

> Let thine heart, O Osiris, who art in the Mountain of Amentet, be content, for thy son Horus is stablished upon thy throne... He leadeth in his train that which is, and that which is not yet... he is exceedingly mighty and most terrible in his name 'Osiris'; he endureth for ever and for ever in his name of 'Un-nefer.' Homage be to thee, O King of kings, Lord of lords, Ruler of princes, who from the womb of Nut hast ruled the world and the Underworld.
>
> Praise be unto thee, Osiris, lord of eternity, Un-nefer-Heru-Khuti, whose forms are manifold, and whose attributes are majestic...thou guide of the Underworld, whom (the gods) glorify when thou settest in the night sky of Nut... Those who have lain down [i.e., the dead] rise up to look upon thee, they breathe the air and they look upon thy face when the disk riseth on the horizon; their hearts are at peace inasmuch as they behold thee, O thou who art Eternity and Everlastingness.[142]

Osiris the World Conqueror

In the years that followed the Greek conquest of Egypt visiting Greek historians attempted to penetrate and solve the mysteries surrounding the history of Egypt and the Osiris cult. The most well-known and comprehensive narratives of

142. Quote from the *Egyptian Book of the Dead*, as quoted by *Tour Egypt*, last accessed January 24, 2012, http://www.touregypt.net/osirhymn.htm.

the life and death of Osiris come to us from Diodorus Siculus and Plutarch.

According to Diodorus, who wrote his *Histories* in the years 60–30 BC, Osiris was the very first ruler to bring civilization to mankind. He turned men from cannibalism and introduced them to agriculture. His first city was the Egyptian city of Thebes (in the Upper Egypt region of Nekhen, original home of the Falcon Tribe). Diodorus also explains how, like the Greek legends of Dionysus, Osiris introduced wine and beer to mankind, and he also promoted the art of writing. Eventually, however, Osiris grew bored:

> Of Osiris they say that, being of a beneficent turn of mind, and eager for glory, he gathered together a great army, with the intention of visiting all the inhabited earth and teaching the race of men how to cultivate the vine and sow wheat and barley; for he supposed that if he made men give up their savagery and adopt a gentle manner of life he would receive immortal honours because of the magnitude of his benefactions.[143]

> Now when Osiris arrived at the borders of Ethiopia, he curbed the river by dykes on both banks... After this he continued his march through Arabia along the shore of the Red Sea as far as India and the limits of

---

143. Diodorus Siculus, *Library of History*, Vol. 1, 17:1–2. For the complete index of the *Library of History* see http://penelope.uchicago.edu/Thayer/E/Roman/Texts/Diodorus_Siculus/home.html.

> the inhabited world. He also founded not a few cities in India, one of which he named Nysa… He also planted ivy in the Indian Nysa, and throughout India and those countries which border upon it the plant to this day is still to be found only in this region. And many other signs of his stay he left in that country, which have led the Indians of a later time to lay claim to the god and say that he was by birth a native of India.[144]

Plutarch, who lived c.46-120 AD, gives an account very similar to that of Diodorus in his biography of Osiris known as *Isis and Osiris*:

> The Egyptians…relate that on the first of [the five intercalated] days Osiris was born, and at the hour of his birth a voice issued forth saying, "The Lord of All advances to the light." But some relate that a certain Pamyles, while he was drawing water in Thebes, heard a voice issuing from the shrine of Zeus, which bade him proclaim with a loud voice that a mighty and beneficent king, Osiris, had been born; and for this Cronus entrusted to him the child Osiris, which he brought up…
>
> One of the first acts related of Osiris in his reign was to deliver the Egyptians from their destitute and brutish manner of living. This he did by showing them the fruits of cultivation, by giving them laws,

144. Diodorus Siculus, *Library of History*, Vol. 1, 19:5–8.

> and by teaching them to honour the gods. Later he travelled over the whole earth civilizing it without the slightest need of arms, but most of the peoples he won over to his way by the charm of his persuasive discourse combined with song and all manner of music. Hence the Greeks came to identify him with Dionysus.[145]

Now according to the Egyptian priest Manetho, who provided the Greeks with a chronology of Egyptian kings, the god Osiris reigned from Egypt at a time *over forty thousand years before King Menes*, the first king of Egypt. However, when we look at the different descriptions of Menes, they seem oddly similar to the descriptions of Osiris. For instance, according to Manetho, Menes had been "an excellent leader" who had led his army "across the frontier and won great glory." Diodorus wrote that Menes was the first lawgiver who also converted the Egyptians into worshiping the gods. The Roman historian Pliny wrote that Menes had invented writing.

All of these descriptions of the historical King Menes are *exactly the same* as the descriptions of the god Osiris. It seems very plausible that the inner circle of Egyptian priests knew that Menes was Osiris, but to protect their secret they promoted a false chronology to the Greeks that pushed Osiris deep into the past.

Confirmation for the identity of Osiris as the biblical

---

145. Plutarch, *Isis and Osiris*, Sections 12–13, last accessed January 24, 2012, http://penelope.uchicago.edu/Thayer/E/Roman/Texts/Plutarch/Moralia/Isis_and_Osiris*/home.html.

Nimrod, whom we equate with Narmer, and therefore Menes, comes from another important piece of evidence given by Diodorus Siculus:

> They say also that the Egyptians are colonists sent out by the Ethiopians, **Osiris having been the leader of the colony**... And the larger part of the customs of the Egyptians are, they hold, Ethiopian, the colonists still preserving their ancient manners. For instance, the belief that their kings are gods, the very special attention which they pay to their burials, and many other matters of a similar nature are Ethiopian practices, while the shapes of their statues and the forms of their letters are Ethiopian... Many other things are also told by them concerning their own antiquity and the colony which they sent out that became the Egyptians... (bold added)[146]

As mentioned earlier, it is entirely plausible that Nimrod, the royal heir of Cush, was born in Ethiopia, the Land of Cush. Whether or not he was truly born there, it is very likely that Narmer's great army that conquered Egypt came from Ethiopia as it swept north into Lower Egypt towards the Mediterranean coast.

What Diodorus relates as being "Ethiopian" is probably better interpreted as "Sumerian" because it was from ancient Sumer that the Falcon Tribe originally came. These conquerors of Egypt also brought with them their burial customs, their system of idolatry that honored Enki (known as Geb

146. Diodorus Siculus, *Library of History*, Vol. 3, 3:1–7.

to the Egyptians), their architecture, and the beginnings of a writing system that can all be traced back to Uruk, the heart of Nimrod's great Empire.

Before we move on to show how the story of the death of Osiris matches up with our hypothetical construct of the events that must have taken place at the death of Nimrod, we need to understand how Osiris truly was a counterfeit Christ to the ancient pagan world.

The "New Testament" of Ancient Egypt

The Pyramid Texts describe Osiris as a dead god who is the benevolent ruler of the underworld. There are no clear narratives that describe exactly how and why Osiris became the "Lord of the Abyss," but there are utterances that refer to his violent death at the hands of the god Set (or Seth). In depictions of the conflict between Osiris and Set the Egyptians often symbolized Set as a hippopotamus. This symbolism occurs in many inscriptions including the depiction of the "Festival of Victory" that is inscribed on the Temple of Horus at Edfu, which remains to this day. When Manetho wrote that King Menes was "killed by a hippo," I believe this is further evidence linking the historical King Menes with the "mythical" Osiris.

Taken as a whole, the Pyramid Texts are a kind of "New Testament" for the religion of Osiris, because they connect the earthly king's hope for a blessed afterlife with the king's devotion to, and identification with, the deceased Osiris who rules over the Land of the Dead.

The very first three "utterances" of the Pyramid Text demonstrate this "New Testament" theme:

> UTTERANCE 1: "The King is my eldest son…he is my beloved, with whom I am well pleased."
>
> UTTERANCE 2: "Recitation by Geb: 'The king is my bodily son…' "
>
> UTTERANCE 3: "…The King is my beloved son, my first-born upon the throne of Geb, with whom he is well pleased, and he has given to him his heritage in the presence of the Great Ennead. All the gods are in joy, and they say: 'How goodly is the King! His father Geb is pleased with him.' "[147]

The king who speaks these spells identifies himself with Osiris, who is the son of Geb, the Egyptian "god of the earth" who is comparable with Enki the Sumerian "Lord of the Earth." The Great Ennead is the "council of the gods," and in Utterance 3, the king, as the representation of Osiris, is welcomed into the presence of the gods.

The two utterances given below show that one of the titles of Osiris is "Dweller in the Abyss;" and Osiris is also named as the "leader" of those in the Abyss:

> UTTERANCE 577: Osiris and the king become one in the Netherworld
>
> "Osiris appears, the Sceptre is pure, the Lord of Right is exalted at the First of the Year, even he the Lord of the Year… 'Here comes the Dweller in the

---

147. *The Ancient Egyptian Pyramid Texts*, translated by R.O. Faulkner (UK: Oxford University Press, 1998), 1.

Abyss,' says Atum. 'We have come,' say they, say the gods to you, O Osiris... The sky has conceived him, the dawn has borne him... You bear up the sky with your right side, possessing life; you live because the gods have ordered that you shall live... You support the earth with your left side, possessing dominion; you live, you live, because the gods have ordered that you shall live."

UTTERANCE 512: The king's son to his dead father identified as Osiris

"Raise yourself, my father... Traverse the sky, make your abode in the Field of Offerings among the gods... Sit upon your iron throne, take your mace and your sceptre, that you may lead those who are in the Abyss, give orders to the gods, and set a spirit in its spirit-state... O my father, raise yourself, go in your spirit-state."[148]

The god Osiris was the Egyptian "god of the afterlife." However, the Egyptian afterlife was not in heaven, but in the underworld, known as the Abyss. Nonetheless the apparent parallels with Christian beliefs about Jesus have been noted by a number of scholars. Many of them have even gone so far as to argue that Osiris was the basis of the "Gospel Story" found in the New Testament, and that the story of "Jesus" is nothing but a myth based on the religion of Osiris in combination with other Near Eastern "Dying God" legends. This seems to be the intellectual position taken by many early mythologists,

148. *The Ancient Egyptian Pyramid Texts*, 232–233; 188–189.

including E. A. Wallis Budge, James G. Frazier, as well as Joseph Campbell.

The parallels between Osiris and Jesus are clearly there, but the academic experts simply cannot comprehend that Jesus wasn't a *copy* of Osiris; He is the *answer* to Osiris.

Here is what Budge wrote at the beginning of his comprehensive study of Osiris:

> The religious literature of all the great periods of Egyptian history is filled with allusions to incidents connected with the life, death, and resurrection of Osiris, the god and judge of the Egyptian dead; and from first to last the authors of religious texts took it for granted that their readers were well acquainted with such incidents in all their details. In no text do we find any connected history of the god, and nowhere are stated in detail the reasons why he assumed his exalted position as the judge of souls, or why, **for about four thousand years, he remained the great type and symbol of the Resurrection.** No funerary inscription exists, however early, in which evidence cannot be found proving that the deceased had set his hope of immortality in Osiris, and at no time in Egypt's long history do we find that the position of Osiris was usurped by any other god. On the contrary, it is Osiris who is made to usurp the attributes and powers of other gods, and in tracing his history...we shall find that the importance of the cult of this god grew in proportion to the growth of the power and wealth of Egypt, and that finally

its influence filled both the national and private life of her inhabitants, from the Mediterranean Sea to the Sixth Cataract at Shablûkah. The fame of Osiris extended to the nations around, and it is to the hands of foreigners that we are indebted for connected, though short, narratives of his history.[149]

The Judgment Seat of Osiris

In the New Testament, the Apostle Paul teaches about the "Judgment Seat of Christ." In Romans 14:10, Paul writes that "we shall all stand before the judgment seat of Christ." In 2 Corinthians 5:10, he writes, "For we must all appear before the judgment seat of Christ; that every one may receive the things done in his body, according to that he hath done, whether it be good or bad."

The Egyptians also believed in a post-mortem judgment of souls, but they viewed it as the "Judgment Seat of Osiris." According to the *Book of the Dead* and other sources, after death every individual was expected to stand before Osiris in the underworld, and have their hearts weighed on a balance against the feather of Maat, which represents righteousness and justice. This was known as the "Weighing of the Heart" ceremony, and its outcome determined whether or not the soul would experience blessing or punishment in the underworld ruled by Osiris.

149. E.A. Wallis Budge, *Osiris and the Egyptian Resurrection* (New York, NY: Dover Publications, 1973 [1911]), 1.

This judgment scene appears throughout Egyptian religion, such as within the papyrus below, which shows the god Anubis leading a newly-deceased individual by the hand while Osiris looks on from his throne:

The Judgment Seat of Osiris and the 'Weighing of the Heart'

Here is a final summary of what the Osiris cult meant for the Egyptian people, as given in the introduction to the translation of the *The Book of the Dead* by E. A. Wallace Budge:

> Osiris was the god through whose sufferings and death the Egyptian hoped that his body might rise again in some transformed or glorified shape, and to him who had conquered death and had become the king of the other world the Egyptian appealed in prayer for eternal life through his victory and power. In every funeral inscription known to us, from the pyramid texts down to the roughly written prayers upon coffins of the Roman period, what is done for Osiris is done also for the deceased, the state and condition of Osiris are the state and condition of the deceased; in

> a word, the deceased is identified with Osiris. If Osiris liveth for ever, the deceased will live for ever; if Osiris dieth, then will the deceased perish.[150]

In the next chapter we will look at the "suffering and death" of the Egyptian god Osiris, which will bring important evidence into our investigation of the past and future careers of the biblical Antichrist.

---

150. E. A. Wallis Budge, *The Book of the Dead—The Papyrus of Ani* (originally published in the UK in 1895), the quote is from a digital version of the original work located at *SacredTexts.com*, last accessed March 13, 2012, http://www.sacred-texts.com/egy/ebod/ebod04.htm.

chapter twenty

A MURDEROUS PLOT

ACCORDING TO THE AVAILABLE SOURCES, the fall of Osiris occurred when he was at the height of his career. It was a wicked plot hatched by a jealous group of murderers that brought an end to mankind's first "Golden Age." Here is how Diodorus Siculus tells the tale:

> Although the priests of Osiris had from the earliest times received the account of his death as a matter not to be divulged, in the course of years it came about that through some of their number this hidden knowledge was published to the many. This is the story as they give it:
>
> When Osiris was ruling over Egypt as its lawful king, he was murdered by his brother Typhon, a violent and impious man; Typhon then divided the body of the slain man into twenty-six pieces and gave one

> portion to each of the band of murderers, since he wanted all of them to share in the pollution and felt that in this way he would have in them steadfast supporters and defenders of his rule. But Isis, the sister and wife of Osiris, avenged his murder with the aid of her son Horus, and after slaying Typhon and his accomplices became queen over Egypt...[151]

The account given by Plutarch is similar, but he gives a different number of members within the conspiracy to kill Osiris, which was led by Typhon, the Greek name for the Egyptian god Set:

> During his absence the tradition is that Typhon attempted nothing revolutionary because Isis, who was in control, was vigilant and alert; but when he returned home Typhon contrived a treacherous plot against him and formed **a group of conspirators seventy-two in number**. He had also the co-operation of a queen from Ethiopia who was there at the time and whose name they report as Aso. Typhon, having secretly measured Osiris's body and having made ready a beautiful chest of corresponding size artistically ornamented, caused it to be brought into the room where the festivity was in progress. The company was much pleased at the sight of it and admired it greatly, whereupon Typhon jestingly promised to present it to the

151. Diodorus Siculus, *Library of History*, Vol. 1, Section 21. For the complete index see: http://penelope.uchicago.edu/Thayer/E/Roman/Texts/Diodorus_Siculus/home.html.

> man who should find the chest to be exactly his length when he lay down in it. They all tried it in turn, but no one fitted it; then Osiris got into it and lay down, and those who were in the plot ran to it and slammed down the lid, which they fastened by nails from the outside and also by using molten lead. Then they carried the chest to the river and sent it on its way to the sea through the Tanitic Mouth.[152]

The number seventy-two is key here, because it connects with the seventy angels who benefited from the death of Nimrod at the Tower of Babel, as described in chapter 9. The original number of *seventy* gradually evolved into the number *seventy-two* in various occult sources, as explained in chapter 12.

The possibility that the death of Osiris was the result of a "conspiracy of the gods" is supported by a subsequent account of the death of Osiris that is provided by Diodorus. It comes within his explanation of the origin of the worship of the male sex organ.[153] According to Diodorus, it all goes back to the story of Osiris who, as Greeks and Egyptians agreed, was the same god as Dionysus:

> We shall at this point discuss Priapus and the myths related about him, realizing that an account of him is appropriate in connection with the history of

152. Plutarch, *Isis and Osiris*, Section 13.

153. Priapus worship is represented today in the USA through the Washington Monument, 6,665 1/8 inches tall by 661 1/2 inches wide at its base. It is a monument to the phallus of Osiris.

Dionysus. Now the ancients record in their myths that Priapus was the son of Dionysus and Aphroditê and they present a plausible argument for this linage; for men when under the influence of wine find the members of their bodies tense and inclined to the pleasures of love.

But certain writers say that when the ancients wished to speak in their myths of the sexual organ of males they called it Priapus. Some, however, relate that the generative member, since it is the cause of the reproduction of human beings and of their continued existence through all time, became the object of immortal honour.

But the Egyptians in their myths about Priapus say that in ancient times **the Titans formed a conspiracy against Osiris and slew him**, and then, taking his body and dividing it into equal parts among themselves, they slipped them secretly out of the house but this organ alone they threw into the river, since no one of them was willing to take it with him. But Isis tracked down the murder of her husband, and after slaying the Titans and fashioning the several pieces of his body into the shape of a human figure, she gave them to the priests with orders that they pay Osiris the honours of a god, but since the only member she was unable to recover was the organ of sex she commanded them to pay to it the honours of a god and to set it up in their temples in an erect position.[154]

---

154. Diodorus Siculus, *Library of History*, Vol. 4, Section 6:1–3. See: http://www.theoi.com/Text/DiodorusSiculus4A.html.

According to this passage, the Egyptians believed that the conspiracy to kill Osiris, which was led by Set (Typhon), also included a group of divine beings—gods—whom Diodorus equates with the Titans. With this revelation we see that the ancient sources are painting a picture that fits more and more with our hypothesis regarding what must have happened to Nimrod at the Tower of Babel, when the seventy angels willingly agreed to put an end to Nimrod and his empire.

The Greeks have much to say about Dionysus, whom they recognized as their version of Osiris. According to numerous Greek sources, Dionysus was killed in a plot involving the Titans and other members of the pantheon of gods. Pausanius was a Greek writer who lived in the second century AD, and in his *Description of Greece* he refers to this conflict:

> The stories told of Dionysos by the people of Patrai, that he was reared in Mesatis and incurred there all sorts of perils through the plots of the Titans.[155]

> From Homer the name of the Titans was taken by Onomakritos, who in the orgies he composed for Dionysos made the Titans the authors of the god's sufferings.[156]

Diodorus Siculus traces Dionysus back to Crete and offers the following remark:

---

155. Pausanius, *Description of Greece*, Volume 7, 18:4, index at: http://www.theoi.com/Text/Pausanias1A.html
156. Pausanius, *Description of Greece*, Volume 8, 37:5.

> This god [Dionysos] was born in Krete, men say, of Zeus and Persephone, and Orpheus has handed down the tradition in the initiatory rites that he was torn in pieces by the Titans.[157]

Zagreus the Mighty Hunter

The Minoan representation of Nimrod is something that is covered in my "Giza Discovery" series. Here is what I wrote:

> The conquests of Narmer and his fame as a great hunter eventually became known on the island of Crete. When the Greeks interacted with Egypt during Classical times virtually all of the Greek writers equated their god Dionysos with the great Egyptian god Osiris. The similarities were obvious, and Minoan Crete was merely a stepping stone between Egypt and Greece for the worship of this great archetypal Underworld "god" who conquered the known world during his lifetime.
>
> German scholar Carl Kerenyi has traced the origin of the cult of Dionysos to the island of Crete, but I believe that it can be traced from Crete back to Egypt and even back to Ethiopia. The Greek poet Anacreon (born around 570 BC) gives one of the titles of Dionysos as "Aithiopias" which simply means "The Ethiopian." Also, one of the many interpretations of the name "Dionysos" is "Dio-Nysa" which means "God of Nysa." According to the Greek historian Herodotus, Nysa was located in the land of Ethiopia:

---

157. Diodorus Siculus, *Library of History*, Vol. 5, Section 75:4.

> … as it is, the Greek story has it that no sooner was Dionysus born than Zeus sewed him up in his thigh and carried him away to Nysa in Ethiopia beyond Egypt.[158]

In Crete the original name for Dionysos was Zagreus, who was often represented as the "lord of the wild beasts." Kerenyi writes that in Classical Greek literature Zagreus first appeared in the sixth century BC in a poetic line that reads "Mistress earth and Zagreus who art above all other gods!" Zagreus is also mentioned twice by the poet Aischylos who gives Zagreus similar reverence, equating him with Zeus and also with Hades. Zagreus was simply the Minoan name for the Egyptian god Osiris, and each was worshiped as the primary "Underworld" god.

The Greeks worshiped Dionysos and they also also had memories of a hero-figure that they knew as Orion, who "threatened to exterminate all the animals on earth" while hunting on Crete. According to Kerenyi, the meaning of the name Zagreus is "Great Hunter," or more accurately "catcher of game."[159] Kerenyi refers to a Minoan seal from Kydonia that depicts this ancient god holding up two lions:

---

158. Herodotus, *Histories 2:146*, viewable here: last accessed January 24, 2012, http://www.mlahanas.de/Greeks/Mythology/Dionysus.html.

159. Carl Kerenyi, *Dionysos—Archetypal Image of Indestructible Life* (Princeton, NJ: Princeton University Press, 1976), 80–83.

> His relationship to the two lions flanking him is clearly expressed in his gesture—he rests his hands on the heads of the erect animals… The god holds fast the lions, two living beasts of prey, with his bare hands. He tames them, as it were, by a "laying on" of hands. He draws them into his sphere of influence and holds them captive.[160]

Kerenyi goes on to ask, *"Why was this great mythical hunter, who in Greece became a mysterious god of the underworld, a capturer of wild animals and not a killer? What are the implications of 'capturing alive'?"* Kerenyi goes on to answer his own question:

> On a bronze shield from the Greek period of Crete… we see the "lord of the wild beasts" with a different gesture from that on the gem from Kydonia. Under the influence of Assyrian art, he is represented here with a beard, but what interests us most is that he is stepping on the head of a bull and seems to be holding up and rending a lion. In this instance the lion is torn to pieces, but on Crete that could also be the fate of a bull. The bull games of the Cretans were a continuation of the bull capture, enacted in the form of a drama. It seems hardly credible that in a wild Dionysos cult such powerful animals should have been torn to pieces alive by the teeth of the participants and devoured raw, but we have

160. Ibid., 81–82.

> express testimony showing that this monstrous rite occurred in a feast of Dionysos repeated every two years… Thus the purpose of the "capturing alive" evidently lay in the rending of the captive animals and the devouring of their raw flesh.[161]

In chapter 12 the idea was introduced that Leviathan was a sort of demonic sacrament for the gods, according to Psalm 74:14, where it says that the Lord breaks the heads of Leviathan and "gavest him to be meat" to the demonic Siyyim, identified as the devil-gods of the nations.

This is interesting because in the Greek Orphic myths, the original Dionysus, known as Zagreus, was actually *eaten alive* by the Titans, after he had taken the form of a bull:

> According to the followers of Orphism, Zeus had lain with Persephone…in the form of a serpent. The result of their union was Zagreus.
>
> Zeus had intended Zagreus to be his heir, but a jealous Hera persuaded the Titans to kill the child. Like the infant Zeus in Cretan myth, the child Zagreus was entrusted to the Titans who distracted him with toys. While he gazed into a mirror they tried to seize him and he fled, changing into various animal forms in his attempt to escape. Finally he took the form of a bull, and in that form they caught him, tore him to pieces, and devoured him.[162]

---

161. Ibid., 84–85. For further information see the online article by Peter Goodgame, "The Giza Discovery, Part Eight: The First Pharaoh," by Peter Goodgame, at http://www.redmoonrising.com/Giza/AfricOrig8.htm.

In this story, supposedly Zeus was able to drive the Titans away from Zagreus at the very last moment, allowing Zeus to retrieve only the heart of the child Zagreus, which he gave to Semele, who re-birthed Zagreus, who then grew up to conquer the world. The chronology of events in all of these Greek myths can be very convoluted, but the kernels of truth at the heart of them remain.

The violent rites of the Dionysian mystery cults were actually a recreation of the Minoan memory of the murder of Nimrod the Mighty Hunter at the hands of the Titans. The modern Spanish bullfight is perhaps a relic of this ancient mystery tradition.

All of these ancient cultural memories point back to Nimrod as the original "Bull," who was known as Narmer to the Egyptians, whose "Bull" imagery survives within various references and artifacts such as the Narmer Palette and the Bull Palette (above). The bull was also a symbol of royal power in Sumer, and in Egypt the living Apis Bull (above)

162. "Zagreus," *Wikipedia*, last modified November 30, 2011, http://en.wikipedia.org/wiki/Zagreus.

became worshiped and viewed as possessing the actual spirit of the departed Osiris. The golden calf worshiped by the Israelites at Sinai was probably an idol of the Apis Bull.

The Lord was not happy to see His people worshiping a representation of the Antichrist, even as He was delivering the Law that would help to pave the way for the coming of the *true* Messiah.

chapter twenty-one

THE MIGHTY ONE FALLS

THE VIOLENT DEATH of Nimrod is revealed through our research into Greek and Egyptian history and mythology. Yet we still have not produced a *biblical* record of this event, which was one of the most important turning points in Old Testament history, unequaled in significance except perhaps for the *Fall of Adam and Eve* and the *Great Flood*.

The downfall of King Nimrod is there in the biblical record. It has escaped notice, once again, because of the translators' misunderstanding regarding the true identity of the figure named as Asshur in the Old Testament. But before we go there we must first clarify the connection between the Egyptian god Osiris and the biblical Asshur, whom we have identified as Nimrod.

In his book, *The Origins of Osiris and His Cult*, Egyptologist John Gwyn Griffiths attempts to uncover the origin and meaning of the Egyptian name "Osiris":

The views of Mercer take us from Libya to Mesopotamia. "There is much", he says, "about Osiris and the Osiris legend which points to some connection with Mesopotamia". He proceeds to urge the identity of Osiris and the Babylonian Asar, a title of the god Marduk:

> In the ancient pantheon of Babylonia the title of the god Marduk was *Asar*... or *Asarri*... Now this word is written with two ideographs one of which denotes a "seat" and the other an "eye"... Compare with this the earliest forms of the name of Osiris... Furthermore, Asar, who was Marduk, was called "the good being", which may be compared to Osiris who is called wn nfr, "the good being."

It must be admitted that the resemblance of the ideographs is a striking fact... But Mercer does not finish here. He wants to identify Babylonian Asar with the Assyrian Ašur... His thesis now becomes rather involved; for three gods [Osiris, Ashur, and Marduk] are equated. He finds the equation of Osiris and Marduk (i.e. as Asar) supported ideologically, for both were "watergods", "vegetation gods", "underworld gods" and "resurrection gods"...

It was Th. Deveria, as we have seen, who first equated Osiris and Ashur, and Mercer is in the main following Sidney Smith's elaboration of the idea, which now includes Marduk in the form of Asar... His own proposal is that a common origin may be

> sought for the Osiris myth and the Marduk-Ashur myth in Syria…
>
> In the Old Kingdom Osiris is written consistently (with one exception) with the throne-sign preceding the sign for an eye. Thereafter there are numerous variations in signs and in the order of them…
>
> Bearing in mind… the [word-play] involved in the early and predominant forms, one is drawn to the conclusion that the true derivation of Osiris is *wsr*, **and that the name means, originally, The Mighty One…**
>
> If the derivation from *wsr*, "mighty", seems too simple to be convincing, it is worth recalling that its simplicity can be buttressed by what is known of several other divine names from Egypt… Among the accepted etymologies are Sakhmet, "the powerful one", Amun, "the hidden one", Horus, "the lofty one", Atum, "the perfected one" and Wedjoyet, "the green one". If Osiris be interpreted as *wsr*, his name will belong to this type.[163]

So there we have it. Griffiths concludes that perhaps the best possible meaning for the name "Osiris" is "The Mighty One." Furthermore, he produces evidence that Osiris is directly related to the Babylonian god Marduk through the symbols used for Asar, as well as directly related to the Assyrian god Ashur.

"And Cush begat Nimrod: he began to be a **mighty one**

---

163. John G. Griffiths, *The Origins of Osiris and His Cult* (Leiden, the Netherlands: E. J. Brill, 1980), 90–95.

in the earth. He was a **mighty hunter** before the Lord: wherefore it is said, Even as Nimrod the **mighty hunter** before the Lord" (Genesis 10:8–9).

We have seen thus far that the historical identity of the biblical "Nimrod" connects with Enmerkar of Sumer, as well as Narmer of Egypt; and we have now shown that Nimrod's other biblical identity of "Asshur" connects with Marduk/Asar of Babylon, Assur of Assyria, as well as Osiris of Egypt.

Nimrod was truly *the most significant figure to walk the face of the earth* after the Flood prior to the first coming of Jesus Christ. He changed the history of the world like no other man. He built the greatest empire the world has ever seen, and then his catastrophic downfall at the hands of the heavenly host set the foundation for the system of polytheistic paganism that ruled the earth until it was broken by Jesus Christ.

The Catastrophic Fall of Asshur

The downfall of Asshur is described in Scripture within a Word of the Lord that was given to Ezekiel for the King of Egypt. At this time King Nebuchadnezzar of Babylon was growing in power and threatening the kingdom of Judah. Jeremiah the prophet warned Judah to submit to Babylon, but instead the king of Judah made an alliance with the king of Egypt, who promised that the Egyptian army would come to the rescue. This rescue never materialized and Jerusalem was taken by Babylon, resulting in the captivity of the southern kingdom of Judah in 586 BC. Because of this treachery against Jerusalem the Lord announced the coming destruction of Egypt, by the hand of King Nebuchadnezzar, in Ezekiel 31.

In this passage, the Lord recognizes that the king of Egypt compares himself to Asshur, but then the Lord declares that the king will fall, just like Asshur fell from his great height, and that the king will end up in hell just like Asshur did long ago. If this Word was indeed received by the king of Egypt, then he would have known that the Lord was speaking to him as the Egyptian heir of the Osiris cult. In other words, in this context the name "Asshur" was meant to be understood as Osiris, which is how the king of Egypt would have understood it. He wasn't comparing himself to the previously great kingdom of Assyria, or to any other king. No, the king of Egypt only compares himself to Osiris, the Mighty One, the great founder of the Egyptian civilization who was worshiped as a god.

As the prophecy of Ezekiel 31 begins, Asshur is portrayed as a mighty tree of Lebanon, the greatest tree in history. This ties directly back to the prophecy against Asshur in Isaiah 10:34: "and Lebanon shall fall by a mighty one." The play on words here is now apparent. Asshur, the "Mighty One," is predicted by Isaiah to fall at the hands of a greater "Mighty One," identified in Isaiah 10:17 as the Messiah, the Holy One of Israel.

In Ezekiel 31, Asshur is portrayed as a great cedar of Lebanon that is even greater than the "trees of Eden, in the garden of God." The Garden of Eden, as Michael S. Heiser has shown,[164] was also the "meeting place of the divine council"

---

164. See "The Meeting Place of the Divine Council," by Heiser located at http://www.thedivinecouncil.com/MeetingPlaceDivineCouncil.pdf. Also see "God's Home Address," at http://www.thedivinecouncil.com/GodsAddress.pdf.

where God would meet with the other "sons of God" who participated with Him in ruling over the earth. We find the same kind of imagery in Ezekiel 28:13–14, where the King of Tyre is shown in the Garden of Eden walking around at the mountain-top meeting place of the divine council. In Ezekiel 31, Asshur is being compared with the angels, "the trees of Eden," that are a part of the divine council. Here is how it begins:

> And it came to pass in the eleventh year, in the third month, on the first day of the month, the word of the Lord came to me, saying, Son of man, say to Pharaoh king of Egypt, and to his multitude;
>
> To whom hast thou compared thyself in thy haughtiness? Behold, **Asshur** was a cypress in Libanus, and was fair in shoots, and high in stature: his top **reached to the midst of the clouds.** The water nourished him, the depth made him grow tall; she led her rivers round about his plants, and she sent forth her streams to all the trees of the field.
>
> Therefore was his stature exalted above all the trees of the field, and his branches spread far by the help of much water. All the birds of the sky made their nests in his boughs, and under his branches all the wild beasts of the field bred; **the whole multitude of nations dwelt under his shadow.**
>
> And he was fair in his height by reason of the multitude of his branches: for his roots were amidst much water. And such cypresses as this were in the paradise of God; and there were no pines like his shoots, and there were no firs like his branches: **no tree in the**

> **paradise of God was like him in his beauty, because of the multitude of his branches: and the trees of God's paradise of delight** [MT- "all the trees of Eden"] **envied him.** (Ezekiel 31:1–9, LXX)

Ezekiel's description of Asshur matches the similar description in Isaiah 14:14, "I will ascend **above the heights of the clouds**; I will be like the most High"

Another important thing to note is the fact that due to his ambition and success the other trees in God's garden *envied* Asshur: "all the trees of Eden envied him." The Hebrew word is *qana*—jealousy, and in the LXX it is a version of the Greek word (2206) *zeloo*, which means "to burn with zeal; to be heated or to boil with envy, hatred, anger."

I think we have right here the origin of the decision made in the divine council of Genesis 11:7, when the angels agreed to descend to the earth and put an end to Nimrod's reign. They agreed because they were *jealous* of his great empire, and they seized the opportunity to rule over their own nations.

Ezekiel's passage continues:

> Therefore thus saith the Lord; Because thou art grown great, and hast set thy top in the midst of the clouds, and I saw when he was exalted; therefore **I delivered him into the hands of the prince of the nations, and he wrought his destruction.** And ravaging strangers from the nations have destroyed him, and have cast him down upon the mountains: his branches fell in all the valleys, and his boughs were broken in every field of the land; and all the people of the nations are gone down from their shelter, and have laid him low.

> All the birds of the sky have settled on his fallen trunk, and all the wild beasts of the field came upon his boughs: in order that none of the trees by the water should exalt themselves by reason of their size: whereas they set their top in the midst of the clouds, yet they continued not in their high state in their place, all that drank water, all were consigned to death, to the depth of the earth, in the midst of the children of men, with them that go down to the pit. (Ezekiel 31:10–14, LXX).

In the Hebrew text, v.11 literally says, "I gave him into the hand of the **god of the Goyim**; to deal with him according to the wickedness for which he was cast out." The word "Goyim" means "Gentiles" or "Nations." In Ezekiel's time there were many "gods" but there was only one *singular* "God of the Gentiles." Ezekiel must be referring to Satan, the ruler of the kingdoms of the world.

The other beings that assisted the "God of the Goyim" are named as the *terrible* (a derivative of the word *ariyts*-6184) *Zurim of the Goyim*, translated as "strangers of the nations." The word *zurim* derives from the verb meaning "to turn aside, to depart," and has a very negative connotation. Could this be a reference to the angels that agreed to destroy the forces of Nimrod before they were given their own nations to rule? A deeper investigation of these beings is certainly called for. In any case, what this text says is that Asshur was handed over to Satan, who, along with the "terrible strangers of the nations," destroyed him and left his "branches" scattered over mountains, valleys, and fields.

But why would Satan destroy his very own son? Well, first of all, Satan faced the inevitable punishment for mating with a woman and producing a Nephilim in the first place, so he was not in a place to negotiate. Secondly, we know that he was given the chance to rule over and possess six more kings in the future, as well as witness the resurrection of Nimrod and a final taste of world domination at the end. For Satan, the only downside was the death of his son, Nimrod. In any case, the decision made in heaven at the Tower of Babel to put an end to Nimrod's reign was undoubtedly quickly acted upon by a particular group of angels, who were themselves led by the devil himself.

Ezekiel's passage continues:

> Thus saith the Lord God; In the day wherein he went down to Hades, the deep mourned for him: and I stayed her floods, and restrained her abundance of water: and Libanus saddened for him, all the trees of the field fainted for him.
>
> **At the sound of his fall the nations quaked**, when I brought him down to Hades with them that go down to the pit: and all the trees of Delight [MT: "all the trees of Eden"] comforted him in the heart, and the choice of plants of Libanus, all that drink water. For they went down to hell with him among the slain with the sword; and his seed, even they that dwelt under his shadow, perished in the midst of their life.
>
> To whom art thou compared? Descend, and be thou debased with the trees of paradise to the depth of the earth: thou shalt lie in the midst of the

> uncircumcised with them that are slain by the sword. Thus shall Pharaoh be, and the multitude of his host, saith the Lord God. (Ezekiel 31:15–18, LXX)

In this passage the Lord is reminding Pharaoh that Asshur's soul is in hell, and He predicts that Pharaoh and his armies will soon meet him there. In effect, the Lord is saying, "Are you sure you want to compare yourself to Asshur (Osiris)? Because very soon you will be destroyed and end up in hell the same way that Osiris did!"

Another strange thing about this verse is that the Lord reveals that there are "trees of Eden" down in hell. Again, this only makes sense if this phrase is understood as symbolic of the fallen members of the Lord's divine council that once met at the Garden of Eden. These angels that are in hell might be the "sons of God" who mated with human women before the Flood. Their current incarceration in hell is revealed in 2 Peter 2:4 and Jude 1:6.

The most important part of this passage, however, is the statement that, **"At the sound of Asshur's fall the nations quaked!"** Finally we have a fitting description of what happened at the fall of the Tower of Babel and the destruction of the world's first superpower.

Slain By the Sword

Following the lengthy Word from the Lord given in Ezekiel 31, the prophet also received two subsequent messages to deliver to the king of Egypt. The first is given in Ezekiel 32:1–16, and the second in Ezekiel 32:17–32. The second one is worth analyzing because it refers to "Asshur and all his host," who were all "slain by the sword." This is the evidence that Asshur was killed in the very same way spoken of the Antichrist in the book of Revelation: "And I saw one of his heads as it were wounded to death; and his deadly wound was healed: and all the world wondered after the beast... And [the False Prophet] deceiveth them that dwell on the earth by the means of those miracles which he had power to do in the sight of the beast; saying to them that dwell on the earth, that they should make an image to the beast, **which had the wound by a sword**, and did live" (Revelation 13:3,14).

The passage from Ezekiel warns the king of Egypt, and once again predicts that he will be killed and end up in hell. The interesting part about this prophecy is the extensive description of the people Pharaoh will meet once he arrives in hell:

> Son of man, lament over the strength of Egypt, for the nations shall bring down her daughters dead to the depth of the earth, to them that go down to the pit. They shall fall with him in the midst of them that are slain with the sword, and all his strength shall perish: **the giants also shall say to thee,** "Be thou in the depth of the pit: to whom art thou superior? yea, go down, and lie with the uncircumcised, in the midst of them that are slain with the sword."
>
> **There are Assur and all his company**: all his slain have been laid there: and their burial is in the depth of the pit, **and his company are set around about his tomb: all the slain that fell by the sword,** who had caused the fear of them to be upon the land of the living. (Ezekiel 32:18–23, LXX)

> And they are laid with the giants that fell of old, who went down to Hades with their weapons of war: and they laid their swords under their heads, but their iniquities were upon their bones, because they terrified all men during their life. And thou shalt lie in the midst of the uncircumcised, with them that have been slain by the sword.
>
> There are laid the princes of Assur, who yielded their strength to a wound of the sword: these are laid with the slain, with them that go down to the pit. There are the princes of the north, even all the captains of Assur, who go down slain to Hades: they lie uncircumcised among the slain with the sword together with their terror and their strength, and they have received their punishment with them that go down to the pit.
>
> King Pharao shall see them, and shall be comforted over all their force, saith the Lord God. For I have caused his fear to be upon the land of the living yet he shall lie in the midst of the uncircumcised with them that are slain with the sword, even Pharao, and all his multitude with him, saith the Lord God. (Ezekiel 32:27–32, LXX)

Will this terrible host of giants, mighty men, and the princes and captains of Asshur, be part of the armies led by Asshur, the King of the Abyss, when he is released back into the world again after the fifth Trumpet of Revelation? The possibility is truly frightening.

chapter twenty-two

WHERE THE CORPSE IS

IN THE STORY OF THE DEATH of Osiris the dead body of the god-king was divided up into many different pieces and scattered throughout the land. I believe this is a metaphor for the division of Nimrod's empire into the hands of the seventy angels. The body of Osiris was divided up, but in all of the accounts his wife Isis eventually succeeded in gathering all of the pieces again and reassembling his dead body. It is even related that she created a magical replica of the lost phallus and was impregnated by the corpse of Osiris, producing Horus, the heir to the Egyptian throne.

According to all of the accounts, the dead body of Osiris was kept by the Egyptians and secreted away in a hidden location. Prior to its deposit, however, the Egyptian priests, with precise direction from the gods, carried out specific instructions to carefully preserve and wrap the body of Osiris so that it would survive through the ages. In fact, in virtually all of

the images of the god Osiris, including his depictions in the tomb of Nefertari[165] (above left) and in the tomb of Horemheb[166] (above right), he is presented in his mummified form, wrapped in white linen, with only his hands protruding, holding his flail and staff.

Yes, this is the absolute truth: according to the Egyptians, *Osiris was the world's very first mummy.* For a specific reason, which is clear to us now that we recognize him as the once and future Antichrist king, the Egyptians wanted to make sure that the body of Osiris would remain preserved and intact. Osiris was the **original case** of mummification after

165. Osiris as depicted in the tomb of Nefertari, public domain art: http://commons.wikimedia.org/wiki/File:Osiris-tomb-of-Nefertari.jpg.
166. Osiris as depicted in the tomb of Horemheb, photo by A. Parrot: http://en.wikipedia.org/wiki/File:La_Tombe_de_Horemheb_cropped.jpg.

death that was to become copied by the kings of Egypt down through the millennia. Those closest to Osiris knew that he would one day need to use his body again when **he returned to the land of the living.**

This fact becomes clear throughout the Egyptian records—in the Pyramid Texts, the *Book of the Dead*, and other sources. For instance, in chapter 64 of the "Theban Recension" of the *Book of the Dead* we find the following declaration from Osiris: **"I am Yesterday and I am Today; and I have the power to be born a second time!"**[167]

The following is a spell from the Pyramid Texts that speaks of the death of Osiris and the preservation of his body. It is classified as one of many "resurrection" texts. These are interpreted by scholars as applying to the king's "resurrection" as a spirit in the underworld, but I believe that many of them actually speak of the return of Osiris to our world. Here is Utterance 576:

> Osiris was laid low by his brother Seth, but He who is in Nedit moves, his head is raised by Re; he detests sleep and hates inertness, so the king will not putrefy, he will not rot, this King will not be cursed by your anger, you gods.
>
> May you wake in peace, may you wake, Osiris, in peace, O you who are in Nedit, in peace. His head is raised by Re… and he will not rot, he will not putrefy, this King will not be cursed by your anger, you gods.[168]

---

167. "Worship of Osiris", last accessed March 14, 2012, http://www.touregypt.net/osirwor.htm.

168. *The Ancient Egyptian Pyramid Texts*, translated by R.O. Faulkner (UK: Oxford University Press, 1998), 231.

The dispute between Osiris and Seth is also mentioned in Utterance 477, which also contains the "resurrection" theme. In fact, R. O. Faulkner, the translator of this text, labels it "Osiris is raised from the dead":

> The sky reels, the earth quakes, Horus comes, Thoth appears, they raise Osiris from upon his side and make him stand up in front of the Two Enneads. Remember, Seth, and put in your heart this word which Geb spoke, this threat which the gods made against you in the Mansion of the Prince in On because you threw Osiris to the earth, when you said, O Seth: "I have never done this to him", so that you might have power thereby, having been saved, and that you might prevail over Horus; when you said, O Seth: "It was he who attacked me", when there came into being this his name of "Earth-attacker": when you said, O Seth: "It was he who kicked me", when there came into being his name of Orion, long of leg and lengthy of stride, who presides over Upper Egypt.
>
> Raise yourself, O Osiris, for Seth has raised himself, he has heard the threat of the gods who spoke about the god's father. Isis has your arm, O Osiris; Nephthys has your hand, so go between them. The sky is given to you, the earth is given to you, and the Field of Rushes, the Mounds of Horus, and the Mounds of Seth; the towns are given to you and the nomes assembled for you by Atum, and he who speaks about it is Geb.[169]

169. Ibid., 164.

There are many other Pyramid Texts that speaks of the "raising" of Osiris. These became the foundation for the religious celebrations of the ancient Egyptians that commemorated his death and looked forward to his eventual return to reign and rule once again over the land of the living:

Utterance 532: "Wake up for Horus, stand up against Seth; raise yourself, O Osiris, first-born son of Geb, at whom the Two Enneads tremble… Your hand is taken by the Souls of On, your hand is grasped by Ra, your head is raised by the Two Enneads, and they have set you, O Osiris, at the head of the Conclave of the Souls of On. Live, live and raise yourself!"[170]

Utterance 498: "**Awake, Osiris! Awake, O King! Stand up and sit down, throw off the earth which is on you!** I come and give you [the eye of] Horus… Go up and take this bread of yours from me."[171]

Egypt's Passion Play

One of the most important cultural celebrations of ancient Egypt was the Festival of Khoiak. This festival included a long procession in the region of Abydos and a five-day reenactment of the death of Osiris (also known as Wesir) at the hands of the Egyptian god Set. Many Egyptologists like to call it the world's first "Passion Play." The summary below is drawn from an ancient artifact, the "Stela of Ikhernofret," from the Middle Kingdom, as related in the online article "Abedjou—The Passion Plays of Wesir":

---

170. Ibid., 200.

171. Ibid., 177.

The First Day—The Procession of Wepwawet: Wepwawet opens the way of the procession. The enemies of Wesir are struck down in a mock battle. It seems an assault was staged by the 'followers of Set,' this was to be struck down, either by priests or by pilgrims acting as the 'followers of Wesir,' or perhaps both. The jackal-god Wepwawet who is walking foremost in all royal processions and conquests, goes by the name of 'Opener of the Ways.' In that context he opens the path for Wesir to gain access to the tomb.

The Second Day—The Great Procession of Wesir: The deceased Wesir, carried on a bark called 'Neshmet' ('night bark which Re rides in every night) is taken from his temple to his tomb. The procession moves through the surrounding cemetery grounds to the tomb (it seems they take a tour out in the desert before ending up at the Osireion). The Lamentations of Aset and Nebt-Het are performed by women impersonating the goddesses. There would be two women impersonating Aset and Nebt-Het, wandering around the temple premises and the village, looking for the body of Wesir. When they found him on the "riverbank", they would sit down and recite the Lamentations… During this night´s reenactment, the enemies of Wesir are slain on the 'banks of Nedyet' (the tomb) and the night ends with the trial of Set before the Divine Tribunal.

The Third Day—Wesir is Mourned and the Enemies of the Land are Destroyed:

> Mourning and weeping are continued. At the same time, there were probably secluded rituals in which a serpent and an ass, symbolizing Apep and Set, were destroyed, thereby making the country safe from their danger…
>
> **The Fourth Day —Night Vigil:**
> During the Night Vigil there were prayers and recitations performed before the statue of Wesir. Priests and priestesses played parts in the reenactment and actual funeral rites were also performed.
>
> **The Fifth Day—Wesir is Reborn:**
> The god was reborn at dawn and crowned with the crown of Ma'at. The statue of Wesir on the Neshmet bark is brought back in triumph to his temple, followed by the jubilant masses. Purifications and reinstallment of the god in his House followed and before the rites were concluded, the ritual of the 'Raising of the Djed-pillar' took place. This last part was not open to the public however.[172]

The Egyptians celebrated the "resurrection" of Osiris (Wesir) in anticipation of the future, but they never viewed Osiris as a "Dying and Rising" type of god. He was merely a "Dead" god, always pictured in his mummified form ruling over the Land of the Dead. Yet the Egyptians did have a clear expectation of his *physical* resurrection. *That is why his body was mummified in the first place.*

172. "Abedjou—The Passion Plays of Wesir," last accessed January 24, 2012, http://www.philae.nu/akhet/APassionPlays.html.

The Day of Awakening

This expectation comes through in the "Story of Setna" involving the magical "Book of Thoth." The main figure is Setna, son of Ramesses the Great during Egypt's New Kingdom (c.1250 BC), who was a legendary adventurer and magician. The story itself was probably written during the Ptolemaic Period (c.300–330 BC) in Egypt's history.

The details of this tale are unimportant, but there is a point in the story when Setna is confronted by the spirit of a long-dead prince, who asks to be reunited with the bodies of his family:

> The ka of Nefrekeptah replied, "Know that though I am buried here in Memphis, my wife and son still lie far away in their tomb at Koptos. I wish for us to be together once more, as a family should be. Bring their bodies to rest here with mine, that we may rejoice together for the first time in many ages. Bring their bodies to rest here with mine, that we may await together **the Day of Awakening when Osiris returns to the world.**" (bold added)[173]

The hero Setna succeeds in his task of reuniting the mummies of the family, as well as the hiding of the Book of Thoth, and then the story ends with the same message:

> The funeral procession left the tomb and closed it up. Setna spoke a word of power, and the door became

173. "The Book of Thoth," last accessed March 14, 2012, http://www.touregypt.net/godsofegypt/thebookofthoth.htm.

> as the stone around it, and the stone became as the hills around it. He spoke another word, and a mighty sandstorm came up and buried the tomb so that none might find it again. There it lies hidden for all ages against its finding by mortals. And there lies hidden the Book of Thoth, held safely by Nefrekeptah, his wife Ahura, and their son Merab. They stand guard over it **and await the Day of Awakening, when Osiris shall return to the world once more.** (bold added)[174]

Abydos

The Egyptians were quite certain that Osiris would return once again to rule the world, and when he came back he would need to use his body. Therefore, after his death his corpse immediately became an important relic that needed to be preserved and kept safe and hidden.

Nimrod was killed around 3100 BC. The evidence seems to suggest that his body was initially taken to the area of Abydos, Upper Egypt, where the tombs of the First Dynasty kings have been excavated. A "Tomb of Narmer" has been identified by archaeologists there, although this identification remains controversial. Seal-impressions indicate that Narmer was at first buried in the area, but it is doubtful that he was buried in a tomb common to other kings of his time, seeing as his life and death was very *uncommon*.

Around 2000 BC the tomb of Djer, a First-Dynasty king, was claimed to be the original Tomb of Osiris. It was refurbished by various kings and turned into a shrine, becoming

---

174. Ibid.

a popular destination for pilgrims and a much-used burial ground for those who wanted to be buried as close to Osiris as possible. It remained a holy site for about a thousand years before fading in popularity.

The 'Tomb of Osiris' at Abydos

During the New-Kingdom reign of Seti I (c.1300 BC) the magnificent "Temple of Seti" was built at Abydos. Next to it was a subterranean complex of monolithic blocks built specifically for the Osiris cult. Some scholars believe that the "Osireion," as it has come to be known, was actually built during the Old Kingdom and was only uncovered and refurbished by Seti. Egyptologist Richard Wilkinson explains why this specific location was chosen:

> The location of the Osireion in the Temple of Sethos I at Abydos, for example, is due to the proximity of a natural spring. This seems to have been used to provide a pool of water around the subterranean "grave" in order to make it a model of the mythical mound of

creation which the Egyptians believed rose from the primeval waters.[175]

I suppose it is possible that this ancient structure of massive monolithic blocks may have been originally built to house the body of Osiris, because it was always known as the "Tomb of Osiris." However, at a certain point its purpose became purely ceremonial and, in fact, there is no hard evidence that a corpse was ever held there. We have to look elsewhere to find the *real* Tomb of Osiris, where the corpse remains to this day.

Orion

One of the most important clues in helping us discover the resting place of Osiris is his connection with the constellation Orion. The Pyramid Texts repeatedly confirm this connection:

> Utterance 219:
> "In your name of Dweller in Orion, with a season in the sky and a season on earth. O Osiris, turn your face and look on this King, for your seed which issued from you is effective."[176]
>
> Utterance 442:
> "This Great One has fallen on his side, he who is in Nedit is felled. Your hand is taken by Ra, your head is lifted

175. Richard H. Wilkinson, *The Complete Temples of Ancient Egypt* (New York, NY: Thames and Hudson, 2000), 36.
176. *The Ancient Egyptian Pyramid Texts*, translated by R.O. Faulkner (UK: Oxford University Press, 1998), 47.

up by the Two Enneads. Behold he has come as Orion, behold, Osiris has come as Orion… O King, the sky conceives you with Orion, the dawn-light bears you with Orion. He who lives, lives by the command of the gods, and you live. You will regularly ascend with Orion from the eastern region of the sky, you will regularly descend with Orion into the western region of the sky…"[177]

Utterance 466:
"O King, you are this great star, the companion of Orion, who traverses the sky with Orion, who navigates the Netherworld with Osiris; you ascend from the east of the sky, being renewed at your due season and rejuvenated at your due time. The sky has born you with Orion, the year has put a fillet on you with Osiris, hands have been given to you, the dance has gone down to you, a food-offering is given to you, the Great Mooring-post cries out to you as (to) Osiris in his suffering."[178]

One of the most recent authoritative studies of Osiris is the book *Osiris: Death and Afterlife of a God*, by Egyptologist Bojana Mojsov. She explains that a common Egyptian word for spirit or soul is *sah*, which is also the name for the constellation Orion.

In Egypt, the constellation Orion disappears from the summer night sky for exactly *seventy* days. This fact eventually became a part of the Osiris cult, with the priests claiming that it took *seventy* days for the soul of Osiris to pass over

177. Ibid., 147.
178. Ibid., 155.

to the underworld after he died. Thereafter, the meticulous mummification process for Egypt's kings was instituted to take place over *seventy* days. Mojsov explains the religious significance of this strange and ancient process:

> Mummification was more than the mere preservation of the corpse; by substituting perishable substances with everlasting ones, the body was transfigured and "filled with magic." It became "an Osiris."[179]

To the ancient Egyptians, the night sky was recognized as a picture of the underworld, and the great constellation Orion was recognized as the image of Osiris himself. The smiting pose of Orion, the Great Hunter, connects with Osiris through the image on the Narmer Palette. In classical depictions of Orion, the figure is often shown holding a bow, a shield, or an animal skin, but Narmer is shown holding the hair of a human victim, ready to crush his skull with a pear-shaped mace.

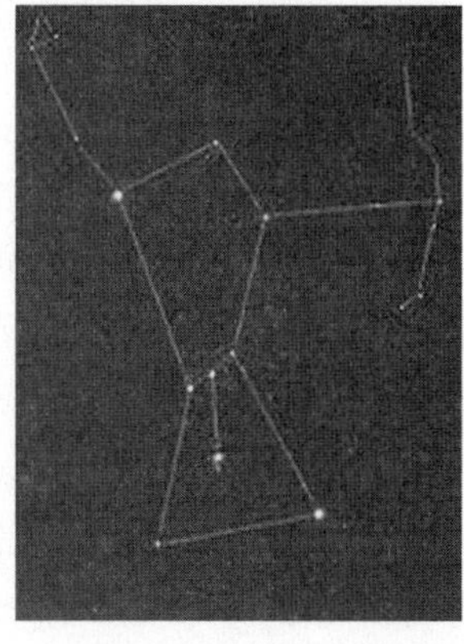

179. Bojana Mojsov, *Osiris: Death and Afterlife of A God* (Malden, MA: Blackwell Publishing, 2005), 18.

In 1995, co-authors Robert Bauval and Adrian Gilbert published a book called *The Orion Mystery*, promoting the theory that the great pyramid complex of Giza was built as an earthly reflection of the constellation Orion. This theory is still resisted by many orthodox Egyptologists today, but the evidence that Bauval and Gilbert presents is very convincing, and their theory is steadily gaining support and popularity.

In 1999, Bauval published a subsequent volume, *Secret Chamber*, elaborating upon his theory that the pyramids of Giza were built as a massive memorial to the great Egyptian god Osiris, and the likely location of his hidden tomb. I summarized Bauval's points in my "Giza Discovery" series online:

> Evidence that Giza was built as a magnificent memorial to Osiris can be found throughout Egyptian history....
>
> For instance, in the *Book of the Two Ways*, which dates to c.2000 BC, Bauval cites a reference to the "Highland of Aker, which is the dwelling place of Osiris," and another that states: "Osiris who is in the Highland of Aker." Bauval then refers to Egyptologist Selim Hassan whose research has concluded that Aker, a lion-figured deity pictured often in connection with Osiris and the Netherworld, is most likely symbolized by the Great Sphinx, and that the "Highlands of Aker" must then refer to the raised Giza plateau upon which the Sphinx and the Pyramids were built. In other words, Giza is the dwelling place of Osiris.[180]
>
> Another reference comes from the inscription on

180. Robert Bauval, *Secret Chamber: The Quest for the Hall of Records* (London, UK: Century, 1999), 82–83.

the Shabaka Stone which dates to c.700 BC. However, the scribe who carved the text states that the inscription is a copy from an earlier original, one that scholars believe may date as far back as the Pyramid Age:

> This is the land ////// the burial of Osiris in the House of Sokar. ////// Isis and Nephthys without delay, for Osiris had drowned in his water. Isis [and Nephthys] looked out, [beheld him and attended to him]. Horus speaks to Isis and Nephthys: "Hurry, grasp him ///."
>
> Isis and Nephthys speak to Osiris: "We come, we take you ///."
>
> ////// [They heeded in time] and brought him to [land. He entered the hidden portals in the glory of the lords of eternity]. //////. [Thus Osiris came into] the earth at the royal fortress, to the north of [the land to which he had come…][181]

According to this text Osiris was buried in the "House of Sokar" after his body had been taken by Isis and Nephthys and brought to the land, whereafter he entered the "hidden portals" and "came into the earth at the royal fortress," which was in the north of the land of Egypt.

The Pyramid Texts explain that Sokar is merely another name for Osiris. Some current researchers believe that Sokar was an ancient deity originally

181. Ibid., 85.

distinct from Osiris but their evidence is thin and based primarily on conjecture and supposition. Sokar may have been a name by which the Egyptians originally knew Osiris, and one of his many aspects, but Sokar was never completely distinct from Osiris.

In Utterance 300 of the Pyramid Texts the king, who is often identified as Osiris, states, "…I am Sokar of Rostau, I am bound for the place where dwells Sokar… " In Utterance 532 the connection is made more explicit: "…they have found Osiris, his brother Seth having laid him low in Nedit; when Osiris said 'Get away from me,' when his name became Sokar." The "House of Sokar" is therefore the very same as the "House of Osiris."

The next question is, what and where is Rostau? …Zahi Hawass [has often referred] to Osiris as the "Lord of the Underground Tunnels." Well the word Rostau means underground tunnels, and "Lord of Rostau" is one of the many titles held by Osiris. "Rostau" was simply another name for the Giza plateau and the many tunnels underneath it.

This understanding is clarified by a stela that once stood between the paws of the Sphinx that is attributed to Thutmose IV (c.1400 BC). Line seven of this stela states that the Sphinx lies "beside the House of Sokar…in Rostau."[182]

Bauval finds further proof that Rostau refers to Giza in the so-called Coffin Texts which were inscribed in burial chambers near the end of the Old Kingdom (c.1800-2000 BC):

---

182. Ibid., 88.

I am Osiris, I have come to Rostau in order to know the secret of the Duat... I have come equipped with magic, I have quenched my thirst with it, I live on white emmer, filling the Winding Waterway..."

"...on the day of concealing the mysteries of the deep place in Rostau... I am he (Osiris) who sees the secret things in Rostau... O you who opens up ways and open up paths for the perfected souls in the House of Osiris..."

"...Sokar...(is) happy and content when (he) sees that this mansion of mine is founded among the waters...while Sokar belongs to Rostau..."

"I have travelled by the roads of Rostau on water and on land...these are the roads of Osiris and they are in the sky..."

"I have passed over the paths of Rostau, whether on water or on land, and these are the paths of Osiris; they are at the limit of the sky..."

"I shall not be turned back to the gates of the Duat. I ascend to the sky with Orion... I am one who collects for himself his efflux in front of Rostau..."[183]

---

183. Ibid., 92–94.

Robert Bauval first made his mark internationally with the book *The Orion Mystery*, co-written with Adrian Gilbert in 1995. This volume put forth the hypothesis, which has steadily gained popular support, that the three pyramids of Giza were laid out and built as a deliberate representation of the three belt stars of Orion on earth. Rostau, Giza, the "Highland of Aker," the "House of Sokar" or "House of Osiris," by whatever name it is known, was built to be a picture of the heavens on the earth. Bauval explains,

> Giza, the earthly Rostau, is located on the west bank of the River Nile. Thus by transposition, we can deduce that the celestial Rostau is a region of the starry sky on the west "bank" of the Milky Way. Furthermore Giza… is a counterpart of a portion of the sky near the Milky Way which contains Orion, Sirius and the constellation of Taurus and Leo. Everything thus strongly points to the idea that we are invited to consider this celestial region as a sort of "guide map"—one, perhaps, that may lead us to the "tomb" or "burial place" of Osiris.[184]

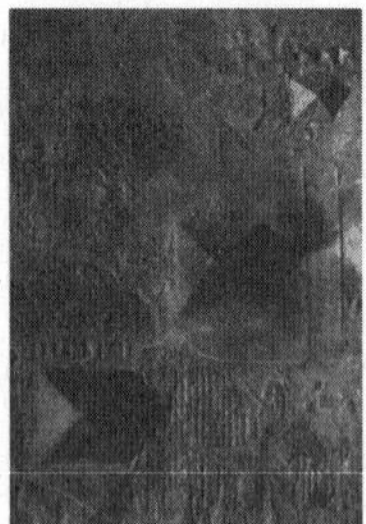

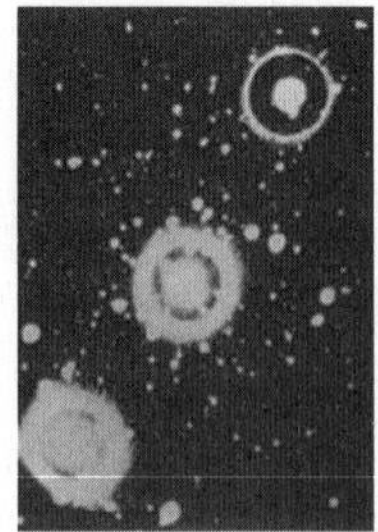

184. Ibid., 95.

chapter twenty-three

THE EAGLES WILL GATHER

THE OSIRIS CULT began with the death of Nimrod around 3100 BC. We don't know exactly where he was killed, although the Egyptian texts may provide an answer. We do know, however, that he was "slain by the sword" and that his body was brought to Egypt. Many different cultures maintained a memory of Nimrod, but only Egypt claims to have always possessed the corpse of this infamous king. To the Egyptians Osiris was always a "Dead" god, revered as their very first mummy, but they continued to maintain the expectation of his eventual resurrection and a return to his former greatness.

Outisde of Egypt, other cultures created a mythology of Nimrod in which he died or somehow descended to the underworld, but then overcame it and rose to become the king of heaven and leader of the gods. This was the memory of Nimrod as it was kept by the Sumerians (Ninurta), Babylonians (Marduk), Assyrians (Assur), and by the Phoenician kingdoms of Tyre (Herakles), Byblos (Adonis), Sidon (Eshmun), and Ugarit (Ugaritic Baal). This story was credible because these cultures had no corpse that would have contradicted their "resurrection" story. We see that through these cultures this version of Nimrod became the basis of the widespread "Dying and Rising God" motif that secular scholars have had so much fun with, at the expense of Christianity.[185]

The Greeks are a completely different case altogether. After Alexander conquered the Near East, the Greeks were inundated with all of these different versions of Nimrod, and they did their best to honor these foreign gods by placing them within their own divine genealogies under the leadership of Zeus. In this way they adopted Apollo from his early Sumerian origins, Dionysus from Crete, Herakles from Tyre, Adonis from Byblos, and then they assimilated the *separate* stories for each of these hero-gods. Twentieth-century mythologist, Joseph Campbell, looked at all of this confusion and created his theory of "The Hero With A Thousand Faces." The historical basis of this hero, unbeknownst to Campbell, was Nimrod, the most influential figure to walk the earth prior to Jesus Christ. Campbell's mistake was in denying the historical Jesus and lumping the "Jesus story" alongside the various accounts of Nimrod. The truth is, Jesus

185. For a good overview of the "Dying and Rising God" debate go to: "The Giza Discovery, Part Three: The Saviors of the Ancient World," at http://www.redmoonrising.com/Giza/DyingandRising3.htm. Also see the book by Tryggve N. D. Mettinger, Professor of Hebrew Bible at Lund University, Sweden, entitled *The Riddle of Resurrection—"Dying and Rising Gods" in the Ancient Near East*, published in 2001.

wasn't a **copy** of the pagan "Dying and Rising God" mythology; He is the heaven-sent **Answer** to this great deception.

Returning to Egypt, we see that the corpse of Osiris was held in Upper Egypt for several centuries at first, but then in the Fourth Dynasty around 2600–2500 BC, three consecutive kings built the massive "Giza Necropolis." The word *necropolis* means "city of the dead." Mainstream Egyptology teaches that each of the three main pyramids were built separately with no unifying plan, as tombs for the kings who built them: Khufu, Khafre, and Menkaure. This "orthodox" belief doesn't hold water, and I believe that the visual and historical evidence is more than enough to prove that the Giza complex was built by the Egyptians using a unified and comprehensive plan to reflect the constellation Orion and to be a great memorial to, *and tomb for*, the "god" Osiris, who was their "King of kings" and "Lord of lords."

The Great Pyramid of Giza was the *first* of the celebrated "Seven Wonders of the Ancient World" to be built, and it is the *last* to remain standing, as all the others have faded away. I believe that somewhere, either within or underneath the Great Pyramid, lies the hidden chamber holding the dead body of Osiris, whom we know as Nimrod, the *first* and the *last* of Satan's seven kings. This chamber waits in silence for the moment when it will be discovered and opened, and its contents will be revealed as *the greatest archaeological discovery in the history of the world.*

The Revealing of the Antichrist

With this possible end-times scenario now firmly in our minds, let's now turn to Paul's description of the revealing of the Antichrist:

> Now we beseech you, brethren, by the coming of our Lord Jesus Christ, and by our gathering together unto him, that ye be not soon shaken in mind, or be troubled, neither by spirit, nor by word, nor by letter as from us, as that the day of Christ is at hand. Let no man deceive you by any means: for that day shall not come, except there come a falling away first, **and that man of sin be revealed, the son of perdition**; who opposeth and exalteth himself above all that is called God, or that is worshipped; so that he as God sitteth in the temple of God, shewing himself that he is God.
>
> Remember ye not, that, when I was yet with you, I told you these things? And now ye know what withholdeth that **he might be revealed in his time.** For the mystery of iniquity doth already work: only he who now letteth will let, until he be **taken out of the way.** And then shall that Wicked be revealed, whom the Lord shall consume with the spirit of his mouth, and shall destroy with the brightness of his coming: Even him, whose coming is after the working of Satan with all power and signs and lying wonders, and with all deceivableness of unrighteousness in them that perish; because they received not the love of the truth, that they might be saved. And for this cause God shall send them strong delusion, that they should believe a lie: That they all might be damned who believed not the truth, but had pleasure in unrighteousness. (2 Thessalonians 2:1–12)

The Apostle Paul is very clear that the Antichrist will not be revealed until the “restrainer” is taken out of the way. He also says that the Antichrist will be revealed before the "Day of the Lord" begins.

There is a lot of confusion as to what the "falling away" refers to, and who or what exactly is the "restrainer." I agree with Bible scholars Allen Beechick and Robert H. Gundry who conclude that the "falling away" does not in any way refer to the rapture of the Church, or to a "falling away" from the faith, or to the removal of the Holy Spirit from the earth, but simply refers to the "stepping aside" of the "restrainer" which will allow for the revealing of the Antichrist.[186] Here is what Gundry has to say:

> "Become out of the midst" [or, "taken out of the way"] does not demand removal from the world. "Midst" more literally means "middle." The restrainer is standing in the middle, i.e., between the *person* of the Antichrist and the *revelation* of the Antichrist. It is as though the Antichrist stands in the wings, eager to break forth onto the stage of history. But the Holy Spirit blocks entrance until the appointed moment when He will step out of the way and allow the man of lawlessness to stride onstage before the admiring eyes of mankind. Perhaps a misunderstanding of the expression "become out of the midst" as passive has aided the pre-tribulational idea of withdrawal from the world. The expression is not passive. Lenski captures

---

186. See Allen Beechick's commentary on 2 Thessalonians 2 within his book, *The Rapture Solution*, at http://www.rapturesolution.com/beechick/Book/2thess.htm.

> the meaning exactly with his idiomatic rendering "get out of the way."[187]

Before the corpse of Nimrod is to be revealed to the world, there is some sort of supernatural force that must first **get out of the way**. This may be the Holy Spirit or it may in fact be an angelic spiritual force. There is a role and purpose for this ancient king and God will ensure his protection, either directly or by allowing him to be *satanically* protected through the ages. I believe this supernatural force is mentioned by the ancient Egyptians as the force that protects the body of Osiris. Consider the following Coffin Texts that speak of his bodily remains:

> Coffin Texts Spell 1080
> "This is the sealed thing which is in darkness, **with fire about it**, which contains **the efflux of Osiris**, and it was put in Rostau. It has been hidden there since it fell from him, and it is what came down from him onto the desert sand; it means that what belongs to him (his body) was put in Rostau… "

> Coffin Texts Spell 1087
> "This is the word which is in darkness. As for any spirit who knows it, he will live among the living. **Fire is about it, which contains the efflux of Osiris.** As for any man who shall know it, he will never perish there, since he knows what shall be in Rostau. Rostau is

187. Robert Gundry, *The Church and the Tribulation* (Grand Rapids, MI: Zondervan, 1973), 127.

> hidden since he fell there… Rostau is (another name) for Osiris… "[188]

I can't say exactly what this fiery "force" is that protects the "efflux" of Osiris, but perhaps it may be similar to the angelic guardian at the gate of the Garden of Eden (Genesis 3:24) who stood watch with "a flaming sword which turned every way." Whatever it is, the Egyptians believed that the body of Osiris was/is supernaturally protected.

The Apostle Paul explains that the restrainer will be removed "in his time." So there is an appointed time for this supernatural protection to cease, which would allow for the Antichrist's "revealing."

What I am suggesting is that we need to adopt a different understanding of the sequence of events given by Paul than is typically presented by Bible scholars. Here is what I believe Paul is intending to convey, which connects with the book of Revelation and other end-times prophecies to give the following timeline:[189]

1. The body of the Antichrist will be revealed when the supernatural force that protects it is removed (2 Thessalonians 2:7).
2. The Day of the Lord will begin at the sixth Seal (Revelation 6:17).

---

188. Robert Bauval, *Secret Chamber*, 88; 94.

189. Also see *Red Moon Rising: The Rapture and the Timeline of the Apocalypse*, by Peter Goodgame, (Xulon Press, 2005). http://www.amazon.com/Red-Moon-Rising-Timeline-Apocalypse/dp/1594679622/ref=sr_1_5?s=books&ie=UTF8&qid=1331868526&sr=1-5.

3. The body of the Antichrist will be resurrected at the fifth Trumpet (Revelation 9:11).
4. The Antichrist will then confirm the Seventieth Week Covenant of Daniel 9:27 which will mark the beginning of the so-called "Seven Year Tribulation".
5. The first half of the Seventieth Week will include the effects of the fifth and sixth Trumpet judgments.
6. The Antichrist will establish his seat in the Temple of God at the midpoint of the Seventieth Week (2 Thessalonians 2:4).
7. The Antichrist will enforce the Mark of the Beast during the second half of the Seventieth Week, and then be destroyed at the end at the Second Coming of Jesus.

The Secret Chamber

The nature of the revealing of the Antichrist is something that I believe Jesus directly addressed, and He contrasted it with the nature of His *own* revealing from heaven.

The possibility that the Antichrist will first be revealed **as a corpse** is introduced by Jesus within His sermon on the end times known as the Olivet Discourse. He is speaking of False Christs and False Prophets, and then He makes a remark saying "Behold, I have told you before!" which in another version is translated as, "See, I have told you ahead of time!" (NIV). In other words, Jesus is saying to His disciples, "Now pay attention! I am giving you some important information that will allow you to resist all of the false rumors about the return of the Christ!"

Here is what Jesus said:

The Timeline of the Day of the Lord

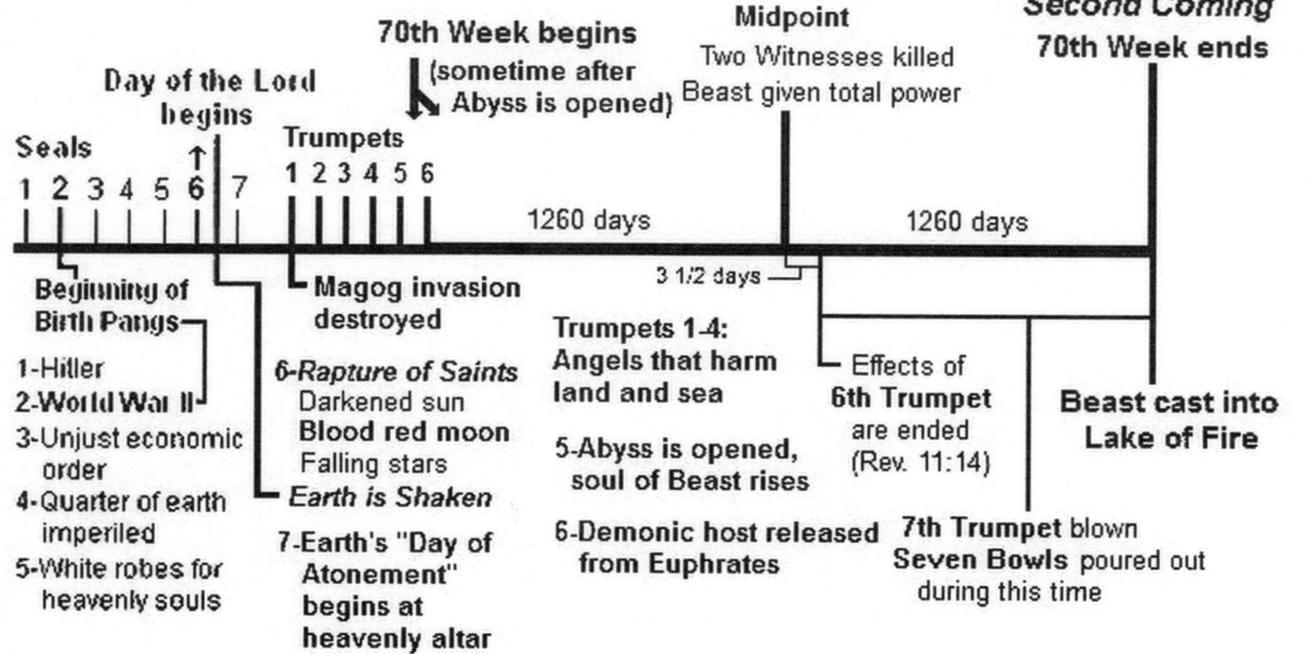

> Then if any man shall say unto you, Lo, here is Christ, or there; believe it not. For there shall arise false Christs, and false prophets, and shall shew great signs and wonders; insomuch that, if it were possible, they shall deceive the very elect. Behold, I have told you before. Wherefore if they shall say unto you, Behold, he is in the desert; go not forth: behold, he is in the secret chambers; believe it not. For as the lightning cometh out of the east, and shineth even unto the west; so shall also the coming of the Son of man be. For wheresoever the carcase is, there will the eagles be gathered together. (Matthew 24:23–28)

In this hugely significant passage, Jesus warns us not to believe it when someone comes claiming that the Christ has been found out in the desert in a secret chamber. He then says that when the true Christ returns, He will be seen by everyone at once, as lightning flashing in the skies, whereas the false Christ will be revealed as a corpse found in a secret chamber in the desert, where the "eagles" will be gathered together.

The symbolism of "eagles" portrays leadership and authority, as understood in the Greek and Roman world at the time of Jesus. Their gathering over the "carcass" as if they were vultures relates to the Antichrist as a demonic sacrament. These are the great men of the earth: kings, presidents, financiers and CEOs, completely given over to the "lust of the flesh, and the lust of the eyes, and the pride of life,"[190] and they are deceived into believing that the corpse that they surround

---

190. 1 John 2:16.

is their Messiah, whom they draw their spiritual sustenance from.

In the pages that follow, we will begin to reveal how this scenario is already being anticipated by the secret societies that have maintained the worship of Osiris down through the ages. These great men truly do expect their "god" to be revealed soon, somewhere in or near the Great Pyramid of Giza.

Dark Reflection #13:

Jesus Christ will be revealed as the Living God from heaven, and every eye will see Him.
The Antichrist will be revealed as a Dead God, hidden in a secret chamber in the desert, where the great men of the world will gather to observe him.

The Resurrection of the Antichrist

The testimony of Jesus parallels the testimony of Paul in several ways. They both speak of deceptive "signs and wonders" in connection with the Antichrist, and they both speak about the nature of the "revealing" of the Antichrist. Paul writes that the wicked will accept the Antichrist "because they received not the love of the truth." He says that because of their rejection of Truth, which happens first, God will *then* "send them strong delusion" that will cause them to "believe a lie."

In verse 11 the Greek the words "a lie," should be translated as "the lie." It is a singular lie that the wicked will believe. This will be brought about by the "strong delusion," which is *energeian planes* in Greek, which literally translates as "an energy of delusion." Throughout the New Testament the word *energeia* always refers to *supernatural* energy.

In other words, God will release *a supernatural energy of delusion*, which will cause those who have already rejected the "Truth" to believe the "Lie." The energy that Paul refers to is, I believe, the energy that causes the body of the Antichrist to be resurrected, after the soul of the Antichrist is released from the Abyss.

It is the resurrection of this five-thousand-year-old corpse that will cause the world to be astonished, and to submit to and worship the Antichrist. Consider Revelation's descriptions of the resurrection of the Antichrist once again:

"And I saw one of his heads as it were wounded to death; and his deadly wound was healed: **and all the world wondered after the beast**" (Revelation 13:3).

"The beast that thou sawest was, and is not; and shall ascend out of the bottomless pit, and go into perdition: and

they that dwell on the earth shall wonder, whose names were not written in the book of life from the foundation of the world, when they behold the beast that was, and is not, and yet is" (Revelation 17:8).

The Way, the Truth, and the Life

In John 14:6, Jesus of Nazareth makes the astounding claim that He is "the Way, the Truth, and the Life," saying that no one can come to the Father except through Him. Jesus claims to be the personification of Truth, and then He goes on to say that after He ascends to heaven He will continue to release the "Spirit of Truth" (John 14:17) to His people on earth.

Paul writes that there will be an energy released from God the Father that will cause those who have rejected the "Truth" to believe the "Lie." Earlier in this book, I referred to the devil as the "Father of Lies." Technically, the verse that was quoted actually names the devil as the father of the "Lie," singular: "Ye are of your father the devil, and the lusts of your father ye will do. He was a murderer from the beginning, and abode not in the truth, because there is no truth in him. When he speaketh a lie, he speaketh of his own: for he is a liar, and the father of it" (John 8:44).

If God is the father of Jesus, the Truth; then Satan is the father of the Antichrist, the Lie. The Antichrist is the personification of "The Lie." He is the one who will be resurrected and empowered to deceive the Christ-rejecting world during the Day of the Lord.

> And for this cause God shall send them **an energy of delusion**, that they should believe **the Lie**: That they all

> might be damned who believed not **the Truth**, but had pleasure in unrighteousness. (2 Thessalonians 2:11–12).

The Good Shepherd

One of the most endearing depictions of Jesus is as a long-robed Shepherd, wearing sandals on His feet and holding a staff in one hand and a lamb in the other. This idyllic picture actually comes from Jesus Himself:

Dark Reflection #14

Jesus Christ is the Truth. The Antichrist is the Lie.

> Verily, verily, I say unto you, I am the door of the sheep. All that ever came before me are thieves and robbers: but the sheep did not hear them. I am the door: by me if any man enter in, he shall be saved, and shall go in and out, and find pasture. The thief cometh not, but for to steal, and to kill, and to destroy: I am come that they might have life, and that they might have it more abundantly.
>
> **I am the good shepherd: the good shepherd giveth his life for the sheep.** But he that is an hireling, and not the shepherd, whose own the sheep are not, seeth the wolf coming, and leaveth the sheep, and fleeth: and the wolf catcheth them, and scattereth the sheep. **The hireling fleeth, because he is an hireling, and careth not for the sheep.**
>
> I am the good shepherd, and know my sheep, and am known of mine. As the Father knoweth me, even so I know the Father: and I lay down my life for the sheep. (John 10:7–15)

This "Shepherd" symbolism was well-known in the ancient world, as I explain within an online series: "One of the most common motifs that was used in the pagan world to describe mankind's relationship to the gods was the metaphor of a shepherd and his sheep. In his dialogue with *Critias* Plato writes, '[the gods] tended us, their nurselings and possessions, as shepherds tend their flocks.' In the Sumerian culture the early kings were viewed as shepherds who ruled the people on behalf of the gods; for instance, King Gudea was a 'shepherd' who ruled on behalf of the god Ninurta, and Ur-Namma referred to himself as the 'shepherd of Enlil.' "[191]

Jesus claimed to be the ultimate "Good Shepherd" who was willing to give up His own life on behalf of His sheep. Jesus then contrasted Himself with the Antichrist, whom He describes as the "hireling shepherd" who deserts the flock. This prediction of the Antichrist actually comes from the Old Testament prophet Zechariah, who wrote:

> For, lo, **I will raise up a shepherd** in the land, which shall not visit those that be cut off, neither shall seek the young one, nor heal that that is broken, nor feed that that standeth still: but he shall eat the flesh of the fat, and tear their claws in pieces. **Woe to the idol shepherd that leaveth the flock!** The sword shall be upon his arm, and upon his right eye: his arm shall be clean dried up, and his right eye shall be utterly darkened. (Zechariah 11:16–17)

---

191. Peter Goodgame, "The Giza Discovery, Part Four: Prophecies of the Assyrian," last accessed January 24, 2012, http://www.redmoonrising.com/Giza/raiders4.htm.

The Hebrew word for "idol" in "idol shepherd" is *eliyl.* It is the same word that is translated as *devil* in the Septuagint translation of Psalm 96:5. What we see is that the prophet Zechariah predicts that an evil, demonic, idol-shepherd will be given power over Israel for a short time, and he will abuse the flock.

An interesting thing about this shepherd, however, is that he will apparently bear on his arm the wound from a sword, and have a blind right eye. Some Bible scholars believe that just as Jesus bears the wounds from His death, so, too, will the Antichrist bear the wounds of his death after he is resurrected. If this is true, then the following Dark Reflection can be applied to Jesus and the Antichrist:

Dark Reflection #15:

Jesus Christ bears the wounds of His death, which include the nail marks in His hands and feet, and the wound in His side. The Antichrist will bear the wounds of his death, which will include a withered arm, and a blind right eye.

The metaphor of a king or ruler as a shepherd can be found throughout the ancient Near East, but nowhere is it more prominent than in ancient Egypt. To the Egyptians, Osiris was the "Good Shepherd" *par excellence*. In fact, in the vast majority of the representations of Osiris he is shown holding (as you may have noticed) two tools related to a shepherd: the shepherd's crook and the shepherd's flail.

Here is the explanation of these implements as given by journalist Jimmy Dunn:

> The crook (heka) and the flail or flabellum (nekhakha), are two of the most prominent items in the royal regalia of ancient Egypt...
>
> The crook was a cane with a hooked handle, sometimes gold-plated and reinforced with blue copper bands. It probably derived from the shepherd's crosier. Its hieroglyphic value was "rule". The earliest example of a crook or heqa scepter comes from Abydos...
>
> The flail was a rod with three attached beaded, strands. The strands could vary considerably, using different types of beads and the lengths between the

beads could be broken up into several segments. The flail appears alone on some of the earliest representations of royal ceremonies… It possibly derived from a shepherd's whip or a fly whisk. However, some scholars prefer to regard it as a ladanisterion, a flail-like instrument used until the present day by shepherds in the Mediterranean region and elsewhere…"[192]

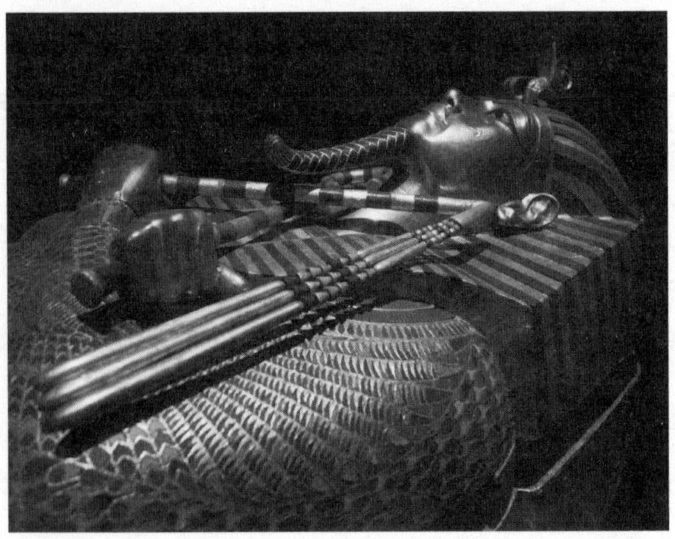

The famous sarcophagus that covered the mummy of King Tut is a representation of the god Osiris, the god that Tutankhamun believed he would "became one with" after his mummification and descent into the underworld. Osiris is the "idol shepherd" of Zechariah, the "hireling shepherd" who cares not for the sheep, whom we are warned about by Jesus.

192. Jimmy Dunn, "The Crook and Flail in Ancient Egypt," *Tour Egypt*, last accessed January 24, 2012, http://www.touregypt.net/featurestories/crooksandflails.htm.

Dark Reflection #16:

Jesus Christ is the Good Shepherd who died for His sheep.

The Antichrist is the Evil Shepherd who cares not for the sheep.

Good Shepherd, painting by Del Parson [193]

"My sheep hear my voice,
and I know them, and they follow me:
And I give unto them eternal life;
and they shall never perish,
neither shall any man pluck them out of my hand."

John 10:27–28

193. Image used with permission. Copyright © 2007 Del Parson: http://www.delparson.com.

chapter twenty-four

HIDDEN MYSTERIES

WITH THE COMING OF JESUS CHRIST, His death on the cross, His resurrection and ascension to heaven and subsequent outpouring of the Holy Spirit at Pentecost, the entire top-heavy spiritual system of worldwide polytheistic paganism *was turned upside down.*

Jesus Christ released the Holy Spirit into the world, and men's eyes were opened to the amazing love and freedom that can be found through a personal relationship with the Creator of the Universe. In only a few hundred years the Christian Church became the most influential spiritual and political power in the world, and the forces of evil were forced to either scatter and re-group, or to attempt to assimilate into it and begin to corrupt it.

The secret cults of Greece and Rome withered away, and in Egypt the inner circle of priests, along with their secret knowledge of the gods, passed from public view. These mysteries, however, were maintained in the teachings of the new pagan systems that appeared alongside the emergence of Christianity in the first few centuries AD. These pagan systems are today known as *Hermeticism*, *Gnosticism*, and the teachings of the Jewish-pagan tradition known as the *Kabbalah*. I cover all of these systems in my online series "The Giza Discovery, Part Six: Domination By Deception,"[194] which I draw from here as we reveal the evolution of the Osiris cult into the present day.

Hermeticism

Hermeticism takes its name from *Hermes Trismegistus*, a legendary figure associated with the Greek god Hermes (symbolized by the planet Mercury); with the Canaanite god Tauthus the secretary of Kronos; with the Babylonian god Nabu (also identified with Mercury) who was the son and scribe of Marduk (Jupiter); and especially with the Egyptian god Thoth, the scribe of Osiris and god of learning to the Egyptians.

The textual foundation of Hermeticism is a collection of dialogues involving Hermes and his disciples in which the major metaphysical questions of life are addressed. These texts date to the second and third centuries AD, but at the time of the Renaissance when they became famous, they were believed to date back much further. Modern collections of the *Corpus Hermeticum* include eighteen Greek texts and one Latin text known as the *Asclepius*.

It is in the *Asclepius* that Egypt's role as the primary home of the gods is highlighted, and within this description there

194. See http://www.redmoonrising.com/Giza/DomDec6.htm.

also appears a prophecy of Egypt's decline and the disappearance of the gods, leaving Egypt destitute and abandoned:

> Do you not know, Asclepius, that **Egypt is an image of heaven** or, to be more precise, that everything governed and moved in heaven came down to Egypt and was transferred there? If truth were told, **our land is the temple of the whole world.**
>
> And yet, since it befits the wise to know all things in advance, of this you must not remain ignorant: a time will come when it will appear that the Egyptians paid respect to divinity with faithful mind and painstaking reverence—to no purpose. All their holy worship will be disappointed and perish without effect, for divinity will return from earth to heaven, and Egypt will be abandoned. The land that was the seat of reverence will be widowed by the powers and left destitute of their presence... Then this most holy land, seat of shrines and temples, will be filled completely with tombs and corpses.
>
> O Egypt, Egypt, of your reverent deeds only stories will survive, and they will be incredible to your children!... For divinity goes back to heaven, and all the people will die, deserted, as Egypt will be widowed and deserted by god and human.[195]

The Hermetic pantheon is described in the *Asclepius* as being led by a group of five major gods who are "hypercosmic"

195. *Hermetica*, translated by Brian P. Copenhaver (Cambridge, UK: Cambridge University Press, 1992), 81.

and "intelligible" who each rule over divine aspects of the universe that are "cosmic" and "sensible." Jupiter is the primary deity, corresponding with Zeus, and he is described as the god of heaven, "for Jupiter supplies life through heaven to all things." Light is second, which rules over its "sensible" divine aspect the Sun. Thirdly, there is a deity named Pantomorphos of Omniform, who rules over the "Horoscopes" or "Thirty-six." These are thirty-six gods, also known as Decans, so-named because they each have authority over ten degrees of the zodiacal circle. Fourth is the deity Heimarmene that rules over the seven planets. Fifth is a secondary aspect of Jupiter that rules over the Air, sometimes known as Zeus Neatos.[196]

The twelve major signs of the Zodiac each include three of the thirty-six Hermetic *Decans*, known as "Horoscopes" and referred to as "stars" in the text. This division of the Zodiac into thirty-six Decans was also doubled to seventy-two Duodecans, a division which gave each of the twelve Zodiacal signs six stars, making each of these Duodecan stars, also known as Quinances, the ruler over five degrees of the Zodiacal circle. From this comes one of the explanations for the occult significance of the Pentagram which is a five-pointed star. Each of the five points represents one of the five "hypercosmic" deities, or five degrees of the zodiac, and each point is created by an angle of seventy-two degrees, with the product of five by seventy-two being 360, which completes the circuit of the zodiac.

In ancient Egypt the priests of the sacred rites were known as **horoskopoi.**[197] The Hermetic emphasis on the astrological

196. Ibid., 231–232.

197. Ibid., 232: citing *Egypte*, by Franz Cumont, 124–5.

relationship between mankind and the stars (who, as we know, actually represent the seventy angelic *Kosmokrator*[198] gods—see Ephesians 6:12) is explained by Frances Yates in her book *Giordano Bruno and the Hermetic Tradition:* "That strange people, the Egyptians, had divinised time, not merely in the abstract sense but in the concrete sense that each moment of the day and night **had its god who must be placated as the moments passed**... They had definite astrological significance, as 'Horoscopes' presiding over the forms of life born within the time periods over which they presided, and they were assimilated to the planets domiciled in their domain... But they were also gods, and powerful Egyptian gods, and this side of them was never forgotten, giving them a mysterious importance."[199]

The return of these gods to an active and outward position as rulers of mankind is predicted in the *Asclepius*, which is said to come after the long period of spiritual decline in Egypt: "Those [gods] who rule the earth will be restored, and they will be installed in a city at the furthest threshold of Egypt, which will be founded towards the setting sun and to which all human kind will hasten by land and by sea."[200]

This text, and the physical location of this divine city, is explained by Garth Fowden in his book *The Egyptian Hermes*:

---

198. Kosmokrators: "World Rulers," as in "the **world rulers** of the darkness of this eon"—Ephesians 6:12.

199. Francis A. Yates, *Giordano Bruno and the Hermetic Tradition* (Chicago, IL: University of Chicago Press, 1991 [1964]), 46.

200. Garth Fowden, *The Egyptian Hermes* (Princeton, NJ: Princeton University Press, 1986), 40.

> …in answer to Asclepius's enquiry where these gods are at the moment, Trismegistus replies (at *Ascl.* 27): "In a very great city, in the mountains of Libya (in *monte Libyco*)", by which is meant the edge of the desert plateau to the west of the Nile valley. A subsequent reference (*Ascl.* 37) to the temple and tomb of Asclepius (Imhotep) in *monte Libyae* establishes that the allusion at *Ascl.* 27 is to the ancient and holy Memphite [Giza] necropolis, which lay on the desert jabal to the west of Memphis itself.[201]

The "mountains of Libya" (which was also the place where Heracles was killed by Typhon according to Greek myth), is simply a reference to the plateau that rises above the desert on the west bank of the Nile, west of the ancient city of Memphis. In other words, according to this Hermetic prediction, when the Kosmokrators are "restored" they will be "installed in a city" **on or near the Giza Plateau.**[202]

201. Ibid., 40.
202. Giza photo by Ricardo Liberato, last accessed March 15, 2012, http://en.wikipedia.org/wiki/File:All_Gizah_Pyramids.jpg.

The Kosmokrators, Egypt, and Freemasonry

The Hermetic text known as the *Asclepius* predicts that "Those gods who rule the earth will be restored, and they will be installed in a city at the furthest threshold of Egypt." This understanding of Egypt's role as the land of the gods and primary seat of the Ancient Mysteries permeates the Western occult tradition and has greatly influenced mystical orders such as the *Golden Dawn* and Aleister Crowley's *Ordo Templar Orientis*. This belief can also be found within the more *mainstream* esoteric organizations such as the Rosicrucians and the Freemasons, as we will now show.

As an independent secret society the Rosicrucians date back to the publication of three famous manuscripts from the early seventeenth century in Germany. Since that time there have appeared a number of groups that have referred to themselves as "Rosicrucian," all with alleged connections to the original group.

In the United States the primary Rosicrucian order is the AMORC (Ancient and Mystical Order Rosae Crucis), which was created in 1915 and is based in California. One of its primary achievements was the establishment of "The Rosicrucian Egyptian Oriental Museum" in San Jose in 1928. On its website the question is asked: "What does the Rosicrucian Order, AMORC have to do with Egypt?" The answer follows:

> The older connection to Egypt is of a Traditional nature. All Rosicrucians from the 17th century onward understood that the wisdom they received had been transmitted through many paths from the earliest times of human civilization, and were consistent with the teachings of the ancient Mystery Schools.

The first mention of the organization of such Schools is associated by mystics with the reign of King Tuthmosis III during the 15th Century BCE. In addition, the 14th Century BCE King Akhenaten taught the ideal that there was one Divine force behind all things, even the many Gods of Egypt.

Thus Rosicrucians trace their Traditional connection back to ancient Egypt because the wisdom and methods they follow are consistent and continuous with those from the Mystery Schools of Egypt through the Rosicrucian Manifestos of the 17th century to the modern-day Rosicrucian Order, AMORC.[203]

The **Rosicrucians** are basically very straightforward in promoting their connection with ancient Egypt, but when it comes to the institution of **Freemasonry**, the subject of Masonic origins is much more controversial and mysterious.

Within Freemasonry there have been three primary study groups involved in researching and publishing material concerned with this question. The foremost of these "study groups" is the *Quator Coronati Lodge* based in London, England, which was created in 1884 by the Grand Master of the United Grand Lodge of England (UGLE), the Prince of Wales, who later became King Edward VII. The first Grand Master of the QC Lodge was Sir Charles Warren, who was the president of the Palestine Exploration Fund (PEF). Another founding member of the QC Lodge was Sir Walter

---

203. Quote originally taken from *Egyptian Museum*, last accessed January 24, 2012, http://www.egyptianmuseum.org.

Besant, who worked under Charles Warren as the Treasurer of the PEF. He was the brother-in-law of Annie Besant who led the *Theosophical Society* after the death of Helena Blavatsky. It should also be pointed out that an early member of the QC Lodge was Dr. Wynn Westcott, who was the primary founding member of the *Hermetic Order of the Golden Dawn*. Perhaps Westcott was involved in the lecture presented at the founding of the QC Lodge which was entitled, "Freemasonry as Seen in the Light of the Cabala."

The primary purpose of the Quator Coronati Lodge was to focus on Masonic origins, to research the Kabbalah and Solomon's Temple, and to promote the creation of a Jewish homeland in Israel. Sir Charles Warren had been the director of British excavations on the Temple Mount two decades earlier, and his Palestine Exploration Fund, which was created in 1865, was itself funded with money from the British Crown, UGLE, the Church of England, and the Rothschild banking trust. The event commemorating the PEF's founding was chaired by the Archbishop of York who proclaimed that the Holy Land was, by divine right, British property.

The Quator Coronati Lodge was therefore intimately involved in the "Jewish" or "Hebrew" side of Masonic origins (and Masonic "destiny") and it downplayed the relationship Freemasonry had with the Ancient Mysteries associated with "pagan" cultures. This was a situation that disgusted several QC members including Dr. Wynn Westcott who, according to one source, "made several attempts to steer the representatives of the prevailing 'authentic' school of masonic historiography into considering the possibility of Freemasonry having more occult origins. That approach was ridiculed then and anyone who has tried to make similar suggestions since then has received a similar response generally from the members."[204]

Perhaps because of the "narrow orthodoxy" of the QC Lodge another Masonic study group, the Masonic Study Society (MSS), was founded in London in 1921 by Alvin Coburn, J.S.M. Ward, and Walter Wilmshurst: "Their aim was to encourage the study of masonic symbolism, to chart its origins and possible interpretations along anthropological lines. Avoiding the methodology espoused by the so-called 'authentic' school, this group is still active and studies Freemasonry in light of cultural phenomena that are broadly similar, in the past and present. They use approaches that have been adopted in the fields of comparative religion and folklore studies. They view Freemasonry as a living organism. Their published transactions are circulated world-wide and devote special attention to the symbolic and mystical interpretation of the various masonic Degrees."[205]

Of the founding members of this group, J.S.M. Ward is the most interesting because he is the author of *Freemasonry and the Ancient Gods*, a lengthy examination of Masonic origins that journeys throughout the pagan world to examine the beliefs of cultures in India, Africa, America, and of course Europe, Egypt, and the Near East. Ward was also a well-

---

204. R. Wy. Frater Trevor Stewart, "A Basic Historico-Chronological Model of the Western Hermetic Tradition, Part VI: Masonic Initiation of Today Viewed as a Process," last accessed March 15, 2012, http://www.themasonictrowel.com/books/a_basic_model_western_hermetic_by_Trevor_Stewart/western_hermetic_tradition_toc.htm.
205. Ibid.

known psychic medium and spiritualist during his day, although he kept up the pretenses of Christianity. His thesis in his study of the origins of Freemasonry reflects the Darwinian overtones of his day and the palpable influence of James G. Frazer's *Golden Bough*:

> Freemasonry originated in the primitive initiatory rites of prehistoric man, and from those rites have been built up all the ancient mysteries, and thence all the modern religious systems. It is for this reason that men of all religious beliefs can enter Freemasonry... Thus Freemasonry is the basis of the mysteries, not the mysteries cut down and mutilated... Therefore it is that to this day, if we look carefully, we can find in our ritual the seed of practically every important dogma of every creed, whether it be the Resurrection or Reincarnation.[206]

The third major study group involved with researching the origins and purpose of Freemasonry is the Dormer Masonic Study Circle, founded also in London, in 1938. It met more frequently than the MSS, and published more papers, but it shared the former group's interest in the ancient mysteries and Freemasonry's occult origins. It's very first paper was entitled "The Pythagorean Tradition in Freemasonry," by the Revelation J. R. Cleland, and begins with the following characterization of Freemasonry: "Freemasonry is closely allied to the ancient Mysteries and, if properly understood, and in spite of

206. J.S.M. Ward, *Freemasonry and the Ancient Gods* (Whitfish, MT: Kessinger Publishing, 1992 [1921]), viii.

repeated revision and remolding at the hands of the ignorant and sometimes the malicious, it contains 'all that is necessary to salvation', salvation from the only 'sin' that ultimately matters, that which lies at the root of all other sin and error, the sin of ignorance of the self and of its high calling."[207]

With this introduction the Gnostic influence upon Cleland and this study group becomes evident. The Egyptian influence comes a few sentences later: "…the usages and customs among Freemasons have ever borne a near affinity to those of the Ancient Egyptians; The Philosophers of Egypt, unwilling to expose their mysteries to vulgar eyes, concealed their systems of learning and polity under hieroglyphical figures, which were communicated only to their chief priests and wise men, who were bound by solemn oath never to reveal them."[208]

An analysis of the most important Egyptian connection with Freemasonry was not published until paper #47, entitled "The Great Work In Speculative Masonry," which begins with the following introduction:

> In this Paper the attempt will be made to present, for the guidance of Masonic students, an interpretation of the Egyptian metaphysical tradition in harmony with the teachings set forth in what are called the Mysteries; the Egyptian tradition will then be briefly discussed in the light of its **transmission and ultimate**

---

207. Revelation J. R. Cleland, "The Pythagorean Tradition in Freemasonry," last accessed January 24, 2012, http://users.ucom.net/~vegan/dormer.htm.
208. Ibid.

> **incorporation in Speculative Freemasonry**; finally, reasons will be given in support of the theory, which we hold to be valid, that the Great Work ("Magnum Opus") of the Rosicrucians and Spiritual Alchemists is **the same as that which is symbolised in our Masonic legend of H.A. [Hiram Abiff]**. Thoughtful students may find in the references to the Old Wisdom and the Mystery tradition an introduction to a great subject; nor should the Mysteries be thought of only as institutions long vanished into the night of time; **rather their re-establishment is to be accepted as inevitable.** In years to come a wiser generation will restore the sacred rites which are indispensable to the spiritual, intellectual and social security of the race."[209] (bold added)

The legend of Hiram Abiff is the basis for the most important ritual within the Masonic Brotherhood, the ritual of "raising" the Fellow Craft initiate (2nd-Degree) to the level of Master Mason (3rd-Degree). According to the myth, which is very loosely based on passages from the Old Testament, Hiram Abiff was a Phoenician master builder who was provided by the king of Tyre to King Solomon to offer help in building the Temple of YHWH in Jerusalem. According to the Masons, Hiram Abiff was murdered by three conspirators after they failed to coerce from him the "hidden secrets" of building, or "masonry." In the ritual, the initiate plays the

209. Dormer Paper #47: "The Great Work in Speculative Masonry," last accessed March 15, 2012, http://www.mt.net/~watcher/greatwork.html.

role of Hiram Abiff and is led along as he is struck once, twice, and then a third fatal time. The ritual ends with the initiate (Hiram Abiff) being resurrected from his dark tomb and into the pure light as an equal and "raised" member of the Masonic Fraternity.

The author of the Dormer paper "The Great Work" goes on to connect Freemasonry with Egypt and, more specifically, he connects the legend of Hiram Abiff firmly and directly with the Egyptian tradition of the death and "resurrection" of Osiris, commenting on the fact that Osiris was the basis for the ancient "Dying God" myth found throughout the pagan world:

> To the earliest period of Egyptian metaphysical speculation belongs the fable of Isis and Osiris, and we find that the myth of the Dying God recurs in many of the great World Religions; also it is an established fact that … the life, death and resurrection of the immortal-mortal have become the prototype for numerous other doctrines of human regeneration.
>
> The fable, as it has descended to us in the account given by Plutarch, the celebrated Greek biographer, has not been much amplified by modern research; nor has any new key been found to unlock this sublime drama, which may well be termed the "Passion Play" of Egypt. Plutarch himself, however, says that "the mystic symbols are well known to us who belong to the Brotherhood," and this intimation suggests that the interpretation of the myth as it is given by him in his *Isis and Osiris* will reveal its hidden meaning to students who are already familiar with the principles of the doctrine…

> The traditional history relates that TYPHON lured OSIRIS into the ark of destruction, stated to be a chest or coffin… Typhon was assisted in his "impious design" to usurp the throne of Osiris by ASO (the Queen of Ethiopia) and seventy-two other conspirators. These conspirators represent the three destructive powers, "the three ruffians," which are preserved to modern Freemasonry as the murderers of *the Master Builder* [Hiram Abiff]; they are ignorance, superstition and fear. Thus the advent of greed and perversion marked the end of the Golden Age, and with the death of Osiris, Typhon forthwith ascended the throne as regent of the world… At this stage, Isis, now represented by the scattered but still consecrated body of Initiates, began the great search for the secret that was lost; and in all parts of the world the virtuous in "grief and distress" raised their hands to the heavens, pleading for the restoration of the reign of Truth. Continuing their search in all parts of the earth and throughout innumerable ages, the congregation of the just at last re-discovered the lost arcana and brought it back with rejoicing to the world over which it once ruled. In this manner, we learn, Isis by magic (the initiated priests were magicians), resurrected the dead God, and through union with him brought forth an order of priests under the collective title of HORUS.[210]

The Dormer study group was not the first, and certainly not the last, to equate the legendary Hiram Abiff with the

210. Ibid.

Egyptian god Osiris. Underneath the surface of mainstream Freemasonry this association has been known and understood as fact probably since the beginning of the organized fraternity. This fact was certainly not lost on the celebrated occult scholar and 33rd-Degree Masonic historian, Manly P. Hall, supports this connection in a paper he wrote on "Rosicrucian and Masonic Origins":

> Preston, Gould, Mackey, Oliver, and Pike—in fact, nearly every great historian of Freemasonry-have all admitted the possibility of the modern society being connected, indirectly at least, with the ancient Mysteries, and their descriptions of the modern society are prefaced by excerpts from ancient writings descriptive of primitive ceremonials. **These eminent Masonic scholars have all recognized in the legend of Hiram Abiff an adaptation of the Osiris myth**; nor do they deny that the major part of the symbolism of the craft is derived from the pagan institutions of antiquity when the gods were venerated in secret places with strange figures and appropriate rituals.[211] (bold added)

The connection between Hiram Abiff and Osiris is also explored in the relatively recent *Harper's Encyclopaedia of Mystical & Paranormal Experience* (1991) under the heading "Freemasonry," which introduces another provocative symbol associated with the seventy-two Kosmokrator "gods":

---

211. Manly P. Hall, "Rosicrucian and Masonic Origins," *Pheonix Masonry*, last accessed January 24, 2012, http://www.phoenixmasonry.org/roscrucian_and_masonic_origins.htm.

In ritual Masons "die" as Hiram Abiff died, and are reborn in the spiritual bonds of Freemasonry.

Philosopher Manly P. Hall compared the Hiramic legend to the worship of Isis and Osiris in the ancient Egyptian mystery schools, another reputed source for Freemasonry. Osiris also fell victim to ruffians, and the resurrection of his body minus his phallus—and Isis's search for it—seems symbolically similar to the quest for the Lost Word of God. Followers of the Isis cult were known as "widow's sons," after the murder of her husband/brother Osiris, and Masons also are called "sons of the widow"...

Speculative Masonry borrowed the tools of the craft as symbols of the order: the square, compass, plumb line, and level. Members wear white leather aprons associated with builders. Ritual colors are blue and gold. The capital letter G appearing in the Masonic compass most likely stands for God. Meetings are held in Lodges or Temples: four-sided rectangular structures decorated with Masonic symbols and black-and-white checkered floors, symbolic of humankind's dual nature.

Another Masonic emblem is the Great Pyramid of Giza, **always shown with seventy-two stones representing the seventy-two combinations of the Tetragrammaton**, or the four-lettered name of God (YHVH) in Hebrew. The pyramid is flat-topped, unfinished, symbolizing humankind's incomplete nature. Floating above the pyramid is the single All-Seeing Eye of the Great Architect, also associated with Horus, son of Isis and Osiris. Both the pyramid and the All-Seeing Eye appear on the United States dollar bill and the reverse of the Great Seal of the United States. (bold added)[212]

So, once again we are brought back to the Great Pyramid of Giza, the first built and last remaining of the Seven Wonders of the ancient world, which is the reputed resting place of Osiris. The Great Pyramid itself is but one structure within a major Necropolis that was designed according to the layout of the constellation Orion, the Great Hunter in the sky. As we have endeavored to show, Osiris is none other than the biblical Nimrod, the "mighty hunter before the Lord," whose death brought about the division of his global empire into the hands of the seventy Kosmokrator angels who descended from heaven to begin their era of authority over mankind. The seventy angelic "world powers" eventually came to be understood as seventy-two, which is the number of "conspirators" who aided Set/Typhon in the murder of Osiris. It is also the number of angels associated with the Kabbalistic *Shem ha Mephoresh*, and the number of stones portrayed in Masonic representations of the Great Pyramid.

212. *Harper's Encyclopaedia of Mystical & Paranormal Experience* (San Francisco, CA: Harper, 1991), 216–217.

Another representation of the Great Pyramid of Giza may perhaps be found in the "square and compass" symbol of Freemasonry. The compass is opened to the familiar number of 72° as the apex of the pyramid, whereas the base of the pyramid appears as the square, while the "G" represents, not "God," or "Geometry," as some have speculated, but perhaps "Giza," the location of the resting place of Masonry's dear departed master, whom they expect to return as their "God."

There is little doubt that Hiram Abiff is but a veiled representation of Osiris, and the Third-Degree ritual of the "resurrection" of Hiram is simply a reenactment of the different pagan Mysteries that ritualized the "raising" of Osiris, the "awakening" of Heracles, or the "resurrection" of Dionysus, all of them looking forward to the resurrection of the Antichrist in the Day of the Lord.

So how did Freemasonry come to portray Osiris as Hiram Abiff, the supposed "master builder" of the Temple of God in Jerusalem under the reign of King Solomon? The fact is that the legend of Hiram Abiff is a relatively late addition to the Masonic tradition which is first documented in Anderson's *Constitutions* of 1723. The little book, *Symbols of Freemasonry*, translated from the French publication *Les Symboles des Francs-Maçons* (1997), reveals that the original "Legend of the Craft" connects directly with our understanding of Osiris as Nimrod:

The date of the construction of King Solomon's temple has not always been the key date in the Freemasons' cosmology. This central role was once given to the Tower of Babel. The *Regius* manuscript, which predates *Cooke* [1410] by twenty years, cites King Nemrod, the builder of that famous tower, as "the first and most excellent master." He it was, and not King Solomon, who gave the Masons their first "charge," their rules of conduct and professional code.

For a long time both King Solomon and King Nemrod played a part in the tradition. A Masonic text known as the *Thistle* manuscript, of 1756, says that Nemrod "created the Masons" and "gave them their signs and terms so that they could distinguish themselves from other people…it was the first time that the Masons were organised as a craft."

It was during the early years of the eighteenth century that Freemasonry stopped seeing its origins in the Tower of Babel and that Solomon alone was considered "the first Grand Master."

The eighteenth-century Masonic texts shed light on the ideas and attitudes at the time of the shift from Operative Masonry to Speculative Masonry… Speculative Masons, who were concerned with social responsibility and had no desire to threaten the establishment, finally rejected the "Legend of the Craft" which honored the Tower of Babel, a pagan edifice constructed in open defiance to heaven. Instead of the Promethean or Faustian Nemrod, they preferred "our

> wise king Solomon," or as *A Mason's Examination* of 1723 puts it: "Grand Master in his time of Masonry and Architecture."[213]

One way or another, the legendary origins of Freemasonry all point back to Egypt, to the Great Pyramid, and to Osiris—the Egyptian version of Nimrod the Nephilim King. He is the original Dying God whose death brought about the era of the pagan gods, and whose resurrection will be accompanied by their return.

---

213. Daniel Béresniak, *Symbols of Freemasonry* (New York, NY: Assouline Publishing, 2000), 26–28.

chapter twenty-five

AN ENERGY OF DELUSION

WHEN JESUS TAUGHT His disciples about the return of the Son of Man, He also warned about false prophets who would appear and claim to have found the Christ. Jesus said, "Wherefore if they shall say unto you, Behold, he is in the desert; go not forth: behold, he is in the secret chambers; believe it not."

In this chapter we will shine a spotlight on a few modern-day voices that are making this very claim regarding the five-thousand-year-old corpse that is buried somewhere in the vicinity of Giza.[214]

---

214. Much of this chapter's material can also be found in "The Giza Discovery, Part Seven: The Second Coming of the Antichrist," at http://www.redmoonrising.com/Giza/SavDest7.htm.

Edgar Cayce and the Second Coming

Edgar Cayce, who lived from 1877–1945, is known as "The Sleeping Prophet." He was famous in the United States and eventually worldwide for his powerful psychic abilities and for the messages that he communicated while laying down in a trance, which were recorded by his secretary. Throughout his life, Cayce was intimately involved in Masonic circles and his career was promoted by fellow Masons. In turn, the channeled messages received through Cayce promoted the Gnostic neo-pagan spirituality that exists at the heart of Freemasonry.

Edgar Cayce

According to the messages given through Edgar Cayce, the most important time in human history, other than perhaps the time of Jesus Christ, was a period in ancient Egypt around 10,500 BC, shortly after the alleged destruction of Atlantis. The whole story, as pieced together from a number of different readings given over several decades, appears to revolve around an ancient Egyptian High Priest by the name of Ra-Ta, who just happened to be a previous incarnation of Edgar Cayce himself. In reading this story it becomes clear that the story of Ra-Ta is simply a thinly-veiled presentation of the myth of Osiris that includes parallels with the life of Jesus Christ.

According to Cayce's messages, the final great work of Ra-Ta was the building of the Great Pyramid, laid out "according to that which had been worked out by Ra-Ta in the mount, as related to the position of the stars about which this particular solar system circles in its activity…"[215] It was to be a prophetic model of human events as well, which was a well-known belief in Cayce's day, promoted by authors such as Piazzi Smith and David Davidson: "As the changes came about in the earth, the rise and fall of nations were to be depicted in this same temple, that was to act as an interpreter for that which had been, that which is, and that which is to be... "[216]

Finally, with the completion of the Great Pyramid, the life's mission of Ra-Ta was accomplished and the end of his earthly incarnation was described: "Then there came the period when all the pyramid or memorial was complete. Ra, having finished his work, ascended into the mount—and was borne away."[217]

The purpose of the Great Pyramid is explained in a separate reading: "In the building of the pyramid, and that which is now called the Mystery of Mysteries, this was intended to be a MEMORIAL—as would be termed today—to that counsellor who ruled or governed, or who acted in the capacity of the director in the MATERIAL things in the land. With the return of the priest [Ra] (as it had been stopped), this was later—by Isis, the queen, or the daughter of Ra—turned so as to present to those peoples in that land the relationships of man and animal or carnal world with those changes that fade or fall away in their various effect."[218]

The story of Ra-Ta does not end with the completion of the Great Pyramid and his "ascension" into heaven. The

215. Hugh Lynn Cayce, *The Story of Ra-Ta*, reading 294–151 from the Edgar Cayce CD-ROM.

216. Ibid.

217. Ibid., "Reports of Reading 294–153."

218. Ibid., reading 5748–6.

spirits behind the messages given by Edgar Cayce were not interested only in the past, they also had a definite agenda for the future. According to these spirits, Ra-Ta would appear again on the earth and he would help to lead humanity into the New Age of Aquarius.

Other readings explain that the "return of the Great Initiate" is associated with the Second Coming of Jesus Christ. However, the relationship between Christ and Ra-Ta remains unclear. On one hand Ra-Ta, a previous incarnation of Cayce, is clearly portrayed as the "Great Initiate" who is expected to return, but then Jesus is also described as the "Great Initiate." Strangely, Christ is also associated with an undiscovered tomb and/or pyramid that allegedly contains records of His teachings. The question is, who exactly is Cayce's Christ?

> (Q) In which pyramids are the records of the Christ?
> (A) That yet to be uncovered.
> (Q) Are there any written records which have not been found of the teachings?
> (A) More, rather, of those of the close associates, and those records that are yet to be found of the preparation of the man, of the Christ, in those of the tomb, or those yet to be uncovered in the pyramid.
> (Q) He said He would come again. What about His second coming?
> (A) The time no one knows. Even as He gave, not even the Son Himself. ONLY the Father. Not until His enemies—and the earth—are wholly in subjection to His will, His powers.
> (Q) Are we entering the period of preparation for His coming?

(A) Entering the test period, rather.[219]

In the quote above, Cayce's source echoes the Bible in saying that no one will know the time of the return of the Messiah, yet in many other readings this return is closely associated with the year 1998. Scholars have since concluded that Cayce's source was merely predicting that a chamber, the so-called "Hall of Records," would be found underneath the Sphinx in 1998. Evidence exists that just such a chamber was found in 1998, although its discovery has not been officially confirmed. Below are a few prophecies of the allegedly momentous year of 1998:

> In 1998 we may find a great deal of the activities as have been wrought by the gradual changes that are coming about...
> (Q) Can a date be given to indicate the beginning of the Aquarian Age?
> (A) This has already been indicated as the period when it should pass, but that is when it begins to affect. It laps from one to another, as is the natural sources, as he holds to that which has been, which is. As has been indicated, we will begin to understand fully in '98.
> (Q) Are there any thoughts along these lines, beyond these, that can be given at this time?
> (A) Holy, holy is His name![220]

---

219. Ibid., reading 5749–2.

220. Ibid., reading 1602–3.

"In this same pyramid did the Great Initiate, the Master, take those last of the Brotherhood degrees with John, the forerunner of Him, at that place...and again is there seen that this occurs in the entrance of the Messiah in this period—1998."[221]

The quotes above seem to refer to Jesus as the Great Initiate, yet another reading also clearly predicts the return of Ra-Ta, a portion of which goes on to describe him as the "Liberator of the World":

> Is it not fitting, then, that these must return? As this priest [Ra-Ta] may develop himself to be in that position, to be in the capacity of a LIBERATOR of the world in its relationships to individuals in those periods to come; for he must enter again at that period, or in 1998.[222]

The relationship between Ra-Ta and Jesus is enigmatic, and Cayce's secretary, Gladys Davis, turned to Manly P. Hall's occult encyclopedia to try to make sense of it. In her notes she explained that according to Hall, the figure Hermes is the same as the biblical Enoch who ascended into heaven in Genesis 5:24. Enoch is named in Cayce's readings as one of the incarnations of Jesus, and so Davis concludes that Jesus appeared as Hermes during the time of Ra-Ta, circa 10,500 BC, to help in the building of the Great Pyramid.

Apparently both Jesus and Ra-Ta are predicted to return to help guide mankind into the Age of Aquarius, which

221. Ibid., reading 5748–5.

222. Ibid., reading 294–151.

corresponds with the channeled messages of Alice Bailey and Benjamin Creme that predict that the "Master Jesus" will appear alongside the revealed "Maitreya" to help usher in the New Age. According to Creme this "Master Jesus" will be based in Rome and his task will be to correct the "false teachings" that have crept into Catholicism and Christianity over the past two thousand years.

It may be entirely coincidental, but it should be noted that the ancient Egyptian holy city of Heliopolis, the spiritual capital of the ancient cults of Ra and Osiris, is presently located underneath a suburb of Cairo that is known today as El-Matariya.

"The Dying God Shall Rise Again!"

It is interesting that Gladys Davis, the secretary of Edgar Cayce who recorded most of his trance-channeled sessions, would refer to the work of Manly P. Hall as an authority on spiritual and esoteric issues. I have not investigated the relationship between Edgar Cayce and Manly P. Hall, but their lives have very much in common. Both looked with interest to ancient Egypt, both endorsed Gnosticism and other occult traditions and beliefs, and both looked to the return of a "Great Initiate" who is often confused with Jesus Christ. Furthermore, while the legacy of Cayce was solidified with the creation of his Association of Research and Enlightenment (ARE) on the east coast in Virginia City in 1931, Hall's was confirmed by the creation of his institution, the Philosophical Research Society, on the west coast in Los Angeles in 1934.

Manly P. Hall was a very ambitious young occultist and his magnum opus, *The Secret Teachings of All Ages*, was published when Hall was only twenty-five years old, in 1928. The first print run of this massive volume included only five hundred volumes that were quickly sold out, and the book remained a collector's item largely unknown to the "uninitiated." It was only in 2003, seventy-five years after the initial print run, that *Secret Teachings* became available as a mass market paperback to the general public.

Manly P. Hall

Manly P. Hall achieved the honorary level of 33rd-Degree within the Scottish Rite of Freemasonry before passing away in 1990, and he was certainly a high-level initiate of many other occult societies. In the early 1920s, before writing *Secret Teachings*, Hall published a small book entitled *The Lost Keys of Freemasonry*, also known as *The Secret of Hiram Abiff*. In this book, Hall presents the legendary tale of the master builder that King Solomon contracted from the King of Tyre to help build the Temple of God in Jerusalem.

The Hiram Abiff myth is the foundation of the most important initiation in the lower levels of Freemasonry—the "raising" of the initiate to the third-degree of Master Mason. In the Masonic ritual the initiate plays the part of Hiram Abiff as he is slain by three ruffians. Afterwards the initiate is regarded as deceased for a period of time prior to his joyous "resurrection" that culminates the ritual and brings the initiate "into the light."

In *The Lost Keys of Freemasonry*, Manly P. Hall dramatizes the death of Hiram Abiff at the hands of the ruffians who, after killing their good master, are startled by a voice from heaven:

The Master fell back, his upturned face sweet in the last repose of death, and the light rays no longer pouring from him. The gray clouds gathered closer as though to form a winding sheet around the body of their murdered Master. Suddenly the heavens opened again and a shaft of light bathed the form of Hiram in a glory celestial. Again the Voice spoke from the heavens where the Great King sat upon the clouds of creation:

"**He is not dead; he is asleep. Who will awaken him?** His labors are not done, and in death he guards the sacred relics more closely than ever, for the Word and the tracing board are his—I have given them to him. **But he must remain asleep until these three who have slain him shall bring him back to life, for every wrong must be righted, and the slayers of my house, the destroyers of my temple, must labor in the place of their Builder until they raise their Master from the dead.**"

The three murderers fell on their knees and raised their hands to heaven as though to ward off the light which had disclosed their crime:

"O God, great is our sin, for we have slain our Grand Master, Hiram Abiff! Just is Thy punishment and as we have slain him **we now dedicate our lives to his resurrection.** The first was our human weakness, the second our sacred duty."[223] (bold added)

---

223. Manly P. Hall, *The Lost Keys of Freemasonry*, 1996, digital edition.

In *The Lost Keys of Freemasonry,* Hall examines the legend of Hiram Abiff on a symbolic level, and he explains that human beings, or more specifically those who are members of the Masonic Fraternity, are in fact the "three ruffians" who must labor to perfect their characters and work for the brotherhood of man that will allow for the inevitable resurrection of "Hiram Abiff," otherwise known, as Hall himself knew, as Osiris.

Hall's *Lost Keys* gives a glimpse of the symbolism behind Freemasonry, but in his book, *The Secret Teachings of All Ages,* Hall explains very clearly what some of these symbols mean on a literal level, and on a level that will eventually affect all mankind. We will pick up his analysis in chapter seven, "The Initiation of the Pyramid" in the section dealing with "The Pyramid Mysteries":

> The Great Pyramid...represented the inner sanctuary of pre-Egyptian wisdom. By the Egyptians the Great Pyramid was associated with Hermes, the god of wisdom and letters and the Divine Illuminator worshiped through the planet Mercury. Relating Hermes to the Pyramid emphasizes anew the fact that it was in reality the supreme temple of the Invisible and Supreme Deity. The Great Pyramid was not a lighthouse, an observatory, or a tomb, but the first temple of the Mysteries, the first structure erected as a repository for those secret truths which are the certain foundations of all arts and sciences. It was the perfect emblem of the microcosm and the macrocosm and, according to the secret teachings, the tomb of Osiris, the black god of the Nile. Osiris represented a

> certain manifestation of solar energy, and therefore his house or tomb is emblematic of the universe within which he is entombed and upon the cross of which he is crucified.[224]

In this passage, Hall connects Hermes with the Great Pyramid, which the medieval Arab sages referred to as the "Tomb of Hermes." The connection between Hermes and Osiris, as previously mentioned, runs deep. In Hall's next chapter, entitled "Isis, the Virgin of the World," he writes that "Plutarch affirms that many ancient authors believed this goddess to be the daughter of Hermes."[225] Cayce's messages claimed that Isis was the daughter and wife of Ra-Ta, while the usual myth of Osiris makes Isis to be his sister and wife. Regarding the Great Pyramid in the quote above, Hall contradicts himself by first saying that it is not a tomb and then immediately explaining that "according to the secret teachings" it was the tomb of Osiris. Hall then continues:

> Through the mystic passageways and chambers of the Great Pyramid passed the illumined of antiquity. They entered its portals as men; they came forth as gods. It was the place of the "second birth," the "womb of the Mysteries," and wisdom dwelt in it as God dwells in the heart of men…
>
> The technique of the Mysteries was unfolded by the Sage Illuminator, the Master of the Secret House.

---

224. Manly P. Hall, *The Secret Teachings of All Ages* (New York, NY: Penguin, 2003), 116–120.

225. Ibid., 121.

> The power to know his guardian spirit was revealed to the new initiate; the method of disentangling his material body from his divine vehicle was explained; and to consummate the magnum opus, there was revealed the Divine Name—the secret and unutterable designation of the Supreme Deity, by the very knowledge of which man and his God are made consciously one. With the giving of the Name, the new initiate became himself a pyramid, within the chambers of whose soul numberless other human beings might also receive spiritual enlightenment.[226]

Hall's references to the "Divine Name" reveals Hall's Kabbalistic inclinations because the seventy-two-letter *Shem ha-Mephorash*, known as the Divine Name of YHWH, is the primary basis for Kabbalists to contact the seventy or seventy-two Kosmokrator angels that rule over the nations of the world. Regarding the number *seventy*, Hall writes that "wherever this round number is used by the Hebrews it really means seventy-two."[227] Hall's commentary on the Great Pyramid continues:

> In the King's Chamber was enacted the drama of the "second death." Here the candidate, after being crucified upon the cross of the solstices and the equinoxes, was buried in the great coffer… While his body lay in the coffer, the soul of the neophyte soared as a human-headed hawk through the celestial realms,

226. Ibid., 188–119.

227. Ibid., 434.

> there to discover first hand the eternity of Life, Light, and Truth, as well as the illusion of Death, Darkness, and Sin. Thus in one sense the Great Pyramid may be likened to a gate through which the ancient priests permitted a few to pass toward the attainment of individual completion.[228]

Again we find that occult doctrines are reinforced with promises of personal metaphysical experience. Both combine to promote the Luciferian lie that death and sin are nothing but *illusions*. Hall continues:

> Though the modern world may know a million secrets, the ancient world knew one—and that one was greater than the million; for the million secrets breed death, disaster, sorrow, selfishness, lust, and avarice, but the one secret confers life, light, and truth. The time will come when the secret wisdom shall again be the dominating religious and philosophical urge of the world. The day is at hand when the doom of dogma shall be sounded. **The great theological Tower of Babel**, with its confusion of tongues, was built of bricks of mud and the mortar of slime. Out of the cold ashes of lifeless creeds, however, shall rise phoenixlike the ancient Mysteries. No other institution has so completely satisfied the religious aspirations of humanity...[229]

---

228. Ibid., 119.

229. Ibid., 119–120.

The reference to the Tower of Babel is certainly interesting, considering the next statement that is perhaps the clearest ever written of occult expectations of the discovery and resurrection of the body of the Antichrist. What follows is precisely the sort of message that Jesus Christ warned us about:

> The Dying God shall rise again! The secret room in the House of the Hidden Places shall be rediscovered. The Pyramid again shall stand as the ideal emblem of solidarity, inspiration, aspiration, resurrection, and regeneration. As the passing sands of time bury civilization upon civilization beneath their weight, the Pyramid shall remain as the visible covenant between Eternal Wisdom and the world. The time may yet come when the chants of the illumined shall be heard once more in its ancient passageways and the Master of the Hidden House shall await in the Silent Place for the coming of that man who, casting aside the fallacies of dogma and tenet, seeks simply Truth and will be satisfied with neither substitute nor counterfeit.[230]

The Stargate Conspiracy

The occult teachings promoted by Manly P. Hall and the very similar messages channeled by Edgar Cayce live on in the twenty-first century as integral components of what can be loosely referred to as New-Age Spirituality. Giza is today viewed as their global spiritual capital and Egyptian religion

230. Ibid., 120.

is seen as a pure form of religion that once had a unique connection with the divine.

In the 1990s, following Rudolf Gantenbrink's exploration of the "star shafts" in the Great Pyramid, and following the great success of John Anthony West's Emmy-winning television program "The Mystery of the Sphinx" (1993), the world became even more fascinated and intrigued with ancient Egypt. Out of this climate two mainstream authors, Graham Hancock and Robert Bauval emerged as important voices that seemed to act as a bridge between the "respectable" world of academia and the bizarre community of New-Age devotees and "pyramidiots."

In Hancock's *Fingerprints of the Gods* (1995) Egypt was looked to as a possible stepping stone to a more ancient and advanced global civilization (Atlantis—which was probably a vague memory of the island of Eridu and the Tower of Babel), while Bauval's *The Orion Mystery* (1994) postulated that Giza was built as a supernatural gateway to the afterlife and to the stars. Later, Hancock and Bauval teamed up to write *The Message of the Sphinx* (1996), *The Mars Mystery* (1998), and recently *Talisman* (2004). The first two continued in their examination of ancient Egypt as the key to the many mysteries surrounding human origins, while *Talisman* promoted Gnosticism and Hermeticism as underground conduits of the "pure" Egyptian religion that preserved these mysteries during the Dark Ages when Christianity rudely dominated the West.

At the same time that Hancock and Bauval were achieving their success and notoriety, a scientist and author named Richard C. Hoagland was making a parallel rise, thanks in large part to his numerous appearances on Art Bell's Coast-to-Coast AM. Hoagland's *The Monuments of Mars* (1987) brought an extra-terrestrial component to the mix, and espoused a belief that allegedly artificial structures on Mars spoke of a connection between the red planet and ancient Egypt. Hoagland believes that an extraterrestrial civilization was responsible both for the alleged monuments on Mars and for the birth of civilization on Earth. He even goes so far as to postulate that perhaps this E.T. civilization was genetically responsible for the emergence of modern *Homo sapiens sapiens*. In other words, Hoagland believes that these "gods" from beyond our solar system are mankind's true creators.

In 1999, there appeared a much needed critical response to the direction in which the hysteria surrounding ancient Egypt was headed. It came in the form of a book entitled *The Stargate Conspiracy*, written by Lynn Picknett and Clive Prince. Their book reveals many strange connections between some of the conclusions reached by Hancock, Bauval, and Hoagland and the messages received by Edgar Cayce that have been posthumously promoted by his Association for Research and Enlightenment (ARE).

For instance, Hancock and Bauval use archeo-astronomical methods to arrive at 10,500 BC as a date corresponding with the legendary Zep Tepi, or "First Time," when the gods supposedly established Egyptian civilization. After arriving at this date using purely scientific methods, Hancock and Bauval then mention in passing the messages received by Edgar Cayce that give the same exact date, which gives the reader the impression of *supernatural confirmation* for Hancock and Bauval's research.

As critics, Picknett and Prince are able to scientifically debunk the 10,500 BC date and then they argue that Hancock and Bauval probably tried to wrap their calculations around this pre-determined date from the very beginning. Picknett and Prince show that Hancock and Bauval are not always upfront with their readers, and they explain that Graham Hancock is even accused by other researchers of "wittingly or unwittingly, following a masonic agenda..."[231]

Edgar Cayce's influence, and that of the ARE, runs much deeper than this, however, and casts a long shadow over the field of Egyptology and over the people responsible for protecting, overseeing, and excavating the ancient site of Giza, as Picknett and Prince reveal:

> Mark Lehner... is the most prominent American Egyptologist stationed in Egypt today. He is highly respected internationally. His 1997 book *The Complete Pyramids* was hailed as a masterly overview of an only too often thorny subject, and was promoted by many major museums, including the British Museum. It is less well known that in 1974 he wrote a book for ARE entitled *The Egyptian Heritage*, based on the Edgar Cayce Readings, which attempted to reconcile Cayce's pronouncements with the findings of modern Egyptology. According to Lehner in his early days, the Great Pyramid was built as a repository of knowledge, and a "Temple of Initiation for the White Brotherhood".
>
> In 1973, Edgar Cayce's son Hugh Lynn Cayce, selected the promising young student Lehner to be ARE's "insider" within the ranks of academic

231. Lynn Picknett and Clive Prince, *The Stargate Conspiracy: The Truth About Extraterrestrial Life and the Mysteries of Ancient Egypt* (London, UK: Little, Brown and Company, 1999), 100.

Egyptology, and it was ARE that paid for his training. They also funded his recent carbon-dating tests of material taken from the Great Pyramid (which seems to indicate that it is about 300 or 400 years older than was thought—but not the 8,000 hoped for by ARE). Today he no longer advocates Cayceism, and appears not to espouse any "alternative" views, now being very much a mainstream Egyptologist...

But Mark Lehner is not the only person on the Giza Plateau to have reason to be grateful to ARE. Amazingly, that arch-enemy of all pyramidiots, Dr. Zahi Hawass—who since 1987 has been in the powerful position of Director of the Giza Plateau and who was recently promoted to Undersecretary of State for he Giza Monuments—was also put through his training as an Egyptologist by ARE. Through fellow ARE members, Hugh Lynn Cayce arranged a scholarship for Hawass at the University of Pennsylvania between 1980 and 1987, where he gained his Ph.D. in Egyptology. Hawass has maintained his association with ARE ever since, and is a regular lecturer at their conferences at their Virginia Beach headquarters.

It is, to say the least, interesting that **the two most prominent and influential representatives of Egyptological orthodoxy at Giza are linked to Edgar Cayce's organisation.**[232] (bold added)

Edgar Cayce died in January of 1945, and with his passing the "spirits" that spoke through him lost a very influential

232. Ibid., 62–63.

voice. The primary "conspiracy" described in *The Stargate Conspiracy* involves what appears to be the re-establishment of contact from these "spirits" with an influential circle of people that included industrialists, businessmen, scientists, and high-level politicians. In this case, the "spirits" claimed to be the nine primary gods of the ancient Egyptian Ennead of Heliopolis, known simply as "The Nine." The figure at the center of the conspiracy was Dr. Andrija Puharich, a physicist and inventor who was closely connected with the CIA and with important scientific research institutes, and who was certainly a high-level member of the Masonic fraternity.

The conspiracy laid out by Picknett and Prince runs very deep and involves groups such as the ARE, SRI International, the Esalen Institute, the Christic Institute, the Institute of Noetic Sciences, the CIA, and even NASA and the UN, and is much too complicated to explore at length here. Let us just say that the predictions from The Nine are very apocalyptic in nature and involve themes such as extra-terrestrial contact, spiritual evolution, and a transition into the New Age. Picknett and Prince also write how these channeled messages from the "gods" of Egypt involve certain expected discoveries in Egypt: "Tom himself—allegedly the god Atum—is emphatic about the importance of the monuments of Giza, in particular the Great Pyramid, but he has refused repeatedly to be drawn on its purpose, saying only that this will be revealed when the landing has happened. However, when asked by Puharich if there were undiscovered chambers in the Great Pyramid, he replied, 'To a degree,' adding, 'The entrance is from the Sphinx.'"[233]

---

233. Ibid.,183.

Picknett and Prince also mention the independent investigations in 1999 of a one-time associate of Richard C. Hoagland, which ties in perfectly with what we can expect if the premise of this book is correct:

> One particularly lurid story was recently posted on the Internet by the independent American researcher Larry Dean Hunter who, as we have seen, investigated claims of tunneling in Davison's Chamber on behalf of Richard Hoagland... It claimed that a massive, 250-foot high chamber had been found inside the Great Pyramid. This they call the Hall of Osiris, which they claim leads to another chamber in which lies the body of the god Osiris himself.[234]

234. Ibid., 101; also see www.larryhunter.com.

conclusion

AWAKE

"NOW IT IS HIGH TIME to awake out of sleep: for now is our salvation nearer than when we believed. The night is far spent, the day is at hand: let us therefore cast off the works of darkness, and let us put on the armour of light" (Romans 13:11–12).

The choice that everyone on earth will eventually be forced to make is as clear as black and white. Jesus stands for life, love, freedom, and holiness, while the Antichrist stands for death, selfishness, bondage, and wickedness. As the time of the new beginning draws closer this stark reality will become even clearer, and the shades of grey will disappear.

Our culture specializes in creating millions of little nimrods[235] out there, each trying to build their own towers. They are all caught up in the lust of the flesh, the lust of the eyes,

---

235. **nimrod**- *noun*, 1: HUNTER, 2: IDIOT, JERK. From *Mirriam-Webster's Dictionary and Thesaurus*, 2006.

and the pride of life, being driven by the love of money and their love of themselves. Self-centered ambition will only lead to destruction. In these last days we can choose to be a nimrod, or we can choose the way of Jesus, surrendering to the Creator and allowing the Holy Spirit to completely possess us. This sounds mystical and hyper-spiritual, and it absolutely is.

Four years ago, I was ready to publish this book, but the Lord spoke very clearly to me in a way that I could not miss,[236] telling me to drop it completely and to focus all of my attention on getting to know the Lord Jesus Christ. You see, I had spent three years researching this material and getting to know the devil's schemes and the identity of the Antichrist, but I still did not truly know Jesus. Sure, I had intellectually accepted that the Gospel was true, but I wasn't becoming a disciple of Jesus and I did not understand what it meant to be obedient to His basic instructions. To put it bluntly, I was practicing an inferior form of Christianity. My book had to wait.

After I made the painful decision to set my dreams aside, I took my wife on a hike up to the mountaintop overlooking the ocean here in Kailua. With tears in my eyes I explained to her that I was putting away my writing and research and was turning instead to pursue Jesus, Himself. This was a moment of great joy for my wife, even as I was feeling as if a part of me was dying. It was hard for me to accept that my immediate

236. I share my testimony of this time in my life in a four-hour interview of *The Iron Show*, Part 7, hosted by John McMahon and Richard White, available at http://ironshow.com/petergoodgame/.

desires were not in line with God's plan for my life at that moment, but I made the choice to follow Jesus.

Over the next few years, the Lord filled two major holes in my life. First, I was introduced to the supernatural power of the Holy Spirit; and second, I was brought into proper relationship with the Body of Christ. Without either of these I believe that the publication of this book would have led to my self-destruction. Followers of Jesus are not meant to go through life without the power of the Holy Spirit and without the support of the Family of God. I now have both, which gives me a profound sense of peace and a confidence that I can fulfill whatever the Lord has called me to do, which is being revealed day-by-day in my life.

This book is important, and I know that the Lord wants it released now, at this very time, but let's keep it in proper perspective. Yes, end-times teaching is something that we should all understand, because Jesus told us what to look for and He told us repeatedly to watch and to pray. But Jesus also told us other instructions that are just as fundamental to what it means to be His disciples.

The "rulers of the darkness of this world" are anticipating the awakening of the body of the Antichrist, but heaven is anticipating the awakening of the Body of Christ. When God's Church, the Body of Christ, turns back to the basic simplicity of the Gospel, and begins to obey the commandments of Jesus, then **the whole world will wonder when they see the awakening of the Body of Christ.** Many of those whose names have been written in the Book of Life from the foundation of the world will be convicted by the Love, Power, and Holiness that they will see displayed, and they will turn away from sin, embrace Jesus, and take their places in the Family of God.

The Last Great Awakening of the Church will precede the awakening of the Antichrist, and you are invited to be a part of it. The Bride of Christ will not go out with a whimper, but with a global explosion of Power and Love!

So what does it mean to follow Jesus Christ? To be honest, most people who claim to be "Christian" give Jesus a bad name. Human beings have a very good built-in "hypocrisy detector," and it seems to ring the louder the closer one gets to a Church; but so what? Jesus set the bar high, and just because so many of His followers fail to reach it should not be an excuse to reject His Call.

Perhaps you have heard that accepting Salvation and receiving the Holy Spirit into your heart is a "free gift" that will cost you nothing. That is absolutely true. Jesus doesn't require anything from you to make this happen. You can be the worst criminal and full of sin, and He will still accept you. Jesus did it all. Just say, **"Yes Jesus, I am yours,"** and He will adopt you into the family of God, taking you under His wing and making you a son or daughter of God.

Jesus died so that He could send the Holy Spirit to the earth as an antidote to sin, freely offered to any and all who will accept it. This free gift of the Holy Spirit is the foundation of what we call "Grace," but it is not the fullness of "Grace."

With the first part of Grace we are saved and brought into the family of God by accepting the offer that Christ extends to live in us. With this foundation we also have free access to the amazing supernatural "spiritual gifts," such as prophesying, healing the sick, casting out demons, and raising the dead.

Most pastors would prefer that "spiritual power" be

connected with "holiness," but God thinks otherwise, and He allows His children to have free access to these gifts, even if they have sin in their lives. Power is therefore related to an individual's boldness and their faith in what Jesus has already done. Power is not selectively "handed out" from heaven based on one's righteousness and holiness, which is a separate track of spiritual growth that must be pursued out of love for Jesus, rather than from legalistic pressures to "follow the rules."

This separate track of spiritual growth must not be ignored, however, because it is the second part of Grace which is actually the fullness of Grace. Unfortunately, in today's self-centered culture, this second part of Grace is not taught very much in Church, which is why Christians often end up looking like hypocrites. This is the part of Grace that gives you the power to consciously turn away from and continually resist sin; to actually become like Jesus, and to pursue the Holiness of God. On our own, we cannot become like Jesus. We can only do this by the power of the Holy Spirit, which is a continual work of Grace in our lives, transforming our minds and changing us into true representations of Christ on earth.

I often hear Christians commenting on the fact that they are "seated with Christ in heavenly places," and that when God looks at them all He sees is Jesus, because Jesus has washed away all of their sins, "past, present, and future." This is the truth, but we should never use it as an excuse to ignore God's instructions to pursue Holiness. You see, Christ's death released not only a Grace that allows us to stand in front of the Father in Holiness; He also released a Grace that will allow the people of God to stand in front of the World in Holiness, bringing a Spirit of conviction upon the world like never before.

Right now God looks at the Church and sees Jesus, but the world looks at the Church and, well…doesn't see Jesus—at least not yet.

Hebrews 12:14 says that without Holiness, "no man shall see the Lord." The Last Great Awakening will be a time when the world will see the Lord merely by looking at His Body here on earth, because there will be a remnant of sold-out lovers of Jesus who will completely submit to the total work of Grace in their lives, realizing the fullness of what was purchased by the death of Jesus on the Cross.

The first part of Grace costs us absolutely nothing; the second part of Grace, which means actually <u>following</u> Jesus, costs us everything…but is entirely worth it! To follow Jesus may appear to cost us everything, but the price we pay is absolutely worth it, because He only wants to take away from us all of our worldly and carnal junk that is only holding us back, and is of no eternal value anyway!

Here is how Jesus explained what it truly means to follow Him: "Then said Jesus unto his disciples, **If any man will come after me, let him deny himself, and take up his cross, and follow me. For whosoever will save his life shall lose it: and whosoever will lose his life for my sake shall find it. For what is a man profited, if he shall gain the whole world, and lose his own soul?**" (Matthew 16:24–26).

So, do you want the world, or do you want your soul? Choose Jesus, die to yourself, live for Him and for those around you, and you will inherit eternity. Why even mention the other option?

The world system is run by nimrods who choose to worship themselves and who relentlessly pursue worldly gain. Even the Church is corrupted with nimrods, whose very ministries are like top-heavy towers of babel, ready to fall. They live for themselves and follow the lusts of their flesh. Their message parallels the message of the "American Dream," and they teach that Jesus died so that we could have the "good life" here on earth, of comfort, consumerism, and overflowing bank accounts. These teachings contribute to a distinctly Laodicean problem here in the American Church. On one hand, many Christians are intellectually convinced of the truth of the Gospel and they try so hard to convince others to agree with them. Yet on the other hand they aren't taught that they must die to themselves so that they can fully live for Christ. Blinded by prosperity, they end up looking like the world while they grow increasingly frustrated, argumentative and judgmental, packaged in a cold shell of self-righteousness. But this blindness is coming off!

I have often heard the end-times awakening of the Church referred to as the "Elijah Revolution." Elijah was called to combat idolatry and to confront Jezebel, and the end-times ministry of Elijah (according to Malachi 4:5–6) is also about healing hearts and mending relationships. Consumerism, materialism, and selfishness have so overtaken our culture today that we struggle to hear God's voice and we find it extremely hard to love our neighbors. The Elijah Revolution will involve massive repentance as we reject our cultural shackles, ask Jesus to heal our blind eyes, and turn our hearts back to our Father in heaven, surrendering to His plan.

This book was all about identifying Nimrod as the Antichrist—the King of Babylon who will rise again during the Day of the Lord. The Church has no business with the <u>King of Babylon</u>, because we are not appointed to suffer the wrath of the Day of the Lord. However, the Elijah Revolution will identify and confront the Queen of Babylon, that great global Jezebel who is described in Revelation 17–18. Like the historical Antichrist, this woman has her origins at the beginning of history, and her true identity can be found in the book of Genesis and in the myths of ancient Sumer. Much of the Church has fallen into her deceptive and alluring clutches, but the Elijah Revolution will bring truth, clarity, and freedom, awakening and sanctifying the Bride of Christ until we are revealed to the earth as the spotless Bride that we were created to be.

The Apostle Paul explains the true source of all freedom: "Where the Spirit of the Lord is, there is liberty" (2 Corinthians 3:17). If you want true freedom, draw closer to God and He will transform you into a Holy son or daughter. Holiness is not a list of rules. Holiness is to be completely possessed by the Spirit of God, and to have the freedom to wake up every morning and to step out into the world knowing that you can do anything you want to, because you have a transformed mind that is completely in line with the will of the Creator of the Universe.

Radical power and love flow from this heavenly freedom. There is nothing else that even comes close to it. No drug, no counterfeit spiritual experience, no intellectual or carnal stimulation, can equal the supernatural lifestyle that we are called to walk out by the power of the Holy Spirit. The end-times move of God will be made up of radical servants of God who will live for nothing else.

"And as ye go, preach, saying,
The Kingdom of heaven is at hand!
Heal the sick, cleanse the lepers, raise the dead, cast out devils:
freely ye have received, freely give."

MATTHEW 10:7–8

Acknowledgements

Thank you Lord Jesus for being the great Example and for giving your life to allow all of us to become children of God. Thank you Father, for all of Creation and for life itself. Thank you Holy Spirit, for drawing us into perfect and fearless love, for revealing your mysteries, and for empowering us for this great adventure.

Thank you Ed and Tracy Bean, the pastors of my home church, New Beginning Christian Fellowship, for allowing me to teach this material at our weekly Bible study. Thank you most especially for your hearts that are open to the voice of the Holy Spirit, that are continually pressing in to the deeper things of God. Thank you also to Louie, for videotaping our Bible study and for constantly supporting me; to Rick for your sincere Berean perspective on all things; and to all the members of my home church.

Thank you Carolina and Shelter of Wisdom, for allowing me to share in our Bible study every Tuesday night in Kalihi. Thank you Mike, Adam, Channing, Sam, Howie, Frank, Arthur, Kawika, Matt, Nito, Gary, Fred, Andy, and all of the rest of you guys who have helped me fine-tune the presentation of this material. You are all blessed and overflowing with the riches of heaven!

Thank you John and Linda Keough of Healing Rooms Honolulu, for showing me how to put faith into action. You are both treasures in the Kingdom of Heaven and a gift of

God to His Church. It is an honor and a privilege to be a part of your ministry and I know that the miracles we have seen are just a foretaste of what is soon to come.

I want to also thank my friend Mike Bennett, who is known as Dr. Future to many. I met Mike back in the summer of 2005 at a conference in Roswell, New Mexico, when I was just beginning to focus on Nimrod. Mike gave me confirmation that I was on the right track, and then supported and encouraged me as I continued to study and write. The interviews we did together on *FutureQuake Radio* were truly epic. Mike, your love of Truth, your Holy Spirit-led instincts, and your gentleness and compassion are mighty weapons for the Kingdom of Heaven. God bless you. I know you will always be on the front lines of battle!

Thanks also to Derek and Sharon Gilbert of *P.I.D. Radio*. You folks have been relentlessly shining the light into darkness since 2005, and I am blessed to have been a part of your adventures into podcast-land.

Thank you John McMahon! Your support has been more important to me than you can imagine. You have an amazing heart and an authenticity that is hard to find these days. Thank you also Richard White. You and Johnny gave me an opportunity to share what was going on in my life as I turned from searching out the devil's schemes to searching out heaven's plan for His people and His Church. Trust me, heaven's plan blows the doors off of anything the devil can even imagine.

Thank you to the people who supported me financially as I took a month off from work to write this manuscript: Jacque, Jeffrey, Murray, Judy, Lucas from Poland, the nameless contributor from the UK, Ann, David, Ben, Mark,

Steven, Mr. Jones, and Wolfgang from Germany. You folks helped me keep the lights on and I thank you very much!

Thank you Tom Horn and Defender Publishing. Thanks Tom, for your consistent reminders and encouragement to write this book. You've made it very easy for me, and it's great to work with someone whose interests are so closely parallel to mine. I have no idea what is in store for us, but I know that our work will prosper in the truly *heavenly* sense. Thanks also to Donna for your corrections and suggestions while editing the manuscript and for patiently dealing with all of the images and footnotes.

And finally, thank you Lori, my amazing wife, for supporting and encouraging me in the writing of this book, and for being *all in* as my partner in this heavenly adventure at the end of the age.

Thank you all, and Aloha in Jesus' Name,
Peter Goodgame
Kailua, Hawaii
May 9, 2012

About the Author

Peter Goodgame lives with his wife and two children in Kailua, Hawaii. Peter and Lori are very active in their local church, and they are the directors of Kahuhipa Healing Rooms, a healing ministry in the town of Kaneohe.

Since 1999, Peter has been the editor of www.redmoon-rising.com, a cutting-edge website that deals with Bible prophecy and the signs of the end-times. According to the Bible there are three signs that will precede the end-times "Day of the Lord." They are:

1: The sign of a darkened sun and blood red moon (Joel 2:31).
2: The revealing of the Antichrist (2 Thessalonians 2:3).
3: The coming of Elijah (Malachi 4:5).

Peter addressed the first issue in his book *Red Moon Rising: The Rapture and the Timeline of the Apocalypse*, published in early 2005; the second in this book, *The Second Coming of the Antichrist*, published in 2012; and the third sign, the coming of Elijah, is related to the realm of personal relationships, economics, and the Kingdom principles of generosity and sharing (Luke 3:7–14), which he is focusing on today.